Dedicated to my sons, Zach and Jeremia.
Always remember your Alaska roots.

Zach & Jeremia at Portage Glacier
August 1980

AN ALASKAN MEMOIR ON TEACHING AND LEARNING

Life at Fifty Below Zero

CHRISTINA REAGLE

wild eagle publishing
wildeagle.co

Copyright © 2022 Christina Reagle

Wild Eagle logo is © 2022 Wild Eagle Publishing. All rights reserved. No part of this book may be used in any form whatsoever without the written permission of the publisher, except for brief quotations included in critical articles and reviews.

ISBN: 978-1-7345021-0-7 paperback
ISBN: 978-1-7345021-1-4 eBook

Printed in the United States of America
10 9 8 7 6 5 4 3 2

Book cover and interior design by Otterburn & Co.
https://www.otterburn.co

Set in Garamond Premier Pro

All photos are from the author's private collection.

TABLE OF CONTENTS

Author's Notes 7

I. Going to Alaska
    Going up the ALCAN 13
    Orientation to Rural Alaska 25
    Moving into bush Alaska 35

II. Teaching and Learning
    Marshall 49
    Summer of 1973 87
    Holy Cross 93
    Allakaket 133
    Nulato 179

III. Back and Forth
    Summer of 1976 217
    Fairbanks and Nenana 223

IV. Juneau, Anchorage and Beyond
    Arriving in Juneau 285
    Working and Surviving 311
    Leaving Alaska 359

Afterthoughts 373

Endnotes 377

Acknowledgements 383

About the Author 387

An Alaskan Memoir on Teaching and Learning

AUTHOR'S NOTES

Freezing is 32° Fahrenheit
or 0° Celsius.

'Below zero or minus' refers
to the temperature below zero Fahrenheit.

50° below zero or minus 50 means it is 82°
below freezing (Fahrenheit).

That is damn cold.

Me in Dawson Creek
July 2, 1972

Life at Fifty Below Zero

An Alaskan Memoir on Teaching and Learning

PART I

Going to Alaska

Life at Fifty Below Zero

Part I: Going to Alaska

Going up the ALCAN

1972

It was a beautiful Saturday morning with the sun filtering through the redwoods around our small cabin in Felton, California. We sat sipping our morning coffee in the beauty and silence of the majestic trees when the phone rang bringing us back to the day ahead. Jed answered it as I sat petting our black lab, Hidalgo. My mind drifted off to the weekend to-do list when I heard Jed say, "Yes, we are still interested." After a few minutes more he hung up and looked at me. "We have been hired and are to be in Fairbanks in two and a half months." The idea of being teachers in a rural Alaskan village sounded so simple when Jed suggested we consider it in mid-March. Now it was April 10 and we were to start an orientation program in three months.

During the final semester of completing his California teaching license Jed had a professor who entertained the class with endless stories about Alaska. He just finished working there and shared experiences of various 'bush' teachers hired to work in remote villages all over Alaska. One week he mentioned recruiters from Alaska would be in San Francisco to interview potential teachers for the Alaska bush. When Jed arrived home that evening he said, "How would you like to investigate the possibility of teaching in Alaska for a year?" I had taught a few years in the Garden Grove area and currently was teaching in San Jose, California. I casually said, "Sure, I am up for an adventure for a year," not really thinking we would be hired.

The following week we drove into the city for the interviews. My five years of experience included teaching grades K–6, which unbeknownst to us made me an asset. There hadn't been any mention about attending a six-week orientation session with new-to-Alaska teachers until the phone call. The pressure was now on since my current school year didn't end until June and I had recently accepted a new district teaching position. As we started planning, I thought we were making a lot of changes for one year. *I still think the reason we were hired was my response to a question during the interview about a honey bucket. I knew what it was and said yes I could empty one.*

Running off to Alaska to teach in a small village on the Yukon River sure seemed like a good idea in March. Now the reality of what that meant was staring us straight in the face. We were interested in a simpler lifestyle but didn't feel we could realistically live off the land. Paid work was necessary to us and Jed had a National Guard responsibility to complete. His first job as an administrator at Los Angeles Airport helped us recognize the corporate world wasn't for us. When we agreed Jed would become a teacher we knew we wouldn't have much money, but would always have jobs. Teaching in Alaska had never been part of the equation.

Life became crazy—deciding what to mail was challenging since we lacked solid information about our living situation. There were conversations during the interview that not all villages with teacher housing had running water. Neither one of us gave much thought to the lack of plumbing. The administrator who called about our jobs said we were hired too late to have items barged into our village. Only twenty percent of Alaska could be accessed by road, which meant most items were shipped by boat or plane. Vessels from Seattle carried items to a couple of key locations in Alaska where they were then barged or mailed by plane to rural communities.

Part I: Going to Alaska

At first, I didn't understand. Naively I thought our boxes would be trucked to our new village home. To become more informed, I headed to the library to find information about Alaska. One of our friends suggested looking at *Alaska* magazines and ordering a *MILEPOST,* whatever that was. At least now I knew we were hired to teach in a village accessed by air, barge or riverboat in the summer and small airplanes or snow machines in the winter. I was in a quandary with lack of solid information.

After the initial shock settled in we realized neither of our two vehicles, a VW hippie camping Van and my sporty MGB baby, were suitable for the trip up the ALCAN. The first decision was to trade both vehicles for a sturdy four-wheel drive Toyota Land Cruiser. The second decision was to follow the *MILEPOST* information for 'Alaska driving.' The preparations suggested a screen mounted across the entire front end of the car with protectors on the headlamps. The final recommendation was traction tires to handle gravel and off-road driving.

Besides the purchase of an adequate vehicle we needed to rent our cabin in the redwoods outside of Santa Cruz. Determining what to take, packing, finishing jobs, preparing for the unknown—so much to do with limited information left us moving in circles for a few days. As we perused the *Alaska* magazines, we began to comprehend the complexities of rural communities in Alaska and our role as teachers.

A week before we left we calculated the travel time from San Jose, California to Fairbanks, Alaska. The distance was less than three thousand miles, but the information about the roads and highways confirmed they weren't the normal interstate.

We left Dawson Creek, British Columbia (BC) early the morning of July 2 to start the big drive up the Alaska Highway, also known as the ALCAN, the Alaska-Canadian Highway. Relentless road reconstruction and modifications in the early years changed MILEPOST 0 several times. Dawson Creek was currently noted as the 'true' starting point of the ALCAN.

The ALCAN was originally constructed as a military highway to connect Alaska with the contiguous lower 48 states. Road repairs were a constant occurrence in rerouting, straightening, and changing sections, sometimes done by Canada and other times the United States. The extreme cold weather often caused gaping holes or major road lakes, which made it difficult to drive through or around.

The ALCAN looped through Canada's British Columbia and Yukon territories, as well as Alaska. Signposts were in kilometers and miles. The accuracy of the miles or kilometers weren't always current with constant repairs, detours, and changes. We started on pavement in Dawson Creek, but it was to change. The *MILEPOST* we purchased was considered the Bible of North Country travel since 1949. Published annually it provided mile-by-mile guidance for Alaska Highway travelers. The price was $2.95 and was worth every penny.

Despite improvements the ALCAN was famous for a rough and challenging drive with many legendary stories. Rocks cracked our windshield three times; the first one at Milepost #230, followed by two more at Milepost #269, and this was day one of a typical four-day ALCAN journey. Despite 'being prepared' another part of day one was a flat tire at Milepost #269! All of this happened while traveling at the break neck speed of twenty-five to forty-five miles an hour.

Part I: Going to Alaska

Thirty-five miles after the flat at Milepost #305 we called it a day at Fort Nelson, BC. We were exhausted and felt it was a good spot to set up the small tent we purchased in Dawson Creek for a night's rest. While paying for our campsite bill the clerk mentioned, "In early July we often get electrical rainstorms." Heading to our tent site I looked up at the high dark clouds and wondered if he was correct in his prediction.

When I awoke in the middle of the night to dripping of water and the buzzing of a mosquito, I swatted at each time it came within ear range I knew he was right. The saturated feeling was getting worse as each drip landed on my forehead, my feet, and three to four places in between. Luckily, Hidalgo, an eighty-pound black Labrador retriever, was cuddled up in the Toyota Land Cruiser with our Siamese cat, Soltar. If he were in the tent more dripping would occur because of the enthusiastic wagging of his tail. He loved water and at this moment I knew he was drier than me.

The torrential downpour we were experiencing was more rain than either of us had ever experienced camping. Maybe the mosquitos that joined us in the tent also felt it was more rain than usual for them. *How can a microscopic size creature be so annoying?* The long night taught me swatting mosquitos in a small tent shared with another adult resulted in constant dripping.

We were both exhausted from a long frustrating day with unplanned events. And now when we needed rest to rejuvenate, mosquitos had other plans. My normal drifting off to sleep tricks weren't working. Each time I heard the aggravating buzz my eyes popped open. I wanted and needed to be the winner over this mosquito invading my privacy.

July in the far north was certainly different than California, Oregon, and Washington. At midnight in Fort Nelson, BC the sky wasn't dark, but maintained a glow of soft light across the horizon that lasted two to three hours. *Alaska* magazines borrowed from the library explained about endless days, but now the reality was more than I imagined. I found it difficult to sleep when it was still light. I loved summer, but this was bizarre and the adjustment was harder than I thought.

Here I lay exhausted and soaked to the core on my way to empty honey buckets in a remote village of less than two hundred people somewhere on the Yukon River. Getting wetter and wetter by the minute, made me realize I agreed to this adventure so it was time to put on my big girl pants and become positive. In 1972 Alaska teaching jobs paid well compared to California and other states, plus we talked about an adventure out of the United States. Many people told us Alaska was similar to a third world country because of its remoteness.

Counting the raindrops and trying to drift off to sleep I figured there were four more days on the road before reaching Fairbanks. I decided it was time to relax, not worry, and enjoy the journey.

The next day a second flat tire happened at Milepost #519. Oh well, the drive was spectacular with a landscape of wild flowers in assorted colors and a backdrop of incredible green trees of British Columbia. I watched the countryside and felt the beauty of the surroundings welcome us to the Northern Country. Somehow my itchy mosquito bites were soothed as I calmly looked around.

Each flat tire cost us two hours of time, as well as the thirty or so miles of nervous driving with no spare. Why had the *MILEPOST* not suggested two spare tires would be a good idea? The ALCAN had little spots in the road every fifty miles or so that assisted motorists with various vehicle problems. Sometimes there was a campground, a gas station, or a motel of sorts that included a tire repair shop.

The second day ended in Watson Lake where we washed muddy clothes and dried out the tent. After a restful night at Watson Lake, we headed for the great Yukon Territory. Not too far into our third day, the ALCAN delivered its third and final flat tire at Milepost #747. The time drain discouraged us, but after observing other people along the highway, our three cracks in the windshield, and three flat tires seemed like nothing.

We arrived in Whitehorse that evening and set up camp. The next morning we had our first peek at the enormous Yukon River that started in British Columbia and moved through the Yukon Territory emptying into the Bering Sea. The Yukon River was 2,300 miles long, the third longest river in North America. Seeing the Yukon intensified our anticipation of the village where we would teach since it was located along this river, only hundreds of miles downstream.

Feeling invigorated and refreshed we were anxious to reach the border. Our excitement was quickly subdued when an unanticipated delay occurred costing us several hours. Despite having papers confirming jobs in Alaska our California hippie appearance made us suspicious looking. Jed had a mustache and shoulder length hair. My hair was long with a leather headband to secure it from blowing around. Although I left my mini-skirts and hot pants in storage in California my current outfit was a tie-dyed, colorful shirt and patched Levi's. I wore an Egyptian bicep arm bracelet.

Part I: Going to Alaska

When the Alaska border delegate saw us he asked to search our car. We showed him papers about our jobs but he still wanted to do a quick search. After securing the cat in her travel box and putting Hidalgo on a leash, *we forgot one important detail*. During the trip we indulged in our final small amount of weed. Being conscientious about not littering the environment with trash and hoping we would have another opportunity to use the pipe sometime in the future we stuck it in the glove box.

When the border cop found the pipe and empty bag a complete turn of events happened. He told us to pull over to the side where three uniformed gun-toting border patrol agents thoroughly searched our car. Everything was taken out and carefully pawed through—suitcases, boxes, camping equipment, dirty clothes, bags of dog and cat food, as well as the cat's litter box. We stood shocked and realized our new life might abruptly end. Our imaginations were dancing about with nervous anxiety. We could lose our teaching licenses. Having spent most of our funds to get ourselves to Alaska we were now concerned about having to call a parent to bail us out of jail. And, what would the border patrol do with Hidalgo and Soltar? It was a tense couple of hours as we watched and waited.

Finally, the customs' agents were convinced we didn't have more pot, so they let us reenter the United States. The border patrol agent told us they would keep the pipe to add it to the contraband display case they proudly hung in their office. As we slowly drove into Alaska, our tires were once again on pavement creating a smoother and more comfortable drive. The warm temperature felt good and the narrow road was thick with trees. There were no buildings, just a road with an occasional house briefly seen down a dirt path. Suddenly a moose walked out of the trees from a side road. Despite the fact I saw pictures of them in the *MILEPOST* and *Alaska* magazine I was struck with the strangeness of his body shape. I knew immediately he was male because of his growing rack. How could his stilt like legs hold up his massive upper body and head? It was nice of him to welcome us to Alaska and not walk into our car. I gave him an appreciative smile.

The long daylight hours helped us reach our destination of Tok. It was 11:00 p.m. We were once again dog-tired beyond description, but pleased the Tok Lodge had a room for our weary bodies. The next morning as we ate breakfast we noticed a couple at the counter. Intuitively, we suspected they were headed to Fairbanks to become Alaska bush teachers. They confirmed our suspicion as we laughed and chatted a bit.

As we walked out of the café heading for our cars I shrieked, "Oh no," and started running toward our car. Soltar was hanging by her collar out the window and standing on her tippy toes. Before going to breakfast we threw our bags in the car, walked Hidalgo, and checked on Soltar. The morning was already warm and there were no trees to provide shade. To keep both animals cool we rolled down the windows for air. We wanted to be sure Soltar wouldn't jump out and run off so we leashed her to a handle in the car. There were a few minutes of concern by everyone, followed by a belly laugh. This terrifying moment was the only hiccup with Soltar's travel.

Part I: Going to Alaska

The Cremation of Sam McGee

There are strange things done in the midnight sun
    By the men who moil for gold;
The Arctic trails have their secret tales
    That would make your blood run cold;
The Northern Lights have seen queer sights,
    But the queerest they ever did see
Was that night on the marge of Lake Lebarge
    I cremated Sam McGee.

—Robert W. Service

Part I: Going to Alaska

Orientation to Rural Alaska

July 7, 1972

When we arrived in Fairbanks on Friday it was eighty-two degrees. The warm temperature surprised me. I had no shorts or summer clothes with me other than a couple of short sleeve shirts and one halter-top. *Alaska* magazine advised the number of mosquitos made clothing that displayed skin a bad choice for Alaskan summers so no shorts accompanied me to Alaska.

Instead of a hotel, the Alaska Rural Schools Project (ARSP) placed us at the University of Alaska Fairbanks campus dormitory for the six weeks orientation program. The dorm was cheaper than hotels and camping in bug territory might not be a good introduction to Alaska. Alaskan mosquitos were known to drive people out of the state before they were even settled.

We dropped the luggage at our assigned room and met other 'newbies' that were part of the bush teacher crowd. Our new friends, John and Mary, mentioned several people were headed to the Malemute Saloon ten miles south of Fairbanks in the community of Ester. Since it was a warm summer day the group decided a trip to Ester for a first Alaska beer was appropriate.

The Malemute Saloon was like stepping back to the Gold Rush days. Ester was an old gold mining camp with a saloon built around 1906.

The swinging doors and barstools were rickety with age, perfect for the atmosphere. The floor of the Malemute was a mixture of dirt and peanut shells. Based on the depth of the mixture we guessed on how often it was swept. The honky-tonk piano player was incredible. Recitations of Robert Service poetry provided occasional breaks for the musician. The music and poetry continued throughout the day and into the evening. Patrons ate their fill of peanuts with a purchase of a fifty-cent dill pickle. The pickles soaked in large wooden barrels scattered throughout the Saloon.

The man reading the Robert Service poetry excelled at creating the illusion of living in the Wild West with a gold miners' timbre in his speech. The voice was spellbinding. I found it had a haunting affect, making the words linger in my mind long after we left. One person in our group said, "Hearing the poetry read in this particular environment was like watching the words speak out loud." Walking to the car I heard another person mumble, "The old Saloon made the poetry come alive." What a mystical place to hear, *The Shooting of Dan McGrew* and *The Cremation of Sam McGee*?

As we left the saloon to drive back there was animated talk about feeling we had stepped into another era. I heard someone getting in his truck say, "I heard Robert Service poetry in college, but it never made me see old miners like I did tonight." The experience and the constant light outside left many of us a bit off balance. It didn't matter if we visited the Malemute Saloon at 2:00 p.m. or left at 2:00 a.m., it was always daylight. Summer in the far North resulted in twenty-four hours of sunshine, a new experience for many of us. It disturbed normal sleep patterns. The warmth of the sun didn't diminish in the late evening. With no air conditioning in the dorms slumber was difficult. People tossed footballs and Frisbees around at all hours as they played in the midnight sun.

Part I: Going to Alaska

Over the course of the first weekend and week of the orientation program I learned Alaska specifically looked for married couples to teach in the bush. This revelation was a new concept to me. California didn't follow this practice, but other states with large rural areas did. The orientation group was a mix of new teachers and individuals with several years of teaching.

In 1972 part of the hiring process for new rural teachers was attending the Alaska Rural Schools Project. On Monday morning, July 10, at 8:00 a.m. the orientation officially started. The Institute for Northern Research, a part of the University of Alaska Fairbanks, was responsible for coordination of the program. The primary goal of the Institute was the preservation of the Native cultures in Alaska. The Alaska Rural Schools Project (ARSP) was a Ford Foundation grant focused on eliminating the constant turnover of teachers in rural Alaska, so it fit into the mission of the Institute. Preliminary results indicated teachers who completed the program stayed in the bush and were more productive with their students.

Previously new educators recruited and hired from the lower 48 states to teach in Alaskan rural communities weren't provided much information. When new hires reported to their assigned village on a specific date they often experienced shell shock. Little information about housing, purchasing groceries, communication, and teaching materials was sent to them before they arrived in their village.

Throughout the time we participated in the ARSP we heard stories about educators who arrived in a village, got off the plane, looked around, and promptly got right back on the plane shaking their head, "No, not for me." There were even more extreme stories about people starting the year and getting village (cabin) fever after a few weeks. It became obvious they needed help when found running naked through the village at below zero temperatures in hopes someone would call for a plane. We all came to think of these stories as village legends shared over a beer. After we heard them repeated multiple times by different people, we wondered about truth to the stories.

When we announced to friends and family in California about being hired to teach in Alaska they were surprised. No one knew much about Alaska and those that did said it was full of mystery and extreme cold. Clearly, cold in Alaska was chiller than I'd ever experienced. Jed and I were no strangers to snow. We were avid skiers in California snow, but had no idea about living in snow. I was surprised to learn that temperatures in Alaska often needed to warm up to snow. All the talk about temperature was confusing. Knowing thirty-two degrees above zero was freezing made the idea of fifty degrees below zero even more confusing. The term wind chill was new for me. I had much to learn. Reading and hearing the discussions helped, but it was still beyond my imagination.

Alaska magazines mentioned most villages in rural Alaska had electricity, but not all had running water. The village we were headed to was in an area of intense cold. I just kept thinking to myself, *I can handle it*. I found out we were going to one of the remote villages, so we would most likely not have running water. I suddenly realized we were entering a part of the United States where many normal services and conveniences weren't available. Communication for emergencies was by a radio connection to one person in the village. This was 1972. What had I signed up for?

We knew we needed cold weather clothing and were told to consider purchasing a snow machine. As all the information began to settle into my brain I remembered a college class that discussed culture shock. The term now had a new meaning. Culture shock happened when a person entered a new environment where the interaction patterns were different than what the individual was accustomed to, their personal norm.

During the Alaska Rural Schools orientation we learned about the importance of helping to preserve the many different Native cultures in Alaska, Eskimo, Indian, and Aleut groups. Sessions included history of Alaska Native groups and language, as well as culturally specific material. We began to understand how different Alaska was from the lower 48 states. There were several discussions about the importance of encouraging Native students to become teachers in villages. None of us realized how much the information we received would increase our abilities to be effective teachers.

Teachers in rural Alaska were hired by one of two systems: Alaska State-Operated School System (ASOSS) or the Bureau of Indian Affairs (BIA). Both were equally bureaucratic and not in touch with bush communities. Alaska Native presenters explained the importance of students' education not being dominated by Western curriculum. The missionaries hadn't allowed children to speak their Native language at school. The repercussions of that action still lingered. With few Alaska Native materials, typical Western curriculum were used in many schools.

Instructors in the orientation program were Alaska Natives or current teachers in village schools. Many of the sessions were organized around ways to utilize Alaska Native history and culture into curriculum. Our orientation sessions were in a Lab school set up on the University campus to mimic a typical village school. Strategies to teach across grade levels and include various content areas were shared since many schools only had three to five teachers. After sessions were done for the day, presenters and new teachers often talked until 9:00 or 10:00 p.m.

A whole day was spent learning to order enough groceries to keep us fed depending on the village location. I never thought about how much flour I used in a month or over a year, or that dried milk powder when mixed with cold water was tasty. The other aspect of ordering food was the time it took to finally arrive and the condition it might be in, depending on the item ordered. I never thought about mailing eggs, fresh fruit, or vegetables and what happened if those items froze along the way.

In the fourth week of the program we were sent to visit our village teaching assignment. The first thing I learned was how to measure distance by the number of airplane rides it took to get somewhere. From Fairbanks we flew to Bethel and then to Marshall (our village destination), only two airplane rides. If we were flying from California, the flight journey would be: LA to Seattle, Seattle to Anchorage, Anchorage to Bethel, and Bethel to Marshall, four flights. That was a lot of up and down. *At least in small airplanes I never worried someone might dance in the aisles.*

Our assignment while in the village was to observe the people in the community, learn about the school, investigate the geographical environment, and orient ourselves to our new home. We didn't realize the opportunity it provided to return with questions and have conversations that helped us gather additional resources.

Our visit to Marshall was great. We met a few students and parents and stayed in our housing. The head teacher was there so we had an opportunity to visit the school and talk with him about the coming year.

We were disappointed to find his teaching philosophy was completely opposite ours. He represented what the Alaska Rural Schools Project was trying to make sure didn't continue. He thought the only thing students needed to learn was how to work as a manual laborer in a big city. He was sure they wouldn't return to their villages and his comment was, "We certainly don't want them on welfare."

There was no art, music or cultural materials to assist in the content areas of reading, writing, math, history, social studies, and geography. Reading textbooks were the standard ones used across the United States depicting middle class families in cities. We dug around the classrooms and found an older collection of basic readers developed specifically for rural Alaska. The mimeographed booklets used to teach reading in grades one through four had pictures of Alaska Native children in villages. I planned to use them for reading and writing lessons.

Textbooks were whatever was left from the previous teachers or distributed to the schools. Sometimes the BIA or ASOSS offices or a school district in the lower 48 sent random textbooks. Alaska villages were treated as missionary projects for churches so the textbooks were old and out of date. Bush teachers had no required standards of what they were to cover.

After we returned to Fairbanks each couple shared their village experiences. Given that teaching contracts didn't start until the third week in August very few of the new bush teachers met any staff during their visit.

We found the six-week orientation sessions stimulating, informative, and surpassed expectations. We felt prepared and ready, even though we still had questions. Most of us were in our midtwenties to midthirties

Enjoying the sun with friends at Mt. McKinley
August 1972

Part I: Going to Alaska

and came from Washington, Oregon, California, Arizona, Montana, Colorado, Nebraska, South Dakota, Minnesota, South Carolina, and New York. We were headed to every remote point of the state. Alaska was large with small villages spread throughout the entire state.

After finishing up in Fairbanks, we had ten days for personal time and tasks before heading into the villages. Several couples decided a visit to Mt. McKinley[1] was a great idea. We gathered supplies and camped for three amazing days while seeing unbelievable wildlife. The weather was clear which provided a view of the mountain in its remarkable splendor.

In 1972 Mt. McKinley wasn't developed into a National Park. At this point the park was raw wilderness with animal trails to follow and few people to share the space. We saw Dall sheep, moose, wolves, bears and caribou. We were so naïve about the wild life. Our dogs were running loose when we saw a Tolkat grizzly bear. Lucky for us the dogs came when we called. The magnificent grizzly with its long, thick hair, remarkable pale golden coat and chocolate-colored legs didn't smell us because the wind was blowing the scent away in a different direction.

None of us knew about hanging food or the need for bear boxes. We were so green and innocent and had much to learn.

Part I: Going to Alaska

Moving into bush Alaska

August 22, 1972

In Anchorage we hoped to enjoy a few nights of dining out. However, we realized—we were broke, groceries were expensive, and restaurants had out-of-sight prices. Ordering groceries and other necessities for Marshall became the priority.

During the Marshall visit I found the one store had very few items. According to the directions I was given the store was down the road, third house on the left. I walked the short distance and all I saw were private homes that all looked somewhat the same. There were no signs or items sitting on a porch to give me the impression of a store. I walked up the steps of the third house on the left and knocked on the door. I heard a response and hoped it was someone saying come in, so I opened the door.

The building was a one-room cabin with scant furniture. The flooring was raw plywood. A toddler was running around giggling in nothing but a shirt. Later I learned this was a typical approach to potty training babies since it saved on diapers. When running water wasn't available many activities were handled differently. The lighting in the room was dim so I sheepishly walked forward and said, "I am looking for the store." A woman stood up and quietly moved toward me. She pointed to the items I walked past, and said, "Store right here." There were six to seven cases of assorted items, red apples, oranges, Spam,

Crisco, green beans, and a few badly bruised bananas. After I introduced myself as one of the new teachers I told her I wanted a couple of oranges. I rattled on that we were here for a few days learning about the school. As I left I thought to myself, *I really talk too much!*

Another reason for a stop in Anchorage was a more direct route to Marshall. It was still two airplane rides, just shorter. Anchorage, the largest city in Alaska, had 124,000 residents, almost a third of the state's total population of 324,464. There were more people in San Jose, California (460,000), where I had taught the previous year than all of Alaska.

Anchorage was small for a city, but certainly bigger than Marshall and it had a few markets. After arriving in Anchorage we stopped at a market for a few items. As I searched for something we needed I overheard a conversation between two women. The visiting mom was aghast at the prices for simple food items and her daughter's response was, "The substance of life—food, housing, clothing, transportation—is more expensive here." Despite being new to Alaska this was not a complete surprise. We were warned about prices for food and necessities like soap, t-paper, lotion, etc. One of the presenters during the summer quoted a statistic that stated, "Of thirty-nine metropolitan areas regularly checked by the Federal Government, Alaska has the most expensive prices for basic items."

That evening in our Anchorage campground, I made lists while Jed hunted down addresses and directions to stores. Even though we knew there was a store in Bethel, our midway point en route to Marshall, the thoughts of shopping with a dog and cat in tow wasn't appealing. Bethel was the primary hub for Native villages in the Yukon-Kuskokwim Delta area. Regional hubs such as Barrow, Dillingham, Ketchikan, Kodiak,

Kotzebue, Nome, were sprinkled around Alaska. Besides shopping, villagers traveled to hub sites for health and social service support. Prices were higher in hub communities, but that was life in Alaska.

The next day we ordered food items, located a few extra teaching supplies, and stored our Land Cruiser for the winter. Thursday evening we packed our luggage to board the jet to Bethel. The Anchorage to Bethel flight wasn't always a 737 jet, but today there was a lot of freight. When there was more freight than people the first 10–12 rows of the plane was utilized for the additional mail, boxes, and other large items. This seemed strange to us, but the differences in Alaska were so many we just accepted this as another part of the new normal. As the flight took off, we looked at each other and knew we were ready to finally settle into the new life. There were so many unknowns to this adventure we were beginning.

As we flew into Bethel the terrain appeared very flat; however, someone on the plane pointed to a 'forest.' Stretching our necks to see we noticed they were chuckling. As we gathered our pets, boxes and baggage to schlep next-door to the smaller airlines, the pilot explained, "Bethel has one tree with a fence and sign stating the Bethel National Forest."

After checking in with the mail carrier for the final leg of our journey we helped load our luggage, boxes, cat carrier, and dog onto the plane. An interesting factoid I learned about travel in bush Alaska was dogs jump on the plane as a passenger. The owner holds the dog and keeps the animal under control. Hidalgo was easy. Being a Labrador he wanted everyone to be happy, including the pilot. Besides, he wasn't constantly meowing.

Arriving in Marshall
August 24, 1972

Part I: Going to Alaska

Flying on a small plane was different than a commercial jet. It always started with the question, "How much do you weigh?" Small planes were based on weight and how it was distributed. *I learned quickly this wasn't a time to take off the five to ten pounds I hoped to lose.* Boxes, bags and freight were weighed on a scale, but people were just asked. You could always tell people who were new to flying in bush Alaska because they whispered their weight. I am a small person, but I always added 10–15 pounds to my weight to make up for the person I knew was lying about their weight.

After everything was loaded and arranged—passengers, boxes and bags, community mailbags, the dog, and a noisy, annoying cat—onto the Cessna 210 Skywagon, we were ready for takeoff. The plane was full and we were glad we didn't need to camp in the Bethel National Forest. The flight was smooth and before we realized it, we disembarked in Marshall or, as some people referred to it, Fortuna Ledge.

Marshall's postmaster, Don Hunter, met the plane with his truck. During our earlier visit we told him we would return the last week in August. Hunter had several jobs in Marshall. Besides being the postmaster he was the Wein Airlines representative, the ticket agent, the village radio operator, the airport manager, and finally, the Vice President of the Village Council. He was a busy guy. News travels fast in small villages and we were the big news. I imagined a town crier ran through the town announcing, "The new teachers arrived!" While we loaded our boxes and gear into Don's truck, kids rode their bikes around and checked us out.

When we visited earlier in the summer, many people were at fish camp so little attention was paid to us. In Marshall the plane arrived on land in the summer and the frozen Yukon River in the late fall, winter, and most of spring. Late August was truck weather, which was lucky for us. Don had the only truck in town and was very generous with multiple trips to get our stuff to our new home. We were appreciative.

Life in small Alaska villages was tremendously different than small communities in the lower 48. Eight months out of the year Alaska villages have lots of snow or ice. During freeze-up and breakup road surfaces were a mixture of ice, mud, snow, and slush. The extreme weather caused difficult road surfaces. Most people trudged along by foot or used an all-terrain vehicle. Alaskan villages in the 1970s had very few trucks or cars. The price of a truck or car was almost double due to the difficulty in getting it into a village. With no television or radio advertisements most people didn't have the itch to even own a vehicle.

Marshall had thirty-three families in the village with a total of one hundred fifty-four people. Everyone was Yup'ik Eskimo except for the two teaching families. We were both Caucasian, as was the head teacher, but his wife was Chinese, from Taiwan.

The buildings in Marshall were composed of a K–8 school, post office, Catholic church, Russian Orthodox church, community hall, and small store. The postmaster had the only radio, which was the only means of connection to a doctor, state trooper, or other government agencies. Village homes were mostly modest single-room structures that might have partial walls or curtained off areas for sleeping. The mail-plane came twice a week from Bethel, weather permitting, one of the big reasons why all the shopping preparations were critical.

Looking at a map to find Marshall confused me, since one map showed Marshall and another showed Fortuna Ledge. Marshall was the original name for the village but when applying for a post office they were refused. Don Hunter was the first postmaster in Marshall when the application was refused. He made an executive decision to apply for the Post Office designation using his oldest daughter, Fortuna, as part of the name. Because Marshall was on a ledge overlooking the Yukon River he added Ledge, Fortuna Ledge. But, as he expected most people referred to the village as Marshall.

Marshall was established in 1913 when gold was discovered. Alaska Native people lived in close proximity to the area before that time, consequently several families settled into Marshall and never left. Our assigned teacher housing was a building constructed for the Bureau of Land Management in the 1930s. It was a two-story house that looked over the Yukon River.

Maintenance on buildings in Alaska was always a challenge with the extreme climate and lack of consistent upkeep. The house looked large from the outside but we were only allowed to use the bottom floor. In August when we arrived we had running water to the kitchen sink, it lasted only a short time. Given there was no bathroom in our assigned housing arrangement we used a honey bucket.

None of the buildings in Marshall had running water, except for the school. Often in rural villages only schools and teacher housing had running water. The school building had three small classrooms, an office closet for the head teacher, a kitchen cafeteria to serve students breakfast and lunch, male and female bathrooms, and a teacher-housing unit. The apartment in the school building had two bedrooms, a kitchen, a bathroom, and living room.

Interestingly, the running water worked only in the teacher apartment and school kitchen, but not in the school bathrooms. Students and staff (Jed and I) used the outhouses located out of the building. When the temperatures hit zero degrees or colder no one lingered outside.

School was to start in a week, so we found ourselves busy. The first few days we focused on unpacking and learning about life in Marshall. The biggest adjustment was related to the lack of privacy. Using a honey bucket when camping was one thing but having it as a daily requirement was quite another. Luckily, we had a mudroom entrance to the house with a closet we used for the honey bucket. Now I understood the question during the interview, "Can you empty a honey bucket?"

Bathing was another issue. The other teaching couple offered us the use of their fully functioning bathroom with shower and tub. Using someone else's bathroom occasionally was reasonable, but quickly gets old when it was the only option. Dragging all the necessary items across a muddy path when it was raining or snowing or the wind was blowing sideways had its own set of challenges. We were determined to figure out another alternative.

In 1972, rural communities in Alaska didn't have high schools. If families wanted their son or daughter to attend high school the student left home in mid-August. Alaska boarding schools were in Anchorage, Bethel, Galena, Mt. Edgecumbe, Nenana, Nome, St. Mary's, or Unalakleet. Some teens even traveled out of state as far away as Chemawa Indian School in Salem, Oregon and Chilocco Indian School in Chilocco, Oklahoma. Many of these young people didn't return to their village until May. A few were gone for the entire four years of high school. If a Marshall family was lucky, their child attended the Bethel Boarding School so periodic home visits were easier. It was understandable that many young people opted not to attend high school.

Part I: Going to Alaska

Life at Fifty Below Zero

PART II

Teaching and Learning

Me in Marshall teaching
December 1972

"*Send not your foolish and feeble; send me your strong and your sane.*"

—Robert W. Service, *Law of the Yukon*

Marshall

August 25, 1972

Alaska had four time zones, Pacific, Yukon, Alaska, and Bering, when we arrived. East of Bering Time was the International Date Line, which meant it was the next day. Facts like this reminded me how huge Alaska was. Settling into Marshall, we realized the many adjustments we were making. Increased daylight as we traveled the ALCAN was just the beginning. The lack of privacy, no running water and access to phones, and few stores were sobering. The lack of newspapers or magazines, TV, and only one radio station resulted in limited information about the world. For some reason a Christian radio station out of Nome came in clear as a bell—the connection to the 'outside of Marshall world.' *Thank you Jesus!*

An itinerant Jesuit priest, Father Petersen, made his monthly visits to Marshall, often joining us for dinner. He didn't try to convert us, but was open to different beliefs. His focus was on nurturing the needs of people along the Yukon. Sometimes he provided news about activities in other villages similar to Marshall. We were hungry for news. When a newspaper was left we devoured it.

Villages of less than three hundred people had few public buildings making the school a hub for health or public service meetings and appointments. They met with people, conducted patient checkups, and even pulled a few teeth using a corner closet of the school building as a clinic during the day or a classroom at night.

We offered dinner to travelers when the principal teacher didn't capitalize on their visit. When a magazine was offered we graciously accepted. We pieced together information about the Watergate scandal and other news events around the world. Because world news was part of our daily existence before arriving in Marshall we found we missed that aspect in our new life.

Both the BIA and ASOSS educational systems controlling education in rural Alaska had structured viewpoints of what *should* be taught to Alaska Native children. Parents weren't included in educational and instructional decisions. For centuries Alaska Native people taught their children by having them observe a task. This teaching and learning strategy was never shared with teachers so it was disregarded unless teachers figured it out. Many students struggled in schools.

Administrators' travel out to rural schools was time consuming and uncomfortable for many. Their visits to schools required an overnight stay. With no hotels or motels in villages, visitors slept on the floor in the school unless the teachers had an extra bed to offer. Some hired a charter, others waited for the next mail plane. The lack of conveniences resulted in minimal school administrative supervision.

Individuals hired to teach in bush schools in 1972 had a considerable amount of autonomy and independence. Teachers primarily came from out of state. Many Alaska Native people and other people who lived in Alaska referred to these states as the 'lower 48' or 'outside.' There were limited opportunities for children in rural Alaska villages and communities to attend school past eighth grade and even fewer Alaska Natives attended college. The few Alaska Natives who completed college seldom became teachers or school administrators. The University of Alaska Fairbanks was developing a program to change this pattern. It was time Alaska Natives were allowed to be involved in local educational decisions.

Unbeknownst to us, a lawsuit against the State of Alaska for failing to provide equal access to education for rural students was brewing. Alaska became a state in 1959 and yet only children living in larger locations of the state had access to high schools. Non-native people made educational decisions with no connection to local communities. Rural students weren't receiving meaningful and relevant education and it was time for that to change.

To make matters worse, many Alaska Native adults had emotional and psychological scars from having their mouths washed out with soap by missionaries for speaking their native language. The cultural disrespect of missionaries created generational trauma for many Alaska Natives. The formation of the Alaska Federation of Natives[2] (1966) and support from a group of educators at the University of Alaska Fairbanks started positive changes in education and other social issues. A major outcome was Alaska Natives began to understand they had rights regarding their children's education.[3]

The number of children in a community determined the number of teachers for a rural school. Marshall had forty-eight children so it was allocated three teachers for its K–8 school. The teachers, not their degrees, guided decisions about who taught a specific content area. A secondary factor that affected teacher workload arrangements was one of the three teachers, the principal teacher, had administrative duties.

During our earlier visit to Marshall, a brief conversation about class assignments took place with the principal teacher. When we returned he told us his staffing decision. He divided the students into three groups:

K–3, thirteen students; grades 4–6, twelve students; and grades 6–8, twenty-three students. His second decision was about content assignment areas. Besides teaching grades K–3, I was to teach reading and writing to all students. Jed would teach grades 4–6, plus social studies to all students. Ben, the principal teacher would cover grades 6–8 and math to some of the students. When we taught his students he had time for the administrative tasks that were part of his job.

We asked about science, art, music, and PE and were told those areas weren't necessary. He felt students needed reading, writing, arithmetic, and some social studies. His attitude was if they remained in the village they didn't need schooling and if they moved they would do unskilled labor. We didn't agree, but managed to keep our mouths shut and thoughts to ourselves. Later we learned this was his third year in Alaska and he hadn't attended any orientation session.

Jed and I talked over how we would weave art, music, science and PE into our classroom groups. We felt confident between our teaching preparation programs and the information from the summer program we were adequately equipped for integrating different subjects. At first the idea of teaching across eight grades was overwhelming. But, thanks to the experienced bush teachers who provided strategies for different grades we felt prepared to meet the needs of the different students.

Not having running water we became aware of the time daily life tasks took, as well as the responsibility of teaching several grades. Jed and I worked together as a team in teaching reading, writing, math, and social studies. We wove science and art into lessons. Combining subjects became easier as we used information from the community.

Part II: Teaching and Learning

One evening we remembered a trip we took on the Yukon River when we first arrived in Marshall. A fellow Jed met offered to take us for a ride in his jon boat. Jon boats were very flat and had squared-off bows. They were efficient boats for rivers and smaller lakes because they could operate in shallow water.

As we traveled on the Yukon he pointed out various landmarks the community used. We decided to utilize those on a map we created for Marshall, which was later expanded to include neighboring villages. These led to discussions about maps to Bethel, Anchorage, Fairbanks, Nome, and beyond. Maps became relevant, meaningful and useful as an educational instrument. Students wrote stories about locations on the maps.

Our interactions with people in Marshall were useful in our lesson planning. Everyone was friendly and open to us. The relationships we established with different community members provided us hope for the school year. Whenever we shared ideas with the principal teacher he said, "We don't do things like that out here in bush Alaska." We stopped offering suggestions and started doing our own planning. We learned quickly it was better to ask forgiveness, than permission.

One evening as we walked Hidalgo, we saw people busy preparing for winter. We asked questions about winter and the differences in the weather patterns. The answers helped us use Native cultural understandings about changes in the environment across the seasons. The local input assisted us in using local history as a starting point to larger historical events. We knew men were out hunting since older students were out of school for a day. I learned from the women about different berries they harvested. Some of the berries I had never heard of like salmonberries and crowberries.

Jed and I discussed a field trip to gather berries. We thought the experience would be a great lesson covering several subject areas. A couple of the village women agreed to help. It seemed to me berries in Alaska were like berries anywhere and would be strong enough to create different dye colors. We made sure the field trip didn't interfere with the regular routine of classes.

The day for the big field trip arrived. It was gray, overcast, and cool with a light breeze. While the principal teacher was busy with administrative tasks, we took off with the students and parents. I was happy the bugs were less aggressive with chillier nights. The light breeze reassured me the bugs wouldn't eat me alive.

Students were grouped into small teams with different assignments: a) collect three different berries, b) write down what elders say about the berries, and c) help younger students pick berries and offer a word about the activity. The two women who assisted in planning the field trip were experts from the village. They reminded us to tell the students to wear boots for tundra walking.

Jed and I knew tundra was challenging to walk through. People twisted their ankles badly trying to walk through arctic tundra if they weren't on the right path. Arctic tundra was different than alpine tundra. Although arctic tundra was found in various places in the world it was more common in Canada and Alaska. It had a unique ecosystem comprised of hardy shrubs, grasses, mosses, and lichen that lived in knee-high communities making it difficult to walk. We didn't want our field trip bogged down with anyone having their boots sucked off their feet or ankles twisted. Our village guides were invaluable in helping us find the right trails to the berries and in many other ways.

When we returned to the school the principal asked where we took the students. We told him about our field trip with the two parent guides. He was surprised and a little perplexed. The next day students developed stories about the berry picking process. No one had ever made dye so all were intrigued and excited. We arranged to use the school kitchen to boil the berries. Hot liquid and kids made me nervous.

With muslin from my sewing supplies students experienced tie-dying a piece of fabric with the finished dyes. Our parent 'berry experts' helped with the berry boiling and tie-dying experience. It was successful and no injuries occurred. The adults and students were pleased with the final projects. Students saw their parents respected as educational teachers. The final task involved writing the science process listing each step. Students studied the charts created and talked about things that happened with each step.

We established respect with community members in Marshall through events like berry collecting. We asked for their advice and opinions. When we asked about their culture they glowed with eagerness to share. We honestly wanted to know what they felt their children should be learning in school. Weaving their culture into social studies lessons made it easier for students to understand larger historical events.

Bush schools held monthly Community Advisory meetings, a requirement of the State Operated Schools system. For the most part this was a 'sit and get' meeting with three-four community members and the school staff. The principal teacher delivered information and asked if there were any questions. We learned from talking to people in the community they wanted a Christmas holiday event. The current principal teacher hadn't held one since arriving in the village. Instead of asking the principal beforehand, we offered to plan and organize the

Christmas Program during the Community Advisory meeting. The three community members thought it was a great idea so the principal reluctantly agreed. It was obvious he wasn't pleased.

Adjusting to food in rural Alaska was difficult for me. I grew up in Hawaii and lived in California during college and my first years of teaching. I was accustomed to plenty of fresh food. As the boxes of food we bought in Anchorage were eaten up I began to get anxious. The darkness limited afterschool berry picking, so I did what I could on the weekends. With no phones to place orders and only two planes a week, the food we ordered was slow to arrive.

My cravings for fresh produce made me like a junkie. On the days the mail plane came in I hoofed it to the store to see if anything fresh was delivered. Eating a salad, a piece of fruit or vegetable was on my mind constantly. When one of the first boxes of food arrived I was home alone. Jed dropped the boxes off and finished delivering the mail to the school. As I began unpacking the box my mouth actually started watering when I saw two heads of iceberg lettuce (*I really didn't even like iceberg that much, but it was all I could order.*).

Before I knew what I was doing I tore off the outer leaves from one of the heads and started stuffing it in my mouth. As Jed walked in I sheepishly looked up and offered him the final leaves from the first head. I didn't even feel guilty. It was a necessary act for my sanity. I sat there innocently on the floor, smiled at him and said, "Here Jed, maybe you would like a bite." He was kind and said he would wait and share it with me later. I thanked him and proceeded quietly to put the remaining groceries away.

The village store got bananas once in a while, but they were generally black. I made banana bread. Unfortunately, it wasn't the same as a fresh banana. I daydreamed of being a child in Hawaii where I sat on the roof picking bananas from a tree next to our house. Oranges and apples that arrived weren't like California produce. Fruit and vegetables were often soft. Dairy products like cheese, ice cream, cottage cheese, yogurt, and eggs were never available at the Marshall store. We learned about powdered Milkman during the summer, which came in quart size packages. It was easy to prepare and tasted good when it was cold, especially with cookies.

The food adjustment required strategic planning. Frozen food orders came from Seattle or Anchorage, at least two airplane rides with stops in between. Alaska would soon be a giant freezer. I just needed to wait. A case of frozen spinach, that I was constantly craving, couldn't be ordered until freeze-up. We brought in cans of green beans and corn that were only so tolerable. (*Now, I can't stomach canned green beans.*) I was definitely learning patience and gratitude. I always took fresh food for granted.

My students were excited about learning and happy to be in school. Discipline wasn't an issue. Kids arrived on time and followed the simple classroom guidelines developed together. They loved recess, even at minus twelve degrees (and colder). Nonetheless, there was one major hurdle requiring a solid directive from me. A culturally accepted practice was that children as young as five or six chewed snuff. I knew nothing about snuff except watching students spit made my stomach queasy.

When indoors they used trashcans as spittoons. Every time someone spit I was sure I was going to participate, only I wouldn't be spitting. For some reason I couldn't stomach watching and made a rule in my classroom 'no chewing and no spitting.' At first students were upset with me, but were good-natured about the rule and agreed. I was relieved, but my stomach was still nauseous. Maybe my mind anticipated the spitting, but it was something different.

After settling into village life, we realized it was time to figure out the Christmas program. Since Marshall was primarily Russian Orthodox, students only had Monday, Christmas Day, off. Jed's parents and my mother were coming for the holiday so initially we were disappointed about the lack of time off. Our new life was difficult to explain in letters. Helping at school and seeing daily routines would be a great opportunity for them. Nothing was sugar coated when people had no running water and everyone used the *same* honey bucket.

School holidays and vacations were different in rural Alaska. The typical school winter break of two weeks and the spring one-week vacation weren't always the norm. Many of the smaller Yup'ik rural villages followed the Orthodox Christian traditions. The Russian Orthodox Slaviq Christmas holiday kept to the older Julian calendar. The celebration lasted three days, and occurred the second week of January. We were excited knowing we would experience this holiday first hand.

To get started with planning for the Christmas program we reached out to the two women who helped us with the berry picking field trip. They assured us the past tradition of holding the program in the Marshall community hall on Christmas Eve at 6:30 p.m. was the best choice. The community hall was a building with two entrances and an oil heater used only when an event was planned. There were folding tables and chairs for the different activities held in the building. Wednesday night Bingo sessions, Friday or Saturday movie nights, and special village potlatches and meetings were regular occurrences.

Everyone was invited to community events when they happened. Children spread the word—Movie tonight!—throughout the village, people showed up, and the movie started within an hour of the start-time. Announcements were also made with a note pinned at the post office or on the door of the building. We went to almost every movie night since we had arrived. The movies were on old 35mm reels and weren't recent releases. No one even knew the name of the movie, but they usually attended anyway.

Seldom did any event start on time. Alaska Native village time was a moving target since there was no other place to go or anything else to do. Another factor was that it was important to wait for everyone to get there. I never understood how the decision about people coming and when to start was made. My patience was often tried in the waiting. I had a lot to learn about Native ways.

Finally, we had a consistent group of people who met three times to talk about the Christmas program. The discussions were good with group ownership. They decided the schedule would include a parent reading the nativity story, children singing Christmas hymns in Yup'ik, and children performing Yup'ik dancing. Eskimo dancing was my favorite so I joined in the practices with the students. Marshall had some of the finest dancing we had seen. A few community events occurred where we saw the adults dance. I loved watching them move to the drumming.

While in Fairbanks we saw the World Eskimo-Indian Olympics[4] (WEIO). It was an annual event held four days in July on the University of Alaska Fairbanks campus. A group of us attended because we heard some of our villages would have dancers. We really didn't know what it was about until we saw it with our own eyes.

Marshall was one of the few villages where both women and men danced. Male elders were generally the drummers. The dancing was a treat to watch. When a couple of the younger men danced their bodies performed similar to finely toned athletes. The difference was they weren't focused on speed or moving the ball. The dancers mimicked the rhythm of the drums and told a story using body movement. Sometimes they were the animal being hunted or the hunter or a bird in flight. It was mesmerizing.

With the Christmas Eve program planned and rehearsals scheduled, we felt pleased about our contribution in the village. Students were learning and enjoyed our lessons. The few extracurricular activities we implemented were well attended by students. With permission from the principal teacher and the Community Advisory group, we held a couple of dances for the 6–8 graders. All the students participated in some way. Mostly they played games and listened to music, but they called it a dance.

The teachers we met in Tok during the trip up the ALCAN invited us to their village for Thanksgiving break. Once we confirmed Marshall had the whole four days off, we arranged for a charter to Togiak. Excitement was in the air with our first outing out of Marshall.

Togiak was 203 air miles almost directly south of Marshall in the Bristol Bay area. The charter saved time and potential delays at each spot. The mail plane route was four flights: 1 Marshall to Bethel, 2 Bethel to Anchorage, 3 Anchorage to Dillingham, and 4 Dillingham to Togiak. The charter was direct, Marshall to Togiak, done. In the short window of four days we wanted to spend time visiting.

Part II: Teaching and Learning

John and Mary were hired as part of the teaching staff to start the small high school program. Togiak was twice the size of Marshall and a much wealthier community because of fishing in Bristol Bay. Eskimos in Togiak were also Yup'ik but opportunities for making money were different from Marshall. One of the community members told John if he fished for two months he would make more money than teaching nine months.

The trip to Togiak was a needed vacation. Besides valuable time spent visiting with our friends we had conversations with other like-minded educators about helping students thrive. We felt revived and content our efforts in Marshall were meaningful. Alaska's famous weather decided we needed a longer break. A huge storm blew in the day we were to leave Togiak with no flights in or out for three additional days. The gift to us was watching the Bering Sea in a turbulent battle with itself.

Time went quickly when we returned to Marshall. Our regular teaching schedule, rehearsals, and holiday baking made the days fly. On Wednesday, December 20, my mother and Jed's parents arrived. Their flight was delayed out of Anchorage so they missed the mail plane to Marshall. Luckily, Jed prepared his dad for obstacles such as missed planes, especially mail planes that only traveled twice a week. With daylight rapidly closing in, the travel gods were in their corner. They immediately called the charter service and were in the air to Marshall within forty-five minutes upon arrival in Bethel. Don Hunter, the postmaster knew they were coming, but we didn't.

Often during lunchtime Jed took Hidalgo for a short walk. When he heard a plane he rushed back home, jumped on the snow machine, and arrived on the river at the same time Don Hunter did in his truck.

Because our parents weren't on the morning mail plane we wondered where they were. Hearing a second plane gave us hope they had connected to the charter into Marshall. *Before going to Alaska I thought only rich people chartered airplanes. In Alaska charters were similar to taxis in New York City.*

    The last few minutes of the Cessna 205 charter flight was a little intense for our precious passengers. Halfway across the tundra a trim fin cable snapped creating a little extra work for the pilot. Our parents were shook up to say the least. The seasoned pilot cut the air speed in half and demonstrated his highly skilled piloting as he gently brought the skis down on the Yukon.

    Their luggage was several boxes and a few small bags (one change of clothes for the week). They hauled fresh produce, ice cream, and eggnog on many flights and one overnight. Their flights started in Los Angeles with a stop in Seattle before flying on to Anchorage. They had one night in Anchorage before heading to Bethel and the charter into Marshall. I always wondered what my father-in-law paid to arrange for the food to be put in a freezer and refrigerator at the hotel. His Cary Grant looks and personality helped him, I am sure.

    When Jed returned to school, he told me about our parents' exhilarating moments during the landing. I was thrilled AND extremely grateful knowing they were safely on the ground. When I arrived home I saw ten heads of lettuce, tomatoes, avocados, cheese, tortillas, grapes, oranges, and apples. My saucer-sized eyes filled with water exposing my excitement. Everyone received big hugs, especially my father-in-law. I was gracious and courteous and didn't start eating the lettuce immediately.

Part II: Teaching and Learning

The next day was December 21, the shortest day of the year. At 7:00 a.m. the local radio station (one and only), two hundred air miles north in Nome stated the sun would rise at 11:04 a.m. and set at 2:58 p.m. It was pitch dark, our new normal, but not for our parents. Daylight would occur at 9:45 a.m. and dusk would be at 4:10 p.m. If we were in Barrow the sun would set in November and not show up again until February. Depending on the phase of the moon the evening light varied. When there was no moon people used flashlights, but when the moon became full the snow reflected light off the snow. Despite our enthusiasm in sharing time with our family, Jed and I hurried over to school for the start of our day.

It was a distracting two days at work but fun. Our parents came over to help each day and, of course, the kids stopped at our house in the evenings. They were in awe of my hair when we first arrived in the village because it was red with blonde streaks. Many little hands were all over my head to see if light hair felt the same as their beautiful dark hair. When they saw Harold's hair once again they wanted to touch it. They had never seen a man with two colors of hair on his head, gray and white. He was good hearted about their need for a tactile investigation.

Visiting in rural villages was different than what I was accustomed to in the lower 48. Children knocked on the door and said the word *visit*; then we were to say *yes* or *no*. When they first visited, I sat down as if to chat, to 'visit' with them. But, the kids sat, maybe raised their eyebrows looked at each other, and read comics or magazines. The visit was genuinely about being in each other's presence. The people visited were to keep doing what they were doing. It was obvious they were comfortable with us because they visited often and usually without any conversation. After my awkward adjustment to this form of visiting, I found I liked it. They wanted to learn about us just as we wanted to learn about them.

We thought our parents would enjoy helping select a Christmas tree so, Saturday morning, December 23 we headed out. The thermometer read minus twenty degrees and the radio confirmed the chill factor hovered at minus fifty-five degrees. Chill factor was calculated by how much wind moved, lowering the overall temperature. Wind chill increased the amount of body heat a person lost when out in the cold. I felt after minus twenty-five what was the difference? It was damn cold, hard to breathe, and finding enough clothes (or maybe the right clothes) to put on wasn't easy.

Our parents put on all the clothes they borrowed and brought, plus items we gathered from village friends. We wore the down jackets I had made, snow pants, fur ruffs (hoods), plus other assorted clothes. Jed drove the snow machine with his father on the sled runners. Many village families still had dog teams and not just 'iron dogs' (snow machines). All three of us, Jed's mother, my mother and I were in the sled. Body warmth was helpful at times and this was one of those times. Hidalgo ran along beside us. Soltar stayed home watching from the sun-warmed window ledge. She was the smartest of the bunch.

Five miles up the Yukon we found trees. It amazed me how quickly a tree decision was made in the extreme cold, especially in an area with limited picture perfect trees. Who cared one side was lean on branches? We agreed once it was decorated, no one would notice the missing branches. When we returned the principal teacher stopped by to say he and his wife had decided to go to Anchorage for the holiday weekend. We were now completely on our own for hosting and ensuring the Christmas Eve program went well.

We spent the rest of the day and evening decorating the tree. The rush of the family's arrival and teaching the first two days had drained us. Knowing the next day would be consumed with the Christmas program, we felt it was time to relax for the rest of the day and evening. We also wanted to announce our big news without any more interruptions. The village public health doctor confirmed our suspicions I was pregnant. It was exciting news for us. There were questions about how often I would see a doctor since the one that came through the village wouldn't be back for six to nine months. The baby was due in June and school was out in May so I hoped to deliver in California.

I was twenty-seven and ready to be a mom. The last six months had been full of surprises, changes, and adjustments—perfect timing. One perk of being pregnant was that I didn't have to empty the honey bucket. Even at two-thirds full a five-gallon bucket was heavy. We learned halfway was a good point. It took one time of being too full and a person understood the limits of a bucket. I was happy to be relieved of that duty. Yippee!

Christmas Eve, time for the big program arrived. At noon Jed and his dad made a trip to the community hall to check if the heat was on. A bingo event had occurred the night before so the heater was left on. Students arrived to arrange the chairs and set the tables to the side. There was anticipation in the community. Kids stopped at the house to ask about the time. They knew we were to be at the hall by 6:00 p.m. When everyone was there it was packed to capacity.

The program started and moved along without any hiccups. Our cultural mentors explained students and adults would wear typical dance regalia. Women wore *qaspeq*[5] (Yup'ik) with beaded and fur-fringed headdresses and dancing fans. Male dancers wore *qaspeq* style shirts with gloves. Men started on their knees before standing to finish a dance. Women always stood. Everyone wore fur and skin *mukluks* (boots). The drummers were in the back. I was excited when one of the Yup'ik dancing teachers showed up at the performance with a headdress and hand fans for me to use. What an honor! I hadn't planned to participate in the Christmas program. The opportunity to practice and learn was wonderful. Now I was part of the program—what a gift!

During the World Eskimo Indian Olympics we learned missionaries had banned Eskimo dancing for a period of time. Alaska Native languages weren't in a written format, so they kept their culture strong through oral traditions, such as storytelling and dancing. The stories preserved the history, geographical locations, and kept cultural traditions alive. Each dance told a story about hunting, berry picking, cultural activities, and everyday life.

While attending the summer orientation program, guest speaker Dr. Michael Krauss shared information about the creation of an Alaska Native Language Center. The Alaska legislature funded the new Center during the 1972 session. The purpose was to document, preserve, and assist in creating a written format of the twenty Indian, Aleut, and Eskimo languages in Alaska. The goal for the Center, located on the University of Alaska Fairbanks campus, was to become the primary institute to study all northern languages.

The Christmas program went well. All of the children received gifts. The church and community council arranged for each child to receive candy, nuts, apples, and oranges. When all of the activities finished everyone went home to rest before the Christmas midnight mass service. Although most people followed the Russian Orthodox Church, they attended the Catholic Church services that Father Peterson held. The midnight Christmas Eve mass was extra special. We were exhausted but knew this was a unique opportunity so we pushed ourselves to attend. It was worth the extra effort because the program included the Russian Orthodox priest presenting his message in Yup'ik. The peaceful blending of the religious leadership was comforting to my soul and a true representation of the meaning of the season.

After the midnight festivities we headed home and indulged in warm eggnog toddies, which helped us fall sound asleep. At 3:00 a.m. we heard Christmas carolers outside the door. One of us managed to open the door, pass out freshly baked cookies, and wish everyone happy holidays before stumbling back to bed. Christmas Day we shared family gifts and attended another big event, the Marshall community potluck dinner, at the hall. Our parents tasted a few new food items: smoked dried salmon, moose head soup, ptarmigan, walrus, and Eskimo ice cream, *akutuq*. I struggled with the Eskimo ice cream especially after indulging in the rich, creamy ice cream from *31 Flavors* brought from California. *Akutuq* was made with ground white fish, whale blubber[6], sugar and wild Alaskan berries. Blueberries and salmon berries were the favorite ones used. All the ingredients were stirred and stirred and stirred by hand since no one had electric beaters or blenders. I felt it was an acquired taste.

Although it wasn't easy we managed to make it to work on December 26. All the students were happy and feeling a bit of the sugar rush, as well as excitement from the events that took place over the three days. Adding to the chaos, our friends from Togiak arrived. Since Togiak was a bigger community and school they had a longer break than we did.

Our parents enjoyed visiting with John and Mary while we taught. The next day our parents were scheduled to leave. When they called Don Hunter about the mail plane he said, "The mail plane might not come. The pilot just radioed it has engine problems." This information wasn't encouraging. The mail plane airline wasn't known for its great service, so a decision to call the charter service was made. The charter airlines had an excellent reputation and were exceptionally reliable. A plane was on its way in five minutes. It was a smooth flight out of Marshall and beyond. They made all of the various connections arriving in Los Angeles at 10:00 a.m. December 28. The luggage going home was much lighter, only three sleeping bags and three small clothing bags, no ice cream or heads of lettuce went south.

Once again we had guests and had to work. John and Mary knew this when they planned the trip, but were interested in seeing our village. Their interest was piqued when we told them how different it was from Togiak.

John and Mary went to the school and helped Jed in teaching social studies. Since they were high school teachers and Marshall didn't have a high school, the students were interested in hearing about their school. John and Mary showed them where Togiak was on the map. They explained about the school and the different classes students took. The 6–8 graders were then given a 'roster of classes,' including information about required classes. Each of the students made a schedule as if they were attending high school in the fall. I believe the questions and discussion were as interesting for the adults as it was for the students.

On New Year's Eve there was a dance at the Marshall community hall, which Jed and I helped plan. The dances for students were held there so the adults asked if we would organize one for them. We were curious how this was going to turn out. Much to our surprise one of the village residents showed up with a record player and square dance records. Wow! Before we knew it we were in the middle of a square dance. Someone used the bingo microphone and called out the steps for various dances. It seemed a bit weird at first, but everyone relaxed and had a great time. We left having a good feeling about ringing in 1973.

Putting on our coats to leave someone said, "Be sure to turn your radio on because Don Hunter will be on the air at midnight." This seemed strange because Don was a quiet man and not talkative. Little did we know New Year's Eve was his special night to shine! The four of us chatted about the dance as we made our way home. I was grateful the moon reflected the snow illuminating our pathway. With no streetlights it was dark. No one wanted to tarry or get lost when it was below zero.

Don's annual message started as we tuned in the frequency. He was more relaxed than his normal self, which was fun. We wondered if he was a little tipsy since his speech seemed a little out of the ordinary. I could visualize him sitting by his oil stove with a cigarette dangling from his fingers as he told everyone, "1972 was a good year for Marshall and 1973 will be even better. Happy New Year everyone!"

Little did we know TVs across the nation people were hearing broadcasts about Nixon stopping the war in Vietnam. Or they were preparing to watch Elvis perform his *Aloha from Hawaii* show. We read later in *Time* magazine his show was big news since he was the first solo entertainer to broadcast live via satellite to over a billion people in forty countries. We knew nothing about either of these news events until early March. I saw Elvis live when I was a teenager growing up in Hawaii. He was filming *Blue Hawaii* and had a concert. I sometimes wondered if my mother was more excited than I.

John and Mary left and we just settled into our normal school routine when it was time for Russian Orthodox Slaviq (Christmas), January 8, 9, and 10. We enjoyed all the company, the welcomed break from our routine, and now there was another week that little, if any, schoolwork was accomplished.

Three school days were designated for Slaviq activities, but the schedule wasn't strictly followed. The shiny star visited each house in the village three times. Some village residents followed the shining star singing carols while others remained home cooking food for the festivities. A designated person carried the shiny, decorated star from one house to the next spinning it as he walked. We learned from a friend in the village the star represented Christ who was born, figuratively, in each house. Generally, the person who carried the star was a young man representing a holy person. Many villages were too small to have an official priest so lay leaders were selected by the village to help maintain these strong traditional ceremonies.

During the Christmas Potluck, we asked about the Slaviq holiday. In the excitement of the holidays, the students kept saying something about a star visiting our house. We wanted to be ready if something was expected of us. It was good we asked because food was expected when the star stopped by the third time. The best part was that we received a present.

Many rural Alaska villages had ceremonial events that included giving gifts. We learned how wise and practical people were because the presents were useful items. Sometimes they presented simple food items, blankets, pillows, gloves, or fabrics to make clothes. The Slaviq experience lasted four and a half days. The large decorated star looked like a sparkling pinwheel when the moonlight or village lights reflected off of it. It was a moving experience that created a sense of community and friendship.

Part II: Teaching and Learning

We learned a typical outcome experienced after Slaviq was that everyone got sick. People had little sleep during the four and a half days. Walking in subzero temperatures and then going in and out of warm houses for short visits wasn't conducive to staying healthy. Even though I wasn't one of the people going in and out of houses, I got sick. With temperatures below zero, it was impossible to leave a window open to bring in fresh air. Germs remained as unwanted visitors after people left and there was no way for them to escape. Visitors from nearby villages were in town. Some people came down with chicken pox and a few others with pneumonia. At least I didn't get either one of those serious ailments.

It was a difficult time for many people. To make matters worse, the weather was so cold no planes made it into Marshall for a full week. The local health aide was sick and flown to the hospital in Bethel. I felt miserable, but didn't feel comfortable taking medications we had because of my pregnancy. The cold I had was annoying, but there was no lingering cough.

School reconvened after Slaviq, but with the low attendance our classrooms were small until the end of January. The students showing up received individualized instruction based on their needs. Most of the one-on-one tutoring focused on strengthening literary skills, which was critical to all content areas. Not having a full class and feeling the need to catch up after the holiday events was frustrating at first, but then we relaxed and made the best use of the time.

Irritated from the lingering cold and wishing for sunshine and warmth, I suddenly felt something strange and realized the baby was kicking. The doctor, who visited in November and confirmed my pregnancy, told me when I sensed internal movement I was to arrange to see a doctor. We immediately took two days off and flew to Bethel to the Public Health Hospital. The doctor said everything was normal and right on schedule. He increased my iron, provided cautionary information, and gave me a schedule of how often I needed to see a doctor. Many women in rural communities didn't visit a doctor until the baby was ready to be delivered. Sometimes the repercussions of not having prenatal medical care ended with problems for the baby, mother, or both. Public Health Service providers were working to change that pattern. I knew it was important for me to be my own health advocate if I wanted a healthy baby.

We were anxious to get back to Marshall. After picking up a few items in Bethel for the school, we hopped the mail plane home. Weather was always an issue when traveling in Alaska and we didn't want to be stuck in Bethel. Plus, in a week the dog sled races started and Marshall was the first village on the race circuit. One of Marshall's residents, Charlie Fitka Jr., hoped to compete in the first Iditarod race in the spring, but couldn't find a sponsor. We knew he was a dedicated sled dog racer. We felt fortunate to be introduced to dog racing by seeing him race.

The dog races brought people from up and down the Yukon River. Over the weekend of February 16–18, 1973, there were an additional 150–200 people in Marshall. That was close to double the population. I had no idea where everyone stayed. People came and went on mail planes, charters, dog teams, and a few snow machines. Despite the dangers of traveling on the frozen Yukon River it was a common occurrence. Sled dogs were the best means of travel because they kept people warm if stops were necessary along the way to the destination. Snow machines were fast but they broke down. Breaking down when it was twenty degrees (or colder) below zero wasn't a happy way to end anyone's day.

We learned Marshall's dog race events included men's, women's, girls', and boys' dog team races. There were other activities: coaster sliding, snow machine runs, and a variety of general fun races, such as gunnysack and snowshoes. With no written program, it was difficult to figure out where the different events happened and starting times. It was a fantastic weekend and we were hooked on dog sled racing, especially Jed.

The weekend ended with a potlatch, an Alaskan Native tradition. We observed potlatches as special gatherings strengthening the social and cultural parts of villages. They always included food, storytelling, and often dancing. With no restaurants, everyone helped feed visitors. People knew when they traveled to other villages the kindness would be reciprocated. During the Christmas and Russian Orthodox holidays, it was obvious how these events reinforced the spiritual connections of the people to each other as well as their families.

School settled back into a routine. People didn't get sick after the dog races like they had after Slaviq. Students focused and we were glad to have a full class again. There was discussion about the Iditarod race about to start in Anchorage, especially by the Nome radio station. The Iditarod was based on a proud history and the dream of several different people.

Many of the students in our classrooms had never been anywhere other than to Bethel to see a doctor or to one of the close villages. Knowing how limited their perspective of the giant state was, we decided to use the Iditarod race for geography and math lessons. The few newspapers we found had articles about the struggles to organize a race

Dog team races on the frozen Yukon
February 1973

such as the Iditarod. Each musher needed twelve to sixteen dogs, a sled, and all his supplies for the epic journey.

Being new to dog mushing, we wanted to understand news hype versus the reality of such an adventure, so we contacted Charlie Fitka Jr. Two of his children were in our classes and Jed often talked to him about dog mushing. Charlie agreed to talk to our students about the Iditarod race and how different it was from the races in the village. After his visit students understood running dogs for a long-distance event was different than the races they saw on a weekend.

We discovered Joe Redington[7], originally from Pennsylvania, helped to organize the long-distance Iditarod Race from a dream to reality. Joe felt snow machines were replacing sled dogs so one of his goals was to save the sled dog culture and Alaskan huskies. The historical significance of the race was to reconstruct the freight route from Wasilla to Nome (1,150 miles), very different from air miles (650 miles). Iditarod mushers traveled as freight mushers did eighty years ago, carrying all the gear needed to reach the destination of Nome. They broke much of their own trail and ensured supplies weren't thrown off the sled. The gear carried included food for the dogs and musher, tools to fix a sled and dog harnesses, as well as an ax and branch cutter for fires or downed limbs along the trail.

The radio stations around the state actively communicated with each other to keep people informed as the mushers raced to Nome. In March 1973 the cold and wind chill factor dipped the temperatures in the minus thirty to minus fifty ranges. Breaking trail wasn't an easy task when the wind blew creating six to eight foot drifts. There were unknown open water spots and icy conditions. No one knew how long it would take the mushers, and if all who entered would reach Nome. It was a tough race. There were no checkpoints or support teams required or available in 1973.

We used information from the radio and newspapers, when available, and travelers who came through Marshall to develop Iditarod lessons. Students calculated the distances mushers traveled as soon as we received a report. Learning math in a relevant concrete approach was different than utilizing a textbook. Even Don Hunter became involved giving us information he heard on the radio. Students came into school in the morning asking if we knew anything or they would come in saying their dad or uncle heard about a musher he knew. It was exciting and stimulating classroom chatter.

In 1973, twenty-two people finished the first Iditarod dog race, nicknamed 'The Last Great Race on Earth.' Forty people entered, twenty-two finished, twelve scratched, and a few didn't get started. Twenty of the people who completed received a monetary prize. The city of Nome collected funds to supplement what the Iditarod committee awarded hoping to give everyone that crossed the finish line something. The winner, a rookie musher, finished the event in twenty days while others took thirty plus days. One dog died. Some mushers broke down and fell in the ice. By the first week of April everyone was glad it was finished. Conversations about needed improvements for the 1974 Iditarod Race started, but the 1973 inaugural event was successful!

The annual Alaska Teachers' Job Fair happened in March. We decided travel to the big city of Anchorage would serve several purposes. It was time to see a doctor, shopping chores were needed, and the idea of eating at a restaurant sounded fun. Even Jed agreed shopping might be a fun diversion.

Part II: Teaching and Learning

The real reason for going was to investigate other villages to teach in. Despite enjoying the students and Marshall the tension with the third teacher was unproductive. Our desire to help students enjoy learning was constantly stifled by the negative interactions. The Job Fair provided a venue to talk with other districts and find out if we were the problem. Our regional superintendent was located in Anchorage, so we could also talk with him.

Anchorage was fun and informative. We saw friends from the orientation program and shopped, real shopping, where we walked into a store, paid for something, and walked out with the product. I saw a doctor (another new one) and we attended the Alaska Teacher Job Fair. We discovered openings in rural villages were plentiful. We liked our regional superintendent and felt comfortable being honest with him. We candidly discussed people we were comfortable working with. We were open to location and the lack of running water wasn't an issue for us.

Returning to Marshall, we realized how long the days were. It was the last week in March and the eleven to twelve hours of daylight felt energizing. We made it through our first winter of darkness! The temperatures didn't feel like spring, but hovered at zero most of the time. With more sunshine during the day it didn't seem as bad.

The big old house we lived in was drafty but had a great view of the Yukon, which changed with the seasons. The Yukon was the third longest river in North America and the longest in the Yukon and Alaska. The word Yukon originated from the Gwich'in language (Athabaskan Indian) meaning 'Great River.' During the Klondike Gold Rush, the Yukon River was a primary means of transportation. In early fall the Yukon was framed with a full assortment of colors generated from the leaves of the different trees. Later when the mighty Yukon froze life along the river changed.

Winter brought out the grays and whites of the snow depending on the light and time of day. After freeze-up planes and other vehicles were allowed to land and travel on the frozen surface. I never thought a river could freeze but there it was out my front window for me to see each day. No plane fell through the ice, so I became a believer. I knew the ice was carefully inspected to ensure the depth was thick enough. 'River taxis,' usually Suburban type cars, out of Bethel traveled to several of the villages on the Yukon. I shook my head at the idea.

One of the visual perks of the old house was watching the activity on the river. It was like living at an airport with aircraft landing every few days. The view most of the year was a landscape of ice covered with snow. Occasionally, the wind blew the snow around so it fell off the trees and bushes, providing a small hint of color between the different shades of white produced by the snow and ice.

We continued to enjoy teaching. Students were easily motivated and appreciated the effort we put into the lessons planned for them. Occasionally, there was a distraction because someone had a family difficulty. Marshall was small and it seemed everyone was related to everyone. But, after we talked to a few families we found out they weren't. When young people reached marrying age there were opportunities to marry from the other forty-plus villages around Bethel and up and down the Yukon.

One thing was clear—everyone knew each other. When a tragedy happened like a death or severe illness in a family everyone was affected. People came together and supported the family most touched. We noticed sometimes when these occurred a student might struggle a bit more and display unusual behavior. Students let us know if something was going on. One of my students, a young seven-year-old named Betty, had an unusual habit of humping the corner of her desk for several minutes.

Part II: Teaching and Learning

When this first happened students called out, "Mrs. Reagle, Mrs. Reagle, Betty is fucking her desk." I was helping students in a reading group. I looked up and there was Betty going to town on her desk. I didn't know what to do. I rose from my kid-size chair and went over to Betty touching her shoulder. My hand brought her back to the 'here and now,' from the trance she seemed to be in. Jed and I discussed this and couldn't really determine a reason it occurred. Her family seemed to be fine, no issues or family problems we saw or anyone mentioned. So when students let me know Betty was at it again, I quietly went to her desk and distracted her to other tasks. There were no counseling services through the district or community at the time.

The regional superintendent, Jerry, made his annual trip out in early April. With the milder spring weather and longer days, business travel increased. During his one-day visit we met as a full staff and individually. Before his visit we told the principal teacher we wouldn't be returning. This information increased the tension but we wanted it out in the open. We also wanted a say in how it was announced to the village.

During Jerry's visit we were told there was an opening in Anvik, a two-teacher school. It sounded perfect. Anvik was on the Yukon, northeast of Marshall. The area had steep mountains, tall timbers, and lots of snow. The current teachers started a cross-country skiing program. Friends in the lower 48 gathered older skis and sent them to Anvik. Students enjoyed the activity so the teachers said they would leave the skis. Jed and I were downhill skiers so we figured we could learn to cross-country ski. No problem! The baby could ride on our backs.

Jerry said the village had alcohol issues, something we hadn't dealt with in Marshall. We agreed we would figure out how to work around the issues. Rural Alaskan villages were usually dry, *no alcohol,* or wet, *alcohol allowed*. Despite being a dry village, bootleggers brought alcohol into the community by boat or air. Some of the airlines wouldn't carry alcohol to villages that stated they were dry. We heard rumors alcohol could be an issue in a village, but felt confident we could handle situations involving the school.

Alaska had a selection system when teachers were hired in villages. The first teachers to be placed in openings were those who taught three or more years in Alaska (had tenure) and wanted a specific school. The next group was composed of teachers requesting a school, but had less than three years in Alaska, and the third group was the new teachers from out of Alaska. We fell into group two. We were excited and frustrated, but realized this was a typical education protocol. We needed to be patient.

As the days became longer everyone was outside walking and enjoying the warmer temperatures. I was amazed at how my perspective of a warm day changed over the year. In Hawaii the weather was always perfect, maybe a little rain on a day I wanted to surf, but nothing to complain about. When I moved to California to attend college, I was cold because the winters dropped into the high forties (above zero). Now it was spring in Marshall and I saw people outside in short sleeves when it was in the twenties and thirties. It seemed crazy but I sure was glad to see the sun and feel its warmth. I admit I wasn't one of the people outside in short sleeves. However, an opportunity to be outside and enjoy longer days was delightful.

The weather on Easter Sunday, April 22, 1973, was sunny and in the midthirties. Knowing our time in Marshall was coming to a close, we decided to hike upriver. The hike was exhilarating and we enjoyed a small lunch sitting by the majestic Yukon River. We were appreciating

Climbing Mt. Pilcher
April 1973

the opportunity to be in Alaska. Before heading back we decided to stop and visit a gold miner we had befriended who had a small cabin near Marshall.

Bill was in his eighties. Some people felt he was a bit crazy, others thought he had great wisdom. He still worked a gold mine located fifty miles away from his cabin that he reached by foot. Gold mining only happened in the summer after the frozen rivers and creeks started flowing in late spring. During the hardest months of winter, Bill left Marshall and went somewhere. No one knew where he went, but he always returned. Jed and I enjoyed his stories, his warm spirit, and his abundant interest in life. I even warmed up to his 'miners' coffee,' which was a required part of the visit. Miners' coffee was water and coffee grounds boiled in a tin pot and poured. There were always grounds in my cup, which I didn't care for, but grew accustomed to.

Two weeks before our outing up river and visit with Bill, we organized a group of students to climb up Mt. Pilcher. Sixteen students, grades third through eighth, agreed to join us. We planned a lunch for all and off we went. Mt. Pilcher was located behind Marshall and was one of the tallest mountains in that part of Western Alaska. The peak was two thousand feet above sea level and provided a commanding view of the tundra. The scene from the top was astounding. The panoramic view was something only a *National Geographic* photographer could capture. Many bush pilots didn't even fly this high.

Being less than two months from my due date I was proud of myself. Many of our students had never hiked up to this spot despite its proximity to their home. We roasted marshmallows and made sure our fire was out before we hiked back home feeling giddy with pride. Our total trip that day was nine and a half miles, mostly on tundra or in knee deep snow. We had no trouble falling asleep that night.

Part II: Teaching and Learning

A message arrived from Jerry letting us know a tenured teaching couple requested Anvik. Although not surprised, we were bummed. A week before receiving the letter we chartered to Anvik to visit the school and talk with the teachers. After returning to Marshall, we chattered all week about plans for Anvik. The village was in a picturesque setting and the school building was in better shape than Marshall.

Jerry mentioned another village, Holy Cross, which would be a three or four teacher school in the fall. The current teachers were a couple we met during the Alaska Rural Schools Program. They had several years of experience in rural Alaska including the Pribilof Islands. They were in Marshall the year before us. *Interesting, they too, only lasted a year.* The next weekend we chartered to Holy Cross to talk with them and check out the village.

A beautiful day and good spring weather made our trip go smoothly. Holy Cross was a village one hundred miles upriver and was the first Jesuit mission on the Yukon River. The population was a mixture of half Yup'ik Eskimos and half Athabaskan Indians. Besides meeting Joe and Rita, the other teachers, we met a few people in the village. We learned the Village Council was more progressive and there was a new store being built by a former village resident returning to Holy Cross. She and her husband had lived in Anchorage, but were ready for a change. The store was to have fresh produce and other items difficult to purchase in a village. When I heard fresh produce my mouth watered with excitement. I knew my baby needed lettuce as much as I did.

We sent a note to Jerry stating we were interested and hoped Joe agreed. We knew he had input on the decision. Once again Jerry couldn't promise us until all of the tenured teachers were placed. Joe agreed so a decision was closer to being made and Jerry sent us blank contracts (Yippee!). When we asked him how we should label our boxes for our next teaching assignment, he said Holy Cross. It was cheaper to barge boxes than mail them, so we hoped for the best. We were encouraged by what he said, but not totally relaxed.

The first week of May arrived and, with it, our final big event at school. We integrated art into many of our lessons during the school year. When students helped with cleanup after school one day in the fall I heard them talking about showing art projects to their parents and aunts and uncles. Jed and I discussed this at dinner and decided we would share an idea we had with the students. The next day we asked them if they would like to plan a Spring Art Show to be held in the community hall. Everyone perked up and agreed it would be fun.

Beginning in the fall we had collected art pieces from each student. In the last week of April we told them to select two pieces they wanted to enter in the show. We found three judges from the community to determine first, second, and third place winners for each student group: 1–2, 3–5, and 6–8. We created many categories of prizes so all students were recognized in some way. Students decorated the hall and baked cookies to be served with juice for those that attended, which of course, was the whole village. It was a big hit. One of the adults came up to me during the show while everyone milled around looking at the different pieces and said, "This show is like in a movie." I thanked her and said, "All the students worked hard for this event to happen." We were pleased the Spring Art Show was appreciated by all that attended.

The planes stopped landing on the Yukon at the end of April and returned to using the dirt landing strip. During the first week of May everyone talked about 'watching the Yukon' and listening for the sound. I kept wondering what they were listening for since they said the noise hadn't started yet. The night temperatures were now consistently in the high thirties to low forties, causing the snow and ice to melt.

In the middle of the second week of May we were out walking Hidalgo when we heard a strange sound. At first we weren't sure what it was but we saw people walking toward the river so we joined them. We leashed Hidalgo so he wouldn't go on the river. The noise was building. We heard stories that sometimes when the river broke it created jams along the way that backed up and flooded villages. If people didn't haul their boats to higher ground the ice could grab a boat and push it downriver.

The sounds made me think something was breaking and falling. We quickly learned it was the incredible noise of the Yukon River breaking up. It was a sound I had never heard. I couldn't determine words for it, other than unbelievable. How would I ever explain this experience to my family or friends? The thickness of the river created giant ice cubes that stacked chunks as big as buildings upon each other as they moved downriver toward the Bering Sea. Some of the giant shards looked like sheets of glass that could cut a person into pieces. We continued to hear the river as we walked home and watched from the window. The mighty Yukon was breaking up and wanted everyone to know.

School ended May 18 and we left Marshall the following Monday. It was hard to say goodbye to our students and their families. As we flew out of Marshall I wondered if our students learned as much as we had during that year. Jed and I felt fortunate to have spent our first Alaskan year in Marshall.

With the dog and cat we chartered to Bethel instead of flying on the mail plane. Jed had to stay in Bethel for the next ten days to complete his Air National Guard commitment for the year. As long as the baby wasn't early, Jed would join me in time for the birth. I flew on to Anchorage with the dog and cat and, after a very long four hours, the three (four) of us flew on to Los Angeles.

Part II: Teaching and Learning

Summer of 1973

Hidalgo had the hardest time adjusting to LA with temperatures ranging in the high eighties and nineties. The noises in Pomona were difficult for him and me. Usually he didn't bark, but the combination of our arrival to a strange place, the fact Jed wasn't with us, and my pregnancy pushed his protective instincts. His bark became raspy. I felt sad for him. He was shedding and looked miserable. My parent's patio was full of black fuzz. I hosed him, and the patio, several times a day, but Labrador fur dries quickly.

Leaving the coolness of Alaska and arriving in warmer climate made my pregnant body swell. To make matters even worse, I ate tons of fresh fruit which created a rash around my mouth. The cat seemed to be the only peaceful Alaskan of the bunch. She just slept in the bedroom by the fan and didn't even try to come out of the room.

The baby was late. Thanks to friends that drove the Land Cruiser to Seattle Jed had a shorter drive to LA. He made it in time for the delivery. The family doctor my mom arranged for me went on vacation three days before the baby decided it was time. A different doctor showed up for the delivery. Six different doctors examined me over nine months—not the ideal birthing experience. Despite the hospital's persistence, I kept refusing to being drugged. While in Marshall Jed and I had studied Lamaze breathing. I was determined to have my baby naturally. The hospital wasn't on board, which complicated the delivery experience. After twenty-four hours of labor, Zach was born on June 23. I was exhausted, but no drugs were involved.

Both our parents had houses in Mexico. They purchased lots next to each other in the late '60s in a small area below Tijuana, but above Ensenada. The houses were modest and right on the beach. It was a little bit of paradise, not a party place for college students. After a hectic two weeks in California trying to see everyone we knew, visiting Mexico was a welcome break. The quiet of the surf rolling along the beach and the gentle ocean breezes made the dog and us very happy. The only cloudy spot in our week was that the sun didn't shine. The pace was slower and relaxing, just what we needed before heading north.

First stop: the Bay Area, to gather belongings from storage, visit friends, and handle personal business. The Land Cruiser was packed to the max with two guitars, an Autoharp, camping gear, baby junk, dog, cat, clothes, and food. We pushed through Oregon, Washington, Vancouver, and most of southern British Columbia in three days. The hours I sat in the car wore on me more than the baby. He slept and then was up most of the night.

The drive was once again spectacular. We noticed a few changes in the scenery because the time was later in the summer. When we reached Prince George we turned left and headed for the coast on the Yellowhead Highway. This route dumped us nearly into the Pacific Ocean at Prince Rupert. We decided to travel a different route to Alaska via the Inside Passage.

We had hoped to camp but a five-week old baby required adjustments on our part. Neither of us liked staying in standard hotels so we looked for unusual or different places to stay. We weren't disappointed. Starting in Prince Rupert we found old hotels with fascinating managers, guests, and systems of plumbing. Boarding the Alaska Marine Highway ferry to travel the Inside Passage, we found unique sleeping accommodations. Some people set up tents on the top deck or solarium of the ferry, while others threw sleeping bags on the floor.

The solarium was the popular space for experienced ferry travelers. We joined the people sleeping in chairs in the reading room, since we didn't know about the comfort of the lounge chairs on the top deck. Little did we know ferry boarding and disembarking along the way occurred at all hours of the day and night. Sleep was unpredictable and definitely not restful.

We wanted to experience Southeast Alaska so we got off several times and occasionally overnighted in a community. In Ketchikan we danced to a blaring rock band as Zach slept on a table in our sight and met a bar wench that taught school during the winter. We also stayed at the Ingersoll Hotel built in 1929, with old fashion toilets that have tanks mounted above the bowl. I was glad they worked. In Juneau we saw the original gold mine and the magnificent Mendenhall Glacier. We had an incredible Alaska King salmon dinner outside while enjoying the beauty and grace of the eagles as they soared above our heads.

Haines was our final stop before heading onto the Haines Highway that joined with the Alaska Highway. Our lodging in Haines was an old army fort, named Fort Seward, built around the turn of the century. The fort had a dozen old mansions complete with stained glass windows, each restored by private individuals. One of the houses was renovated into the Halsingland Hotel. It was hard to believe this house was a single family dwelling since we had a room on the fourth floor. In fact we were the only guests on the floor and one of four guests in the hotel for the night.

After a hearty breakfast of coffee, juice, cackleberries, sausage, and toast we headed to Anchorage. The Haines Highway connected to the Alaska Highway through Canada before we returned again to Alaska soil. We visited friends in Montana Creek, had a hectic day in Anchorage buying last minute items, stored the Toyota, and boarded a plane for Holy Cross with a quick stop in Aniak.

Part II: Teaching and Learning

*"I am the land that listens,
I am the land that broods."*

—Robert W. Service *about his Yukon home*

Part II: Teaching and Learning

Holy Cross

August 16, 1973

Jed and I were happy to board the plane to Holy Cross. All the expenses over the summer wiped us out. We looked forward to settling into our new home and finding someone to care for Zach. During our visit in May we saw our housing—a singlewide trailer with three small bedrooms. The exciting news was the trailer had running water that worked.

In the 1970s Alaska school districts used mobile homes for teacher housing in many villages. These units were barged up or down the Yukon River, and placed in many locations throughout Alaska. Sometimes a huge military transport airplane flew them in if the runway handled that size of plane. Some type of machine moved the trailers from the airport or the dock to the housing site. These delivery methods were often primitive and not always smooth. Many times mobile homes were damaged and needed attention they never received. With repairs not completed the trailers were drafty and not airtight.

During the spring visit when we heard about the new store I hoped it wasn't a pipe dream. After having access to fresh food all summer I looked forward to it continuing. The thirty-minute flight in a Twin Otter from Aniak to Holy Cross was picturesque and smooth. Twin Otters were standard planes used for mail because they were adaptable to outfit with wheels or skis and carried eighteen to nineteen passengers.

We arrived and unloaded the dog, the cat, the baby, and endless luggage and supplies carried on the plane. The boxes barged might be there and the ones mailed over the summer would arrive in the next couple of weeks. Holy Cross received four mail planes each week. Joe met and delivered us to our trailer, next to his. Joe was the principal teacher. He and his wife, Rita were beginning their second year in Holy Cross. They had a thirteen-year-old son who helped with our stuff from the plane. Their experiences in Alaska covered the Pribilof *Islands* and Marshall.

Located in Alaska on the west bank of Ghost Creek Slough off the Yukon River, Holy Cross was 279 miles upstream from the Bering Sea. The direction was 40 miles northwest of Aniak and 420 miles southwest of Fairbanks. There were several different types of trees—spruce, diamond willow, birch, and aspen—surrounding the village, creating a stunning location. During the landing approach we saw trails that wandered through the tree areas into open meadows that seemed to go on forever.

Over the years many Alaskan villages were given numerous assorted names. Holy Cross was no different. In the 1840s Russian explorers traveled the Yukon and called Holy Cross Anilukhtakpak. Later in 1880, when Father Aloysius Robaut arrived, the village was referred to as Askhomute. Father Robaut carried a cross as he hiked over the Chilkoot Trail to Alaska with the purpose of establishing a Catholic mission and school. The cross[8] formerly belonged to a retired bishop in Idaho. Despite a post office that opened in 1899 under the name of Koserefsky (no one seemed to know where that name came from), the village name changed once again in 1912 to Holy Cross. This name remained.

Shortly after arriving in Holy Cross, Joe stopped by with some news. A family with five children had moved to Anchorage the week before we arrived. The school was now at the number of students that made it a three-teacher school. This unexpected news meant Jed was the third teacher and I had no job. No one could have predicted this change since it was unusual for families to leave rural villages. They just up and left; life happens. Joe was working with the administration to see if he could hire me as a teacher assistant. If we were in most school districts throughout the nation this wouldn't happen. In most communities other jobs would be available, but we were in rural Alaska. There were few jobs in rural Alaska villages, especially for non-Native people.

Jed and I sat there for a few minutes thinking. It was too late to switch to a different teaching assignment. With only five days until the start of school where would we go? We continued to unpack boxes, but the feeling of *now what are we going to do?* lingered in the air. Traveling in and out of Alaska was expensive and not covered in teaching contracts. Furthermore, we learned from other teachers over the summer that Alaska's State-Operated School System was in turmoil. The tentative contracts we received from the regional superintendent in May weren't verifiable agreements because the state operated school system was crumbling apart. At the time we received the contracts, we didn't know about any of the issues confronting the state. We knew the lack of education past eighth grade had created a stir. We agreed it was a problem, but figured nothing would happen soon. We were wrong.

A lawsuit, The Tobeluk Agreement against the State of Alaska, was happening. The lawsuit claimed the state failed to provide equal access to education for rural students. This grievance, referred to as the Molly Hootch[9] case, presented to the 1973 Alaska legislature was argued on the grounds of racial discrimination. During the legislative discussions a decision was agreed to dissolve the ASOSS and the BIA school systems. A second decision focused on giving villages more local control over their children's education. Conversations across the state, villages and communities in Alaska talked about how the new system would be structured. One proposal was to divide the rural areas into twenty-one Regional Education Attendance Areas (REAAs).

The Molly Hootch case was a major step in changing the way rural schools were organized and education implemented. Finally, the time was here for Alaska Native people to have a voice in their children's education. Alaska Native people experienced similar patterns affecting other American Indian and indigenous people across the nation—everyone knew what they needed without even asking them. The new REAA system was to change this flawed structure and provide opportunities for local involvement in educational decisions.

A huge plus to the proposed changes was Alaska Native students were able to stay in their home community and continue their education until they graduated from high school. The REAA system supported the building of small high schools in rural communities with eight or more high school students. The cost of building high schools was projected to be high since building materials would need to be flown into villages. A major factor in building the hundred-plus small high schools was the short building season.

Fluctuating student enrollment was the argumentative point against building high schools in small, rural communities. Based on normal birth rates of children in rural communities, one year twelve to fifteen students were of high school age, followed by a few years of six to eight students, or less. Looking at our precious baby the thoughts of putting him on a plane for boarding school when he turned fourteen and not seeing him again until school was out in the spring was unimaginable.

Zach sensed the tenseness in the air because he was restless. He needed to sleep but was awake and crying. I knew if I put him in his carrier pack that snuggled him close to my belly he would fall asleep. I asked Jed if he wanted to go for a walk. Since school was starting in a few days he declined and said he was going to find Joe and ask him about classroom arrangements. After strapping Zach in the carrier I leashed up Hidalgo and we headed out. The wonderful thing about small villages was the way they were laid out. As we flew in, I saw the Yukon and knew if I headed back along Ghost Slough I would be close to the Yukon. The road would lead me through the village toward the airport.

Hidalgo, our Labrador retriever, weighed eighty-five pounds and loved to run free. I learned the hard way the importance of exercising big dogs. Our first Lab, Mr. Jack (Daniels) wrapped his leash around me and took off after another dog. The result of that experience was knee surgery. Rural airports were typically flat, open fields, a good location for dogs to run as long as there weren't any planes landing or taking off. The mail plane had come and gone and I would hear if a plane approached. We headed toward the airport, so Zach could nap, Hidalgo could run, and I could think.

A few people in the village waved to me as we walked along the road. Holy Cross was a mixture of Athabaskan Indians and Yup'ik Eskimos. The impact of the Catholic Church and missionaries over the years resulted in Holy Cross having running water, a sewer system, electricity in homes, and Western cultural influence. Marshall's modernization was limited in comparison, which created a slower paced community than Holy Cross. During our earlier visit to Holy Cross we learned people traveled to Anchorage and occasionally on to Seattle.

As we walked along the Yukon River smoked salmon hung and dried in the sun on poles. I loved the smell of the oily salmon fish jerky, often referred to as fish candy. The wood smoke wafted across the road as I walked along singing quietly to Zach and holding Hidalgo. I took a deep breath and pulled in the crisp smoky air.

In full view was the mighty Yukon. I thought I knew it well from watching it the year before from the window in the Marshall house and from my classroom. Now, in another location, it looked different, even bigger and vaster. We couldn't see the river from our new home, so I knew walks to the Yukon would be necessary. As my father-in-law stated after seeing the Yukon last year, "There is something mystic about the Yukon that draws one." During my stroll, a comfortable feeling settled over me. I realized not being a full-time teacher allowed more time with Zach and visits to the Yukon.

Hidalgo had a great run at the airport and was ready to head home when I called him to leash up. Zach woke and watched Hidalgo come to me as we headed back to the trailer. I saw something on the Yukon that puzzled me. It was difficult to clearly define. The closer we got I saw it was a raft with a sail, only it was huge. It was larger than the fish wheels I saw on the Yukon gathering the last fish of the season.

Zach was restless. My focus returned to the present moment, which included feeding a two-month-old, unpacking boxes, figuring out dinner, and trying to settle into our new situation. I was overjoyed to turn on a faucet for a glass of water and to clean the kitchen. After living without running water my appreciation for having it had greatly increased.

The next morning I told Jed about the vessel on the Yukon that looked like a giant Tom Sawyer raft. He was interested in seeing what I meant, but needed to return to the school to assess his teaching materials for the grades Joe had assigned him. Since my purpose at the school was undefined I decided I would join him later. After unpacking several boxes I decided to take Hidalgo for a short walk. My curiosity about the strange, floating craft drew me back to the banks of the Yukon. Holding firmly to our water dog so he didn't jump into the powerful current, kept me slowly moving forward.

As we approached, I saw four figures on the raft moving around. After a quick 'good morning' and introductions we chatted about their journey down the Yukon. They arrived the day before in the afternoon. They planned to stay a few days and hoped to find a place to wash clothes and shower. Understanding the need for a shower and clean clothes as well as the lack of places to do that, I offered our washing machine and bathroom. We made a time to meet at 12:30 at our trailer, which I explained was the closest to the school. After introducing Jed to them, Zach and I followed him to school while the fellows cleaned up and washed clothes. They offered dinner the following night on the raft in exchange for our hospitality.

The next evening we boarded the raft and were stunned at the size and stability of it. The four men were on an assignment for *National Geographic* magazine[10]. Each of them was interesting in their own right. Their adventure had begun a year earlier in July 1972 by hiking the Chilkoot Pass to Bennett Lake, the headwaters of the Yukon. Their final destination was the mouth of the Bering Sea. All four of them had experiences and backgrounds valuable for the trip. Their adventure was full of hard work and challenging surprises. One fellow was a third-generation logger originally from Oregon, one was a native Alaskan who shared his time climbing mountains and skiing on the US Olympic Ski Team, and the other two were land surveyors from the backwoods of Alaska.

The Yukon drew many river travelers each year. The raft adventurers were our first encounter and they set the bar high. After hiking the Chilkoot Trail the year before, they felled spruce and pine trees to build a sturdy, seagoing raft. The rough timbers were set crosswise, fastened by wooden pegs and joined together to create the 32-by-22-foot platform of rugged logs. The raft was strong enough to maneuver through the canyons and rapids, as well as face the forces of wind encountered along the way. In order to ensure consistent movement down the Yukon, they built a thirty-six-foot mast from tree trunks. They attached a surplus parachute for a sail. To make the raft habitable and guarantee some comfort they added a four-man wall tent, a small cast-iron stove, and room for the needed gear.

When they reached Whitehorse in September of 1972, they took the raft apart and stored it for the winter. As soon as the 1973 spring weather allowed, the raft was reconstructed and they headed down the Yukon. The intended final destination was in Piamute, an old abandoned Indian village fifty miles below Holy Cross. In Alaska the start of winter could be as early as mid or late September. This didn't happen every year but it did occur. Finishing a trip on the river before it froze was critical to their lives and the usefulness of the raft.

The plan when they reached Piamute was to take the raft apart and build a small cabin. The final stage of the adventure was to hole up in the cabin as they waited for the Yukon to freeze. After the Yukon was solid, they planned to ski the remaining miles to the Bering Sea. Wow! We were envious and in awe.

Dinner on National Geographic raft
August 1973

The raft was comfortable enough to accommodate the six of us for dinner. Wooden boxes suddenly appeared for us to sit on. Someone in the village distributed meat from the first fall moose, which was shared with the rafting group. We were fortunate to be included in this traditional gift of moose steaks, too. The communal distribution of food happened in Marshall and once again in Holy Cross. When village residents went hunting and fishing they proudly spread the bounty. Freezers were more common in Holy Cross, but the habit of sharing food was a strong cultural practice. Drying fish and meat into jerky was a traditional way of preserving food we observed in both villages.

Although not much of a meat eater, I did enjoy the moose steak. The meat was tender and had a wonderful smoky taste. The big treat for me was cornbread smothered in butter and honey. It was made in an iron skillet on top of a cast iron stove. I had heard about making cornbread that way, but hadn't seen it done. The logger from Oregon learned the method while in one of the logging camps. It was a great evening and we hoped we would see more of them.

The school year began. It was strange not to start the school year in a classroom. I worked two years as a teaching assistant while getting my teaching certificate and five years as an elementary teacher in California before our first year in Alaska. Maybe this was what a duck felt like when out of water. I just didn't feel right. I loved the excitement of beginning a new year with students who seemed just as enthusiastic as me.

The third, fourth, and fifth grade combination was not Jed's favorite age range. I offered to volunteer a few hours each afternoon to help him with reading and math. We needed Joe's approval for me to bring Zach.

Part II: Teaching and Learning

We didn't want costs associated with my time. Joe agreed and asked if I might think about working with all the students in some way. The hope was that the volunteer work might lead the head office to consider me as an aide, especially since I was a fully qualified teacher.

We began to settle into a pattern in our second village. One morning in mid September a parent showed up to talk with Joe. They had a short conversation and the parent left. Soon after Joe visited his wife Rita's classroom, and then Jed's. The conversations were identical—school would end right after lunch. When Jed looked puzzled, Joe explained, "The elders need the students to help their families gather potatoes because tonight is to be the first freeze."

Holy Cross produced the best produce anywhere on the Yukon and was known as the 'garden of the Yukon.' Decades earlier the church started gardens to provide for the village. They even ground fish to use as fertilizer. The magnificent bounty reaped was sold up and down the river. At one time there were farm animals and different pieces of machinery. The animals were long gone and the machines sat rusted, weathered away. Despite finding the land plentiful, the short growing season discouraged the continuation of the garden produce. Potatoes were one of the few items left still grown. Village residents needed help from their children to gather the potatoes and help watch younger siblings. It was satisfying to see the family work together. The school was supportive. When Jed told me about the early release I wondered if our previous principal would have allowed school to get out early.

The fall weather was so pleasant. The mosquitoes in Holy Cross were far less than Marshall. The autumn colors painted a breathtaking picture. Colors of the various trees exploded into a palette of golden amber to a rich flaming red. The only negative thing about the perfect fall was the lack of berries. Bummers. I had planned to make jam and meat sauce. The local residents said the lack of mosquitoes wasn't normal. Weather patterns with fewer bugs usually meant fewer berries. I was torn between this being good and bad.

Joe had a boat and asked Jed if he wanted to help with a project. During his first year in Holy Cross, he discovered an old cabin a few miles upriver. He inquired about it in the village and found it had belonged to an old German trapper who had disappeared thirty years ago. Joe asked permission to disassemble the cabin and bring it back to the village to create a steam bath. Jed was interested and I was intrigued. We heard about the various types of saunas built across Alaska depending on the resources available.

In Togiak, Jed went with our friend John to the men's sauna, called the *maqiq* (Yup'ik), which you crawled into. No one could fully stand up in it and when heated up it was very hot. Eskimos have a wonderful, mischievous sense of humor, nothing evil, just fun. They loved to heat the *maqiq* up to the point a new person, especially a *gussuk*, would be more than a little uncomfortable. It was a bit of a rite of passage before being asked to return. Many old stories were told by the elders when 'steaming or *maqiqing*,' so there was a strong incentive to return.

The reason saunas were small and compact in Togiak was because there were few trees. In Holy Cross there was an abundance of wooded areas. Joe and Jed carefully took the old cabin apart and loaded it in the boat. Going up river to take the cabin apart and bringing it back to Holy Cross took three trips. When all the materials were in Holy Cross they built a tight, small, sauna cabin next to Joe's trailer. The sauna was large enough for an inner steam bath with an outer room for cool down and changing. Three to six adults could be in the sauna at a time depending on how cozy the group wanted to be. There were two sitting benches, one low and one high, for those who liked it hot.

The sauna was heated using a Yukon stove, a fifty-gallon drum with fittings for a door and the chimney. The stove was placed in the corner and surrounded by rocks. Wood was then shoved into the stove. As the stove heated, water was thrown on the rocks to intensify the heat producing steam. I was amazed how clean I felt after steaming and taking a cool shower. We joked about rolling in the snow but never did. Walking to the sauna at twenty degrees below zero was cold, but returning was an enjoyable stroll breathing in the cool, refreshing air.

Women were generally the first to use the sauna. There were three of us that often shared the time together: Rita, Mary (the school cook), and I. It was a treat to have a break from the baby and an opportunity to be with these women. This cleansing experience was my social time. The two women had an established friendship from the year before and were helpful in opening my mind to many things. Rita was a forward-thinking person and aware of the changes happening with women's rights. Mary had twelve children, ten of whom were still alive and seven still in the village. Both were independent women with viewpoints and opinions. Besides cooking for the school, Mary was considered one of the best skin sewers in the village. Her ability to provide mothering advice without judgment was helpful and greatly needed. She handled situations with confidence and nothing seemed to bother her. I had no family or friends I could talk with, so I worried about everything.

The location of the sauna made it convenient. After it was built the only cost involved was time to gather and chop wood. Joe and Jed shared the tasks. After a steam I felt refreshed and my skin glowed. What we would have given for that sauna in Marshall!

The first visitor from the school system was Mike, an administrative director of some type. He arrived in the middle of October unannounced, something not uncommon. Since schools were the only public building in a village, people were always traipsing through checking equipment, providing a social or health service, conducting an investigation on the land or about someone in the village. Most of the time there was no knowledge someone was coming. Principal teachers were always dragged out of the classroom to answer questions or provide information.

When Mike visited Holy Cross he mentioned to Joe there might be funds to hire me as an aide. Since he was overnighting, sleeping in the school, Jed asked him to join us for dinner. As we were chatting after dinner, we mentioned a problem with one of the typewriters we found in the school. Jed and I used the typewriter to create lessons for his students. Mike offered to take a look at it. We were skeptical since the typewriter didn't really belong to us. Joe said Mike was extremely resourceful and loved tinkering with machines so we agreed. Legally blind, Mike wore thick glasses with a small magnifying glass for one of his eyes that allowed him to look at something closely. He certainly taught me never to assume when someone was legally blind they weren't able to repair machines. The typewriter was fixed and he said he would let Joe know about the funding possibilities. We knew decisions moved slowly in school systems, especially during turbulent times.

Mike filled everyone in on the 1972 Indian Education Act, a landmark decision to provide additional opportunities for American Indian and Alaska Native students. The federal funds depended on the number of American Indian and Alaska Native students in a school. The funds schools received were used to strengthen cultural activities.

Joe talked with elders in the village about different needs. The first one was setting up a trap line that students could check. The pelts would be used for skin sewing projects. With only a few sled builders left, some of the funds were targeted to help students learn to build sleds. When the trap line yielded furs, women were hired to teach skin sewing. When Joe received the funds, people were hired to work with sixth to eighth grade students.

The skin sewing in Holy Cross was different from Marshall. It was more decorative and even utilized calfskin ordered from Seattle. Cows were certainly not native to Alaska. Most skin sewing was done with moose and caribou. My sauna friend, Mary, offered to make me a pair of fancy boots using calfskin. She created a fur pattern at the top that was decorated with beads and trimmed with red fox. They were striking plus kept my feet warm and cozy. In Marshall they would be considered extravagant. It amazed me how no scrap of fur was wasted. Fur pieces as small as my thumbnail were stitched together. When the fur pieces were seamed correctly they looked smooth and perfect on both sides.

Fall was busy with adjustments to Holy Cross. The big school event was a Halloween carnival. The plan was to have the carnival on Halloween, but the school board insisted the date be changed. Joe explained to us later that nothing, absolutely nothing, interfered with bingo. Wednesday night was and always would be bingo night. Next year Christmas would fall on Wednesday so that would be interesting. Students built carnival activities such as a beanbag toss, dart-throwing area, pin the nose on the witch, bobbing for apples, and an amazing, creepy, terrifying spook house. Most of the village residents came and participated. Some students also worked with Mary to make refreshments they sold. The financial outcome was a start toward raising funds for a year-end trip to Anchorage for the sixth, seventh and eighth grade students.

Many things were different in Holy Cross. We came to think some of the differences were because of the missionaries. Movies were shown to children and adults separately. The dances in Holy Cross were adults only with live fiddle music. An element to the dances we found unsettling was the impact of 'fire water.' We enjoyed a drink but not to the point of intoxication. People unfortunately showed up drunk. When musicians played drunk sometimes things got out of control.

The holidays were a few months away. We actually had a whole week of vacation. Jed's parents wanted to see Zach, so they asked to visit. Jed was an only child and Zach was the first grandchild. My mom couldn't make it. She was the breadwinner of the family and couldn't get the time off. My dad had been in the military. Despite being a captain and flying B-52 bombers, after fourteen years of service he was asked to resign. While living in Hawaii his gambling and drinking caught up with him. He dabbled in restaurants and then ended up driving a cab. Besides, my sister had two little children Mom wanted to spend Christmas with. I was happy she visited us in Marshall.

We knew flight arrangements into Holy Cross were easier than Marshall. Jed's dad asked us to make a list of items we wanted. The first thing Jed put on the list was a female black Labrador for Hidalgo. Dog teams were almost non-existent in Holy Cross. The influence of the missionaries disrupted many cultural activities and dog mushing was one of them. Jed had a plan to develop a dog team of Labrador retrievers, but when his dad talked with a breeder the plan was squelched. According to the breeder pulling sleds wasn't a good use of Labs. They had weak hips that would become strained in the cold when pulling weight.

One thing off the list for them to haul from Los Angeles to Holy Cross was ice cream. We purchased an old-fashioned, hand-crank ice cream maker during our time in California. I said it was an investment in feeding our baby. I reasoned my chocolate chip cookies and ice cream were necessary to keep producing milk so making ice cream was a necessity. The new Holy Cross store had real milk most of the time and when they didn't, I used powdered Milkman and sweet condensed canned milk. I had my priorities when it came to ice cream.

In early December, the Santa Claus plane, a good-Samaritan effort by the National Guard, was scheduled to visit Holy Cross. The goal of the National Guard was to travel to as many rural villages as possible each year. We had heard about this in Marshall but they didn't make it. Seeing the disappointment on the children's faces from last year still penetrated my memory.

This year, despite the weather hovering at zero degrees, the plane arrived. Snow machines rushed toward the airport when they heard the plane. Cold temperatures didn't decrease the excitement children held to receive a gift from Santa. Alaska's definition of cold continued to amaze me. My Hawaiian and Californian background made me think I should be inside if temperatures were below freezing, and definitely when it hovered close to zero. Alaska was different. You dressed and out you went. I continued working on getting the hang of it.

As the plane approached the airport, the pilot decided the field was too short for a safe landing. I felt confident that everyone on the ground was wondering, "how did previous planes land the other years?" Military personnel were always trained to have a plan B. This year four pallets of presents were air dropped into Holy Cross. A much different crew was in charge than on the Marshall plane the year before. The two yellow parachutes didn't open but the two red parachutes did.

(*We decided if we were to parachute out of a military aircraft we would ask for the red parachute.*) Most of the children did receive a present, but once again no one sat on Santa's lap.

The Christmas program happened the week before Jed's parents arrived. The students did a fantastic job putting it together and made everyone proud. Joe told us that the year before a few people from the village had shown up drunk and were very disruptive. Everyone in the village knew if that happened again this year Joe would stop the program and send people home. There were no problem people this year and all of us were relieved.

Peggy and Harold arrived with fresh vegetables and fruit. This year their luggage was one suitcase and seven boxes of varying sizes, which brought the total weight to 280 pounds. Besides the food items, the boxes included fifty pounds of chickenfeed, chicken wire to build a fence, a chicken feeder and watering trough, and a few baby items I had requested. Jed and I had raised chickens in California, so we developed a plan to help the community of Holy Cross learn how to raise chickens. We knew it would be challenging, but we discussed it with Joe and he said "Why not?" We were friends with the owners of the new store and they agreed to sell the eggs when produced.

A dozen of California Redwing Hatchery's most fertile chicken eggs were included in the carry-on items. The eggs were placed in a plastic egg carton and wrapped in newspaper to protect them from the elements along the way. The rough calculation of how many times the eggs were passed back and forth between Peggy and Harold was one hundred fifty times. "Here, hold these while I..." The flight attendants and passengers were quite interested in the unusual package that traveled back and forth between them.

Part II: Teaching and Learning

They overnighted in Anchorage before heading to Aniak and into Holy Cross. The Anchorage airport had an overnight baggage area where the boxes were left, except the precious eggs. The Anchorage Airport was accustomed to storing items due to the length of time it took to fly to places in the state and weather conditions that delayed flights.

After a restful night of not passing the eggs back and forth, they were up early. It was clear and cold (six degrees above zero) in Anchorage. They returned to the airport and boarded the flight to Aniak. As they flew to Aniak they enjoyed a view of Mt. McKinley, a gift since clouds often hid it. The agent in Aniak knew they were coming and had a Cessna 180 all warmed up ready for departure to Holy Cross. The pilot, a former bush teacher, had retired from teaching a few years earlier.

This year the flight into Holy Cross had no airplane glitches. The picturesque landscape was surrounded by hills so the landing didn't have the wind they experienced in Marshall. They even saw a few moose move slowly along in the snow. Unless it was a scheduled mail plane, pilots announced arrival by circling the village. There was no way to call into town, no buildings at the airport, and no taxis to pick up people. The seasoned pilot circled the village and explained the geographical points of interest.

Their visit was very different from the previous year. They immediately fell in love with the various trees and the beauty of the snowy Christmas card image in Holy Cross. None of the eggs were broken and all of the welcomed fresh produce arrived with no blemishes. The new, local store had done pretty well, but California fruits and vegetables were still fresher. At least this year I hadn't succumbed to stuffing lettuce in my mouth like an addict.

Each village was different and had its own personality. The social activities and interactions in Holy Cross were more westernized than Marshall. Peggy and Harold enjoyed meeting the other teaching couple and their son. There were also a couple of evenings with the new storeowners, Jim and Betty Johnson, Mary, from the school, and her husband, Bob, who was a trapper.

Betty Johnson grew up in Holy Cross, but left as a teenager to attend high school in Anchorage. While in school she met and married Jim. They raised their children in Anchorage, all of whom were graduated. Betty still had family and land in Holy Cross she missed. She and Jim decided they were ready for a slower pace, so they visited Holy Cross. Jim was a contractor prepared to build them a comfortable home wherever they went. When family and village residents heard they were considering a move to Holy Cross, Jim and Betty were encouraged to open a well-stocked store like in Anchorage. Jim ordered lumber, some equipment, and other materials to be delivered on the first barge of the season. He was thorough when ordering because there was no hardware store to pick up extra nails and other incidentals forgotten.

The building he built served as a home and store. During the digging of the basement Jim found sawdust four feet down. The discovery of the sawdust confirmed they were on the land where the old sawmill was back in the late 1880s. Betty had twenty or more old pictures of Holy Cross they hung around the store and their new home. The pictures depicted her family's early involvement in the church, school and community of Holy Cross. The final outcome of the structure he built was a small, modern, well-supplied store and a modest comfortable home.

Part II: Teaching and Learning

During Peggy and Harold's visit there were several holiday activities to attend. With temperatures hovering at zero, Peggy and I decided to let Jed and Harold go tree shopping. The thought of bundling up a six-month-old baby made the decision easy for me. Peggy and I created holiday goodie boxes for the students' families. There were sixty students in the school, which equaled twelve family boxes. I loved to bake, so for several weeks I made holiday breads, cookies, and fudge.

On Christmas Eve there was a mass at the church. Jed, Rita, and Mary played their guitars and sang with Sister Agnes. The music added an extra element to the traditional ceremonial festivities. Christmas was spent eating too many holiday goodies. I even made the special iron skillet cornbread to impress Jed's parents. It was great!

A major task Jed and his dad worked on during the visit was to build an incubator for the eggs carefully transported to Holy Cross. When the egg idea was conceived, it was thought of as a business experience for the students. The first goal was to get the incubator to a constant temperature of 102 degrees that could be maintained for twenty-one days to allow the eggs to hatch.

After hatching we all hoped the chicks would grow and become egg layers themselves. None of the students had seen a baby chick or hen. They saw eggs in the wild close to small water areas around Holy Cross. However, the concept of how eggs arrived in a nest was never discussed. The ultimate plan was for students to watch eggs hatch, become chicks, and grow into laying hens. The eggs produced would become a resource for the community to purchase at the local store—a full farm-to-table experience.

After one final sauna and a good night's sleep Jed's parents left Friday morning. Their return went well, which was a good sign when many connections needed to be made. It was a long way from Holy Cross to Los Angeles.

In early January the village electricity acted up. The current alternated from too hot to too cold. *Can electricity become menopausal?* The poor eggs! With no signs of a crack in any of the twelve eggs Jed couldn't stand it any longer. It had been twenty-five days, longer than it was predicted for chicks to hatch. Jed cracked five of the eggs. None had begun to grow into a chick. We were devastated. After another week we checked the remaining seven eggs, with no luck. We sat at the school deflated. How would we explain this to the students? Everyone was excited and eager to see the baby chicks. The disappointment was difficult and left us unsure of what we could have done differently.

Despite Joe and Jed's efforts, the electrical issues continued. School was closed for a few days and several partial days because of boiler difficulties. Long hours of working on the boiler and many hours of stress left them both on edge. They were concerned the boiler might blow. As we cleaned up the chicken-egg equipment, we made notes for a possible future attempt. We weren't sure Jed's parents would be into passing the eggs back and forth on another flight. We knew we had the wild card—the only grandson, so anything was possible.

Long, dark winters increased the intake of alcohol and rural villages didn't escape this reality. One of the unfortunate outcomes of Holy Cross's westernization was a greater awareness of alcohol, which resulted in more consumption. It was an accepted norm to imbibe at adult village activities. The drinking contributed to a higher rate of accidental deaths. Jed and Joe brought a body back from a hunting accident during a fall outing. The rumor, later confirmed, was that the accident involved alcohol. A sixteen-year-old was shot in the back because people were drinking and not being careful.

We heard of deaths in the community where people were drinking and then decided to go to another village by snow machine. They were found dead along the trail because the snow machine broke down and the person was inadequately prepared. The weather wasn't forgiving when it was twenty to thirty degrees below zero. One tragic accident that shook me up was when a nineteen-year-old beat his own mother to death because he was drunk. She wasn't found for four days.

These were hard stories to hear. They created a counter productive environment in the entire community and especially at school. We understood when students found it hard to focus at times. Alaskan villages didn't have police to monitor drinking, accidents, enforcement, and other community issues. In the mid 1970s villages and the Alaska State Troopers discussed the development of a new system to help with 'bush justice.' Alaska was a large, young state and needed new systems to help with all the changes occurring. Prior to statehood, Alaska Native Indian and Eskimo groups took care of their problems based on cultural and historical systems.

With no infrastructure to provide health and safety services to citizens in villages, it was impossible to collect dependable data, as well as to understand and to mediate when a problem or death occurred. A 1970 report noted accidental deaths in rural Alaska were three and one-half times the national average. Stories were confusing, especially after the fact. One thing seemed to be consistent—alcohol was involved, but no one would confirm it.

Alcohol changed the landscape of villages, interaction patterns, and cultural norms. The Alaska State Troopers decided to pilot a new system to assist communities. Villages were to select a person trained as a Village Public Safety Officer (VPSO). The training provided information and techniques of how to manage situations dealing with alcohol and violence. Each village had a small room that held a person until picked up by the State Trooper. Depending on the amount of training and comfort level of the village, the person might even be provided a gun.

When a State Trooper and village leaders met in Holy Cross to discuss a plan for their VPSO, it was held in one of the classrooms. The meeting was open for the community, but limited information was provided. We were curious about two things: the selection criteria and the training they would receive. It seemed everyone was related in some way, so how could a neutral person be chosen? We heard in one of the villages a relative with a drinking problem was selected as the VPSO, which created a whole new level of problems.

Many changes happened in rural Alaska, some for the better and others were questionable. Health aides were paid to travel out for improvement training, but received little compensation for their time. Telephones began to show up in a few locations, but access to them was difficult. There were no fire hydrants in villages so a fire in a village was devastating. Running water wasn't consistent and if it was improperly installed, it froze.

In February Jed made a trip to Bethel for his National Guard commitment. His return flight didn't go as planned. The winds were dangerous to the point the plane made it to Aniak when the pilot said, "Done." The wind blew so hard it was difficult to taxi to the normal tie down. A jeep was used to anchor one side of the airplane and a five-hundred-pound propane tank wheeled to the other side. The plane and passengers were stuck in the Aniak Lodge for three days. Jed felt he was transported back to the days of Jack London or Robert Service. They sat around the stove, drank way too much coffee, swapped stories, read every book in the building, and played poker until the sun came up. It was a true blizzard, not an experience many wanted to repeat.

The long Alaska winter was dragging me down. The occasional warm day that melted the ice sheets increased my cabin fever attitude. I wanted to see beyond the trailer's blurred views. Each storm added a layer of ice, further distorting the hazy picture of what lay beyond the window. It was late March and the windows of the trailer were still impenetrable through the thick frost and ice build up. I wanted to look out of the window and see light.

Holy Cross was colder than Marshall. As I walked around the village I observed that when temperatures dropped way below zero people covered the lower portion of their faces loosely with a scarf so they could breath. Light blankets hid children's faces so their eyes barely peeked out. Often I felt so confined when I walked, it reminded me of the tire advertisements of the Michelin Man I saw on TV.

Extreme cold canceled mail delivery flights, as well as all plane travel. When planes didn't fly, rural villages were more isolated. It didn't matter if help was needed in an emergency. If the weather was bad, travel didn't occur, end of story. Sometimes medical personnel could provide information over a satellite radio. Distance-based assistance required willing participants, detailed explanations of the situation, and limited radio static so an audible conversation could happen.

Life at Fifty Below Zero

The days started getting longer, always welcomed in the interior of Alaska. People began checking on the Yukon even though the calendar stated it was barely spring. My cold bones guaranteed it wasn't spring. I needed the sun to penetrate my skin. This Hawaii girl longed to see thirty to forty degrees above zero, not zero to minus twenty.

April 1 began like many other days. It was 7:45 a.m. I was still in my pajamas and had just stuck my head outside to read the temperature. The thermometer read twenty degrees below zero. Zach was moving around in his walker. I loved hearing him laugh as he jabbered to himself. I was scrambling eggs for Jed when suddenly there was a piercing scream. I turned around and saw Zach crying and looking straight at me. As my eyes focused I realized he had tipped a freshly poured cup of extremely hot coffee down the front of his chest. Jed walked into the kitchen just as the screaming began. How could this happen on our watch?

Overwhelmed by the shock we were frozen for a split second before moving into action. Our minds knew too well the nearest doctor was at least one plane ride away, maybe three plane rides. We looked at each other and knew we were both focused on finding help for Zach. Knowing Jed was trained as a medic in the National Guard, I looked at him for guidance. He told me to hold the walker firmly as he pulled Zach out. Jed carefully removed his little turtleneck and t-shirt. Later we learned if we had waited the shirts would have stuck to his burn sores making them more difficult to remove. We saw several red oozing blisters already bursting on his bare chest.

Seeing the open sores shocked me. Moms are supposed to protect their children and know what to do. I felt powerless when Jed handed our son to me. When Zach looked at me I could feel him say "Mommy, help me!" His screams of discomfort penetrated my heart. I saw his little arms reach for the seeping lesions as Jed cautiously placed Zach's right arm behind my left side and said, "Hold him firmly so he can't touch the blisters."

Jed grabbed his heavier coat, hat, and gloves and asked me if I knew how cold it was outside. I told him the thermometer was at twenty to twenty-five below. He walked out the Arctic entrance mumbling, "I hope the snow machine starts." Zach continued to cry in pain as I tried to soothe him. Jed popped his head back in the door, to say, "It started. I will check with Agnes to see how quickly a plane can get you and Zach to a hospital. Don't let him touch the sores in any way."

I know I heard him, but all I could think about was soothing our son. All of the normal tactics of singing nonsense songs, walking and rocking him, and turning on his favorite lullaby toy didn't work. He fought to move his body and tug at the pain that continued to rage. His sores became redder and burst. Zach felt strong in his struggling, but I was firm in my hold and gentle in my grasp.

If Jed was able to get a plane into Holy Cross, where would it take us—Bethel, Fairbanks, Anchorage, Seattle, Los Angeles? The Bethel Hospital was a Public Health Service Hospital, which meant it primarily served Alaska Native people, so I was unsure they would help us. Thoughts raced around in my head when I realized I would need to put something on my body other than a nightgown. At that moment, I felt so incompetent as a mother and as a person. Deciding clothes to put on was a challenge.

My guilt was out of control and impacted my ability to breathe and think. Everyone told me I was an overly protective mother and needed to relax more. Zach was a fussy baby, colicky, and still woke several times during the night. With no family or close friends around me I lacked confidence as a mother. Jed walked through the door "A plane left Bethel ten minutes ago so we need to get you to the airport." I was relieved thinking everything would be OK. Then I realized he said something that made me know he wasn't going with us. How could I handle this by myself? My feelings of panic returned.

There was no time to think. Jed took Zach as I quickly dressed, grabbed my toothbrush, a few items of clothing for Zach and myself, and threw everything in my daypack. Maybe this was a bad dream, a hallucination or a nightmare? Jed asked what we could wrap Zach in that would keep him warm, but not rub his open wounds. As I put his rabbit fur hat on his little head, I thought of the down comforter I made. We used it when we walked or went to the store. His overall bottoms and tiny fur boots were still on him so the lower half of his body would stay warm. We changed his diaper, bundled him in the comforter, and dashed outside.

Sitting behind Jed with my arm wrapped around his waist holding Zach and keeping myself upright on the snow machine was a challenge. I held tight as we sprinted to the airfield, arriving as a Cessna 185 landed. Agnes, the health aide, was there and told us she alerted the hospital a nine-month-old burn victim was on his way. She assured me someone would be at the airport to drive us to the Bethel Public Health Hospital. I thanked her, reluctantly said goodbye to Jed, and climbed into the small airplane. My gratitude for this first step of help for Zach filled me with tears.

As the plane rose I realized how lucky we were it was warmed up when the call was made. Motor vehicles needed extra time to adjust when temperatures were twenty degrees below zero. When I looked out the window I wondered when we would see Jed again. Bethel was a primary hub that served forty-plus villages in the Yukon Delta area with some medical and social services. Chartering a flight to Fairbanks or Anchorage usually happened only in life and death situations. I felt fortunate we were on our way to Bethel for assistance, whatever that meant.

The skies were calm and the flight went smooth and easy. Zach wore himself out crying so he fell asleep to the drone of the airplane engine. His little nap provided me a short and welcomed reprieve. As I looked down at my quiet, peaceful child my calm was interrupted with more anxiety. I began to wonder if the hospital would take him and tell me they would call when they knew his status. I read stories about babies needing to go to a hospital for a variety of reasons and parents not being able to stay with them. The concern was overwhelming. This couldn't happen. I knew Zach needed me and being part of his care was critical for me.

Intuitively, I knew I would be firm and gently assertive. My communications with everyone needed to ensure I wasn't separated from my son. I hoped his need for breastfeeding would help. Most rural Alaska Native moms breastfed their babies, so medical care people were accustomed to that situation.

I looked at my watch as we landed in Bethel; it had been two hours since this horrific accident began. Knowing the distance to the hospital and the lack of traffic, I felt certain we would arrive at the hospital in ten minutes so long as someone was there to take us. I smiled thinking we could have sat on the LA freeway for that long driving to the hospital.

As the plane rolled along the ice the pilot turned to say someone was coming to help me to the waiting taxi. Zach stirred and gently twisted in my arms. I checked his hands to ensure he couldn't grab at his chest. The comforter kept him warm without sticking to the blisters. My Sorel boots felt toasty as I shivered from the cold breeze when the door was opened. Someone outside offered welcomed kindness in the simple words, "How can I help you?" I was grateful for the hand that reached up to help me out of the plane.

This guardian angel assisted me along the slippery runway, as well as grabbed my daypack, which was thrown in the back of the plane. My focus was on Zach so the pack could easily have been left. This anonymous helper gently held my elbow and walked me toward the hanger. The air service had a small waiting area in a closed off corner of the building. The hanger was where normal maintenance tasks were done and people waited.

I saw exhaust fog coming from several cars in the parking area next to the building. Taxis in rural Alaska were cars with no distinguishing marks to alert a person their taxi arrived. Vehicles idled while waiting for a passenger. Sometimes an empty car sat with the motor running as someone dashed into the building to take care of a quick errand. Locations accessed strictly by airplanes in the winter didn't worry about someone stealing their rig. Limited roads went nowhere, causing a person to circle around, and easily be caught.

When we were close to the entrance of the office, my friendly assistant diverted me to one of the cars. The driver put down his newspaper as we approached and jumped out of the car to open the door. He steadied me as I settled into the car and held my treasured bundle.

Part II: Teaching and Learning

I thanked both of them and within minutes the taxi came to a stop at the hospital. I was guided into the building and told to keep walking straight down the hallway. When I arrived at the desk, a nurse inquired if I was the woman with the burned baby. I nodded and was prepared for them to say, "Please hand us your baby and we'll take it from here." Just at that moment a second nurse appeared and told me to follow her.

I was relieved as I followed her into the intensive care room adjacent to the nurses' station. It was a sterile room with a crib, chair, and rolling hospital tray table. Two women in uniforms taped plastic to the walls starting at the floor and working up the wall above my head. I heard one of them say something about an ointment put on burns that stained everything. Another nurse walked in and said the doctor would be here in a few minutes. She lowered the crib and asked me to set Zach down. She told the nursing aides they had done a good job. As they left she asked them to turn the heat up.

I carefully uncovered Zach. He appeared confused maybe because he didn't recognize anything or anyone other than me. I assured him everything was OK, "Mommy isn't going anywhere." I said the statement out loud more for the adults in the room than the baby. My thinking was that if I kept saying it would continue to be true.

As the nurse began looking at his wounds, the doctor walked in and joined in the examination. I continued to hold my son's little hand to comfort him and me. The doctor began to ask how the accident happened, where the coffee landed on his body, and whether the coffee had sugar or cream in it. We didn't use cream or sugar in our coffee, which kept the burns from being worse. The nurse said it was a good thing we had taken his shirts off. Clothing absorbs liquid and sticks to the burns. The longer the cloth absorbs the harder to get it off and more skin is removed in the process. She added the air helped to relieve some of the pain Zach felt. Her words helped me feel better and I wished Jed could have heard them.

The doctor explained burns were characterized by severity of the skin damage, which caused some of the affected skin cells to die. Zach had a few first-degree burns, the most minor, but the bigger concern were the second-degree and potential third-degree burns. He hoped the worst lesions would respond to the treatment process limiting damage and future difficulties.

Hearing all of this I was even more frightened and unsure of the next steps. The doctor explained the first step was keeping the wounds clean and soaked in a liquid called silver nitrate. I learned later silver nitrate was the substance put into a baby's eyes soon after they were born.

The beginning treatment was critical in assisting the skin to rejuvenate and repair itself. To ensure no infections occurred, Zach remained in the intensive care room. With his wounds primarily on his chest he needed to be monitored carefully to ensure pneumonia didn't become a complication. To begin the treatment silver nitrate was poured all over Zach's chest and down the area of his burned arm. The next step involved wrapping sterile gauze over his burned wounds followed with another soaking of silver nitrate. He was dried off and wrapped in sterile blankets for me to hold. Someone brought in a wooden rocking chair and asked if I thought I could feed him and get him to sleep for a while. I asked for a glass of water and everyone left.

Finally, I had quiet and Zach took the nourishment and comfort of Mommy. He ate and fell asleep. I sat there for a while content to rock him before I moved him to the crib. The peace and calmness allowed me to reflect about the last few hours. Next was to stay focused on ensuring his healing went well. The rocking back and forth calmed me, something I really needed. I wanted to cry and be held, but that was a luxury for another time.

No one explained how long it took for burns to heal. I was nervous and a little scared. I had no idea where I would stay or what would happen next. Moms can do anything when they need to and I was no different. I felt sad I couldn't call his father and tell him we received help in Bethel. For all he knew we might be in Seattle or Los Angeles or a burn unit anywhere.

With limited services for people in most rural villages and definitely no telephones, sharing or explaining news, good or bad, was difficult. The only communication for families was via a radio station in Bethel that provided messages to the villages. Most of the time the radio station worked. If the family didn't hear the message someone in the village did and made sure it was passed along. I heard the messages about babies being born or someone was OK after surgery, but now I needed to send a message to Jed. I wanted to let him know we were in Bethel and Zach's status. It would need to be brief and basic with few details. At least he would know we were still in Alaska.

The next sixteen days of my life and Zach's was spent in the Bethel Public Health Hospital. He remained in the intensive care room for twelve days. The hospital staff was very kind to me and allowed me to stay in a room down the hall. His crib had a sign: 'Breastfed baby, mother down the hall.' I was continuously involved with my son's care and learned how to clean burn wounds.

April 18 we went home. I was grateful we returned to a home with running water. Cleanliness was more challenging when hauling water. The nurses taught me to clean the burn areas. I stood over Zach telling him a story while they did the cleaning and now I would be both nurse and storyteller. Wound cleaning was tedious but essential.

Zach didn't need skin grafting in spite of having sores that took six to eight weeks to heal. The damage did leave small scars that I watched carefully for years. The heat from the coffee penetrated many layers of skin, but the doctor didn't think nerve damage occurred.

We were fortunate the attending doctor arrived from the Los Angeles burn unit. Several hub communities had young doctors out of medical school completing their residencies in public hospitals. Rural Alaska had endless types of medical situations, so their time was well spent.

Jed was glad to have us back and many village friends stopped by to see how we were doing. I didn't return to my school assignments until Zach was ready. No one said another word about being an overprotective mother. Returning in mid April meant spring arrived—the snow was melting, the sun was warmer, the windows were beginning to thaw, and I could once again see out into the world.

During my stay at the hospital one of the nurses talked about the importance of taking care of my emotional needs. She felt confident Zach would be fine, but was concerned about me. She hinted the responsibility and guilt a parent feels when a child has a serious injury lingers long after wounds have healed. She was right. That moment in time when the accident occurred can never be changed. I spent many hours rehashing that moment and wishing I could talk to my sister. I knew she would understand.

Sled built in Holy Cross
April 1974

While Zach and I were gone Jed and the other two teachers mutually agreed that Holy Cross needed a new staff. It was a difficult year, very different from Marshall. All three of them felt the residents of Holy Cross had major struggles with the influences of mainstream culture and its effects on traditional Native ways. It was hard to define and certainly not an open, easy conversation.

Only one elder spoke his Athabaskan language, only two men could build sleds, only three-four people performed Native dancing, and very few women did skin sewing. The traditions, culture, and customs were strong with the elders, but disappearing in younger generations. The missionaries had meant well, but left confusion about what was appropriate and acceptable. There were many group factions, people gossiping, and loss of community spirit that led to counterproductive actions with few positive results.

Despite the difficulties in Holy Cross and Zach's accident, our year had been personally rewarding. The greatest gift was the opportunity to be outdoors more. We cross-country skied and spent time on the snow machine. Being in the woods and peaceful forests marked with tracks of many species of wild animals was incredible and unbelievable. One weekend in March we left Zach with a babysitter for the afternoon while we traveled to a friend's trapping cabin twelve to fifteen miles out of Holy Cross. It was a fantastic 'almost spring' day! The cabin was eight feet by ten feet with a small stove that heated up quickly. We sat there with a cup of hot coffee and enjoyed the quiet while we soaked in the silent language of the wilderness around us.

One of the few sled builders left in Holy Cross constructed a small sled that was perfect for Zach, as well as picking up packages from the store or post office. The sled was built from birch wood. He cut and milled it with only a handsaw. It was a work of art that we knew we would use for years to come.

When I returned to school there were only a few weeks left. I helped a few students with their final social studies assignments and coordinated the sharing of the art projects they started earlier in the year. In early May twelve students and three chaperones traveled to Anchorage. The students worked on fundraising activities all year to make the trip a reality. Only a couple of them had been to Bethel, let alone Anchorage. It was an exciting learning adventure for them. They glimpsed a different world and lifestyle.

During one of Jed's trips into Anchorage to attend a required school meeting, he met the School Board President from a village close to the Arctic Circle in the Brooks Range, Allakaket. Jed was impressed with the village's commitment to their culture. The school population was composed of a mixture of Athabaskan and Inupiaq Eskimo students and required three teachers. One of the current teachers was leaving. The remaining couple we met during the Alaska Rural Schools training. They were experienced teachers who gave us valuable information on teaching in small rural Alaska schools. One of them wanted a year off, which meant the school needed two teachers. This opportunity looked like a good fit for us. After a couple of letters back and forth, the Allakaket school board president vowed he would fight the State of Alaska tenure policy if they didn't allow us to be hired.

We weren't excited about moving again, but we were hopeful. We needed two paychecks to help us get back on our feet financially. Alaska was expensive with so many unexpected costs. The crucial detail we worried about was finding someone to take care of Zach while I was teaching. The Brooks Range intrigued us and provided a fresh perspective of Alaska. The magnificence and magic of the mighty Yukon created a lingering hesitancy in our departure.

The plan was summer camping in Alaska and the Canadian Yukon Territory. No trip to the California to visit family because of the costs involved. With hope, we looked forward to being in a new home by early August.

Part II: Teaching and Learning

"Looking at the story of my life and that of my family makes me overwhelmed.

How can you write about the storm if you are still in it?

—Velma Wallis, *Raising Ourselves*[11]

Part II: Teaching and Learning

Allakaket

August 5, 1974

We chartered a Twin Otter plane to fly 190 air miles northwest of Fairbanks to Allakaket. Flying over the Sawtooth and Ray Mountains meant we were at greater elevation than regular bush flights. My preference was close to the ground. I enjoyed seeing the terrain. Mount Tozi, the tallest of the Ray Mountains, was 5,519 feet and required the pilot to fly even higher. Again the plane was loaded with groceries, furry family members, all of Zach's necessary paraphernalia, and a few items to keep us going until our boxes arrived. Reading about crossing the Arctic Circle prepared us for fireworks. Reality demonstrated it was just another day.

Allakaket sat at the junction of the Alatna and Koyukuk Rivers. The Athabaskan name for Allakaket, Aalaakkaakk'et, meant, 'mouth of the Alatna River.' When we arrived the weather was incredible, warm and sunny with a light breeze. The area surrounding Allakaket resembled Holy Cross with birch and spruce trees galore, as well as rolling hills below majestic mountains. Regrettably, the muddy Yukon River wasn't there to greet us.

While the plane circled and started to land, we glimpsed the Alatna and Koyukuk Rivers. Both flowed with clean, clear, blue waters bordering the areas around the village. The headwaters of the Koyukuk River were above the Arctic Circle in the Endicott Mountains, a part of the Brooks Range. The Koyukuk was 425 miles long, the last major tributary entering the Yukon before it emptied into the Bering Sea.

The School Board President, Sam, explained the school population was a mixture of Athabaskan and Inupiaq Eskimos students. On the north bank of the Koyukuk River, was the Inupiaq Eskimo village of Alatna situated on the upper side of the river with a bluff behind it. Getting across the river from Alatna was a daunting task at times; nonetheless, residents needed access to the Allakaket airstrip and school. Allakaket was originally an Athabaskan village. Over time people became a blend of both groups. Students who lived in Alatna traveled to school in a boat or snow machine except when the weather had other plans. Fall freeze-up and spring breakup caused gaps in attendance. Teachers gave students extra work during these times of the year in case they were stuck in Alatna.

Similar to other villages when a plane circled, someone showed up. I never understood how the decision happened, but it usually was someone with a truck. We introduced ourselves as the new teachers to David, the driver of the truck. We learned from him there was one truck in Allakaket, and it didn't always start. Looking at all of our stuff I was happy the truck started that day. Schlepping boxes and bags in and out of airplanes and trucks was enough work. The thought of adding a three to four mile hike for each trip wasn't appealing.

A few people in the village had ATVs for hauling mail, freight and people when the truck didn't work. After the snow arrived travel was easier since many people had a snow machine or dog team. Snow was generally on the ground for seven to eight months out of the year.

Part II: Teaching and Learning

David was surprised of our arrival in early August. Many times teachers didn't show up until the day before school started. Nevertheless, he offered to load up our stuff and take us to the teacher housing area.

Sam informed Jed there was no running water in the village or at the school. He added, "Allakaket is a traditional, 'no frills' village and school with modest teacher housing and a store with minimal groceries." I wasn't looking forward to returning to no running water, but I was tough. *I made it through Zach's burn accident so I could handle anything.*

During our time in Fairbanks before flying to Allakaket we visited with the couple that taught in Allakaket the previous year. We knew them from our first summer in Alaska. They had a small cabin in Fairbanks where they spent the summer. Genie was the third teacher to this year's team, while her husband, Dan took a year off.

When we showed up to visit in Fairbanks they were a bit frazzled from hosting and chaperoning fifteen students from Allakaket in their cabin for a week. Plus, they had two children under the age of eight. The previous year, Dan and Genie had helped students raise funds for travel to Fairbanks to attend the Indian-Eskimo Olympics. Their two-room cabin was small so I am sure it was wall-to-wall sleeping on the floor at bedtime.

The additional information Dan and Genie shared helped us shop and be prepared for the year. As we left they mentioned our apartment might be messy since workers were camped in it to finish school maintenance projects. With no motels or hotels in villages, school buildings, including teacher apartments, were frequently used in the summers. The various work crews didn't have good reputations for tidying up. They sometimes left trash for the next person to smell and deal with.

The state-provided teacher housing was generally the only option for rural teachers and very basic. Furniture was ordered from Sears in bulk and randomly sent to village housing units on the barge or plane. There was no regular inventory taken and no one coordinated what was ordered. Most places were a mish-mash of furniture. We heard stories about people arriving and finding only box springs, no mattress or a couch with missing cushions. New teachers hoped a housing inventory was done at the end of the school year, but that was the exception.

David dropped us off and helped unload the items into the apartment, which wasn't locked. It was dirty, but the trash was empty. We looked at each other knowing we had work ahead before we would sleep the first night. I found a broom and knew a bucket was in one of the luggage boxes. Jed found other buckets in one of the school buildings and the new thirty-gallon barrels Dan and Genie mentioned. The plastic barrels stored clean water after it was hauled from the river. Jed brought water up the bank from the river and I cleaned. Zach was content on my back in his baby carrier. His burn accident delayed his walking and the thought of him crawling on the floor didn't set well with me.

I was good at organizing a box of immediate cooking and cleaning supplies, such as one pot and pan, a few plates, cups and silverware, plus food for a few meals. It was similar to preparing for a camping trip, only I never knew exactly how long I needed to feed us before boxes arrived. I wished the water camping canteens were available, but they were left in Fairbanks. I was thirsty and it took time to find and unpack cups and haul water. Zach would soon need milk. The only milk was a dry

Milkman packet that needed to be prepared and cooled. Of course, the refrigerator was dirty. It was going to be a long day.

Our housing was a two-bedroom apartment with a non-functioning bathroom. At least it had a mirror and was easy to clean. There was basic furniture in the apartment covered with summer dust despite people being there. One bedroom had a double bed and the other room had two twin beds, all mattresses were intact with no stains. Thank goodness for small miracles. I found a small vacuum that worked.

A few people stopped by and introduced themselves. When Jed was down at the river getting water, he learned where to go for even cleaner water for drinking. One of the village visitors brought us fresh fish already cleaned. Yeah, dinner! Despite the dirty apartment we felt welcomed.

While in Fairbanks stocking up on groceries we purchased a seventeen-foot Grumman canoe. We heard the area around Allakaket had rivers that were great for canoeing. It was a white-water canoe selected more for the strength and durability than the white-water aspect. The aluminum was efficient in the Arctic weather conditions. Since we missed the spring/summer barge the only way to get the canoe to Allakaket was to fly it from Fairbanks to Bettles. From there someone needed to canoe it down the river since it was too big to be transported on the smaller flights that flew into Allakaket. Jed offered to fly to Bettles and bring it down river to Allakaket. We had no idea how Zach would take to the canoe so it was the best decision.

When Jed trudged up to the school after coffee the first afternoon, he discovered someone had broken into the school and vandalized it. The maintenance people left two weeks earlier so the incident was recent. With no one checking the school, people in the village didn't know about the break-in. The school was a mess. Jed was assigned the principal teacher position, so it was his responsibility to handle. He called the regional superintendent who gave him authority to hire four people in the village to do the immediate cleanup, but a mechanic would be needed to inspect the generator. Jed and the workers from the village estimated repairs and replacement damages to be at least $3,000, maybe more. Three students were serious suspects, but with no proof, nothing was done. Continuous daylight equated to little supervision of kids who played outside all hours of the day and night.

The regional superintendent, Joe, declared Allakaket School a disaster after Jed explained the full scope of the damages. We thought the action a little overboard, but knew too well the slowness of state systems. Joe said in order to get state funds allocated to correct the issues and make the school safe for students and staff the 'disaster statement' was necessary. Students started school in less than month and winter was close behind. A full assessment of the school's main boiler and generator was required, materials ordered, and maintenance workers arranged. None of these steps were easy in a rural village.

Bettles was thirty-five miles north of the Arctic Circle just south of the Brooks Range. Several services were in Bettles, such as an FAA office, school, grocery store, and a liquor store. It was a destination for F-27 airplanes and mail service center for several villages. F-27 airplanes had seats for fifty-six passengers, with a large cargo area between the cockpit and the passenger cabin. Mail for the various villages in the Bettles surrounding areas filled the plane from Fairbanks to Bettles on a regular basis. Cargo and mail were unloaded into a warehouse and then sent on to the villages via regular Cessna 207 mail plane runs. Bush flights were always based on weight so mail could be slow if there were more passengers traveling.

Jed enjoyed his two-day float from Bettles to Allakaket. Before leaving he gathered information about the waters of the Koyukuk River and animals he might see on his trip by talking to people. When he arrived in Bettles he found the canoe in the airport warehouse, close to the southeast bank of the Koyukuk River. He loaded his daypack, put on his life jacket, and launched the canoe headed for Allakaket. After a hectic week getting us settled into our new housing and dealing with a school incident he deserved a quiet respite. Neither of us had ever canoed so it was a great learning experience and relaxing sojourn with breathtaking scenery.

The day Jed flew up to Bettles to get the canoe I decided to look for the woman Genie said was interested in caring for Zach. When visiting Dan and Genie in Fairbanks I inquired whether they knew about a sitter for Zach. Genie immediately said Marie Henzie. She told us Marie and her husband, Moses were wonderful people and they didn't drink. It seemed odd she added the comment about drinking, but I didn't say anything.

Marie and Moses Henzie lived close to the airport with their daughter, Catherine. It was easy to find someone in Allakaket because the houses had the name of the family above the door. People in Allakaket refused government housing, which we felt was a smart decision. The Bureau of Indian Affairs (BIA) in New Mexico was the contractor for building government houses in Alaska. The weather in New Mexico and Alaska were quite different so many of the BIA houses built in villages had problems. The small log homes designed locally and constructed by village residents in Allakaket were tough, well made, and built with pride. They were basic and intended for the Arctic weather, with limited electricity, and heated solely by wood.

I knocked on Moses and Marie's house. Marie opened the door. I introduced myself and she asked me to come in. Their home was minimal, with a table, four chairs, and a small couch. There was a wooden counter held up by several Blazo boxes that served as shelves. I knew Blazo boxes were universal in village houses. Blazo, a brand of gasoline, was shipped from Seattle to Anchorage and out to villages either on the barge or on an airplane for snow machines. Two five-gallon cans fit in sturdy wooden boxes that were almost as important as the gas.

Marie had just returned from fish camp with Moses and their daughter. They planned to be home for a few days before heading back to finish summer fishing. She helped me get the baby carrier off my back. At first Zach was content to sit on my lap while we talked. When he was ready to get down and do some toddler investigation, I observed Marie as she carefully watched him. Zach didn't always warm up to people easily. His accident had made him stay close to Mommy. Marie's quiet manner was comfortable to him. Their interactions made me feel at ease and assured that my baby would be in good hands.

As I was leaving, Marie offered to show me the traditional Native way to carry babies. I was interested so she brought out a sheet blanket, a type of blanket I had never seen. It was a thin, flannel blanket ordered from the Sears catalog. She folded it into a triangle, laying the long end over the back of her couch. I was told to sit on the couch as she placed Zach on my back. The next step was for me to grab the two pointy sides, cross them around my chest, and tie the ends under Zach's bottom. It took a couple of times before I was able to get him tight enough for my comfort level but it was fantastic. My hands and arms rested under his bottom, which was comfortable. The metal baby carrier often dug into my lower back and this method seemed so much easier. Zach giggled and thought it was funny. I made a note to add a sheet blanket to my Sears order. She offered to lend me the blanket, which I accepted.

Marie and I agreed on a time she would come visit our home. Genie guided me about the appropriate amount to pay her. When I asked Marie what she would charge she suggested a price much lower. We agreed on a price closer to Genie's suggestion. Before I left Marie told me she and Moses didn't drink. I was again surprised this issue was mentioned.

Despite the school break-in, Jed and I enjoyed the slower pace and relaxed entrance to Allakaket. The canoe rides on the rivers and sloughs were remarkable and vital to our desire to be outdoors and enjoy the pristine environment surrounding the area. The water was clean and blue. The aesthetic pleasure of drifting into a new area created a tranquil feeling of bliss. Was it the sound of a bird flying off announcing our arrival or seeing a fish jump that created comfort for us? Even Zach seemed to sense the opportunity for silence.

During our walks through the village and occasional visits with people we learned Allakaket's history. One evening we walked past a church assumed to be Catholic when we saw a sign saying it was Episcopalian. Jed saw Tom, a fellow he ran into when hauling water. Tom explained in the early 1900s, Archdeacon Stuck founded the Episcopal mission in Allakaket and named it St. John's-in-the-Wilderness. His reason for selecting this site was its physical location of the two rivers. At that time the area was an important trail from the Yukon to the mining area around Wiseman. After the mission opened, people came from Arctic City and beyond to make Allakaket their home.

A memorial potlatch happened the last week in August, marking the end of summer. Potlatches were different based on the Alaska Native group hosting the ceremonial occasion. The definition of a potlatch was a social gathering to honor the spiritual, social, and cultural aspects of a community. Potlatches sometimes occurred to thank people who helped during a period of grieving a death or helped with the burial process. Everyone brought food to share and there were traditional ways food was distributed. If the potlatch included gifts they were given out in a customary manner. Sometimes people danced and sang songs. In Allakaket there was an added element—devil water or whiskey. The potlatch became 'party time' and went on until the bottles were empty. When we saw things getting out of hand, we quietly returned home.

Fall was a busy time. People gathered wood. We saw boats return in the late afternoon full with wood moving slowly through the deep water. The teacher housing was heated with oil, which we felt was unfortunate. What if we ran out of oil and the village had none? Allakaket had acres of woods and forests surrounding it. Why did the housing not have a wood stove?

Allakaket was different from Marshall and Holy Cross. Daily chores such as gathering firewood, hauling water from the river, emptying honey buckets, and cooking for dog teams were critical to existence. The Arctic temperatures were known to consistently dip well below zero and remain there for weeks. It was important to keep dogs warm and well fed. With no place to buy straw, local grasses were cut and stored in a cache for the winter. Seining for fish to feed the dogs over the winter was important and a timely task.

Seining occurred after the temperature dropped below freezing, but before the rivers froze up. It involved a net known as a seine net that hung vertically off the side of the boats in the water. When we first arrived we observed people repairing their nets. We visited with Marie and Mo while she wove a new net. Mo carved a moose bone Marie used as the netting needle. In Holy Cross we heard people talk about buying nets because no one knew how to weave a net anymore. Many old crafts were lost there because of the strong missionary influence. We were grateful to see cultural traditions still practiced, but felt they were on the cusp of being gone.

Enough of the school repairs were completed to allow school to start on August 29. A few students were at fish camp, but that was the date we were told to start. The student population was fifty-two students. Genie taught kindergarten, first, and second, I taught third, fourth, and fifth, and helped Jed with the sixth, seventh, and eighth graders. Jed's responsibilities as principal teacher were greater than expected. He was to teach, be principal and maintain the generators and overall maintenance of the $750,000 school building and teacher housing. There were twenty school staff members, mostly part-time, but each required a piece of Jed's time.

We felt personally overwhelmed, but confident we could do the job. Both the regional superintendent and school board promised to support Jed in his decisions and the staff in implementation. The nineteen-member school board had three students who took their responsibilities seriously. The educational changes occurring in Alaska gave school boards additional power, which included hiring teachers and having students on the board. The Alaska Federation of Natives was working with the first Commissioner of Education for Alaska to write the regulations for structuring village schools. One thing was clear—Native people's voices weren't ignored anymore and they were asked to be involved. Time would tell how these changes in responsibility and local authority would affect the students and the communities.

A few days before school started we walked past an area where dog teams were staked. Jed wanted to buy a few sled dogs to start a team, so he started talking to people to learn more about dogs. On another walk a few students came up and said, "I remember you. We saw you in Fairbanks at Dan and Genie's cabin." Soon after that interaction students stopped by our apartment to visit. They came in and sat to observe us, similarly to how kids were in Marshall. One of the students noticed a bottle of Jack Daniels sitting on top of the refrigerator. He looked at Jed and said, "You get drunk tonight?" Jed and I looked at each other perplexed. We assured the students we weren't going to get drunk.

The fall weather was so enjoyable—crisp and cool. One afternoon Genie and her daughter took Zach and I out to pick high-bush cranberries. I was reluctant at first because I was afraid the no-see-ums would eat me alive. Genie told me how to prepare for them. I had never heard of a no-see-um until I arrived in bush Alaska. They were much tinier and meaner than mosquitos with a bite that was extremely more impactful. Each bite caused a red wound that irritated the skin for days. I hated those annoying insect creatures because they crawled up my pants legs and lodged themselves at the top ridge of my socks, and then nibbled around the sock line. Later when I was back indoors the intense itching began. When I checked my leg I discovered bites around the rim of my socks. I couldn't believe I hadn't felt them until it was too late. For some reason if I did as Genie suggested and wore higher socks up to my knees, the little devils didn't make it up that far. I never understood, maybe they were lazy, I wore high socks and I didn't get bit. At least when a mosquito buzzed I had a fighting chance to swat at it, not so with a no-see-um. They were ruthless.

As school started I began to relax about all the non-teaching responsibilities. Jed was still constantly checking the electrical generators.

I knew he felt stressed with the new responsibilities. The power for the school building, plus the two teacher apartments came from two Allis Chalmers 100 kW Diesel generators. There was also an old 90 kW Witte generator or backup system that Jed called the saving grace to ensure consistent electrical output. When the mechanic came to do the school repairs, Jed spent hours learning everything he could about the two AC Diesel plants and the Witte. Continuous electricity was a constant challenge. It was especially important because the electricity powered the oil heaters for the school building and the teacher housing.

During the first week of September, the Allakaket School Board held their first meeting for the year. Jed shared information about the school break-in and the process for getting repairs completed in time to start school. The board thanked Jed for his efforts and nothing else was said about investigating who caused the damage. It was done and over with, time to move forward. The student school board members reported plans for a Halloween carnival, a pancake breakfast, and making gifts to sell for Christmas. The positive interactions from the students were well received by the board members. As parents everywhere, they were proud of the students' enthusiasm and anxious for positive student reports. This type of information was easier to hear and more welcome than the destructive summer behavior.

Before the meeting adjourned, Jed explained that Allakaket had a satellite television system installed in the school over the summer. This communication system was to help strengthen students' education and was available to the community one night each week. People in the village knew something was added to the school over the summer, but not what it was. Jed received training on the system because he was the principal and it was in his classroom.

The community knew of the ATS-1 broadcasting system that provided radios to villages, one at the school and one for the health aide. The satellite radios were the only communication to the 'outside world' when an emergency happened. The health aide had one in her home for these events. A nurse or doctor on the other end gave medical advice to help in emergency situations. Land radios were tried with no luck, maybe because of the mountain ranges or the extreme cold in the winter; we really didn't know.

The second ATS-1 radio was installed in the school so the principal teacher had regular contact with the regional superintendent. Access to the radio was vital when Jed needed to call Joe about the break-in to get repairs started. It would have taken three weeks to let Joe know about the incident if a letter had been mailed and who knows when work would have started.

A year prior to our arrival the federal government launched a nation-wide program, the ATS-6 television system. Three regions of the United States, the Appalachian Mountains, the Rocky Mountains, and fifteen rural Alaska sites were designated for "The Experiment," the name given to the project at the federal level. The TV broadcasting system was to last for one year, a super shock to anyone who knew the cost of setting it up across the nation. We felt confident after the one-year 'experiment' the TV equipment would be added to the pile of other never-to-be-used-again, broken items in buildings and back rooms of schools.

The weekly schedule consisted of two programs for students, one for family and community, and an in-service training for teachers. They were educational-focused television, not sitcoms, news stories, or even *National Geographic* specials. The satellite system cost the federal government $111 million and was to be used in remote areas where there was no access to telephones and daily airplanes. Of the fifteen Alaska sites, only three were really remote; the others had access to phones and airplanes on a regular basis.

The school staff, both full and part-time, met before the school board meeting to discuss having a coffee shop open during the family TV evening. We all agreed students would operate it. Jed wanted to be sure the part-time staff were willing to help with the coffee shop idea since he knew how much work the three of us had on our plates. Genie suggested the funds could be used for another end-of-year trip. The students were thrilled and motivated, asking if they could also sell food. Jed found funding to order a popcorn machine. We were excited about the community plans and felt it would build pride in the school, business skills in the students, and community involvement. Our hope was the ordering and math used selling their products would help with their academic work.

One perk in the satellite radio for Jed was the opportunity to hear conversations and even join in on some in other countries. The satellite gave him an escape and the ability to talk to people in the lower 48 states. He listened to programs from the South Pacific, Australia, Fiji, and even the British Isles. Wellington, NZ and Fiji were especially interested in Alaska, and asked about problems living in such a harsh cold environment. This fringe benefit helped Jed de-stress from the endless maintenance and supervision responsibilities. He shared the conversations and interactions with me from his bi-weekly chats. Keeping Zach entertained in the evenings, fixing food, and cleanup were never-ending evening tasks for me. I did enjoy hearing what was going on in the world. Once in awhile Zach and I joined him at the school.

Knowing the village store was limited to bare necessities and seldom had fresh food, I placed a large food order. The cases and boxes of food arrived slowly, which made it easier to organize. One of my passions was baking. I enjoyed the wonderful aromas of fresh baked bread, muffins, various sweet breads, and cookies. I ordered a case of one-pound boxes of raisins. When they arrived the raisins were in bags of one-ounce boxes. The small boxes were perfect for a small child. One little snack box entertained Zach for at least an hour. He toddled around or sat on his toy snow machine eating raisins one at a time. Sometimes he put the box in the back compartment of his snow machine.

The dog watched him carefully knowing there was food to be eaten. While Zach played, the dog sat patiently, drooling over the morsels of food. When released Hidalgo cleaned up the raisins and I cleaned up the dog drool.

Students in Allakaket had positive and strong self-images. We attributed this to the previous teachers' concentration on a Native culture curriculum. While this approach was a welcomed change from other villages where we taught, we observed an interesting drawback. Many of the students had no interest in academic skills or books at the school. In a way we understood about the textbooks. They weren't relevant to their lives and had no significance to them. Another problem we encountered was lack of respect for any school structure and self-management skills when in school. Genie, Dan, Jed, and I had many discussions about the balance of western education and respect for Native culture.

Based on their first year experience, Genie provided some guidance. She found many students struggled to read, so she paired older and younger students together for reading. This approach helped both groups of students. The benefit resulted in different levels of reading skill development. It was a great idea. Students didn't feel belittled. Genie and I worked as a team with reading, language engagement, and story writing lessons. Students moved between classrooms with focused tasks and created storybooks about village life. Word lists related to students' environments were developed and used to build vocabulary in the three classrooms.

The coffee shop and food preparation sparked an interest in math skills. Work tasks for the weekly menu preparations became math exercises. Progress was slow but encouraging. When setting up my classroom, I discovered some education catalogs. I noticed the date and discovered they arrived during the past summer. With the school in disorder I kept finding surprises.

As I plowed through the catalogs, I found a comic book reading program. We knew kids enjoyed comic books, so I ordered the series. It wasn't expensive, which made it easier to find funding. With Jed busy with the maintenance responsibilities Genie and I included his students in our reading program. We decided older students could read the comics to younger students. While waiting for the series to arrive and to generate enthusiasm we created bulletin boards about them. The comic books worked across all grade levels and improved reading.

Changes were rapidly happening in Alaska. Less than ten years after Alaska had become a state and a few years before our arrival, oil was discovered in Prudhoe Bay. Money and greed pushed many groups and individuals to want a piece of Alaska's oil profits. The 1973 oil crisis stirred up debates about the need for new energy sources, such as the Trans-Alaska Pipeline System (TAPS), or 'the pipeline.' Again, the newly formed Alaska Federation of Natives was needed to ensure Alaska Native people received some benefits from the pipeline.

Building the pipeline wasn't easy. The engineers dealt with many obstacles. The extreme cold, the isolated terrain, and permafrost made the construction challenging. Several of the men in Allakaket worked on the pipeline. When they came home they were fat with cash and not sure what to do with it. New kickers (boat engines), ATVs, the latest snow machines, and rifles were purchased and still money was leftover. Union wages and the cash economy produced a new experience. No one could have predicted this problem, and it got worse. Living a subsistence lifestyle hadn't required a lot of cash.

One day a Cessna 207 plane arrived with a pilot, no seats, and cases of Calvert Whiskey and beer stuffed in every nook and cranny of the plane. We read the plane could handle as much as fourteen hundred pounds when we first chartered one. No food, gas, or mail—just whiskey and beer—filled this five-passenger plane. It was a charter from the liquor store in Bettles. It wasn't a weekend, but the attitude was "Let the party begin. And it did!" Students weren't fed and children ran around the village sleeping wherever they could find a quiet spot to lay their heads. People drank until the bottles were empty and the beer was gone. Jed and I were stunned.

Genie and Dan hadn't mentioned the whiskey/beer runs, but agreed it was a problem. Students' behavior was more agitated when people drank. We thought maybe food would help since many arrived at school hungry. Lunch was part of the daily school program, but not breakfast. Federal food was sent to the villages, such as large cans of peanut butter, Tang, cocoa, coffee, and large blocks of cheese. Additional items purchased included dry milk, spam, tuna fish, and boxes of pilot bread.

Part II: Teaching and Learning

I knew pilot bread and Tang were staples in fish camp. Pilot bread and dry fish were essential to hunters and dog mushers. Both were easy to stick in a pack or pocket and didn't freeze. Pilot bread was new to me, but quickly became a favorite of mine. It tasted great with peanut butter or dry fish. I couldn't stomach Tang but drank it during visits to village homes.

We decided to offer peanut butter, pilot bread, Tang, and cocoa for morning snacks when they arrived at school. We found a convenient location in the school that worked for the three classrooms. At first students were surprised but after a few days they were on board with the breakfast program. It was messy at first, but no one overindulged. The atmosphere at school was less agitated, students were more focused, and the importance of breakfast reaffirmed.

December was a great month in Allakaket. Students sold holiday gifts and held a bake sale. Jed's parents made it for our Christmas break and had a true Arctic experience. We were grateful that during their visit no whiskey runs from Bettles occurred. Everyone in Allakaket was engaged in the fun of the season's activities creating laughter and good times. With a full week off we were able to relax and enjoy our family.

Alaska's crazy weather wasn't the fault for Harold and Peggy's frustrating experience getting into Allakaket. Their flight from LAX to Fairbanks was delayed with fog in LA, followed by a blown tire and punctured right wing in the airplane, all while sitting on the runway. When they arrived in Fairbanks it was minus thirteen degrees. With barely five hours of sleep, they stuffed their luggage and boxes into a Frontier Flying Service Cessna 185 charter directly into Allakaket. As they headed north and then west, they flew over two Pipeline camps and the Arctic Circle. Harold was ready for fanfare during the Arctic Circle crossing. Gary, the pilot politely told him some pilots pull back the stick abruptly, forcing a small bounce or jerk action. When asked, "What was that?" the pilot smiles and says, "We just crossed the Arctic Circle."

Gary buzzed the village and, of course, there were several of us out there to welcome the guests of honor. Students wanted to see what Jed's parents looked like. *Kids are the same everywhere.* The temperature was minus twenty when they arrived at noon on December 22. The shadowy daylight reminded us all, the shortest day of the year just occurred. Everyone was amazed once again the different food items made it. Boxes sat who knows where while the airplane issues were figured out. Harold remembered dry ice for the ice cream and hand carried many of the priceless veggies I requested. I couldn't believe the ice cream was still hard. We were all grateful to whoever created dry ice!

The next morning the temperature dropped to minus thirty as Jed, his dad, and Hidalgo ventured out for the tree. On Christmas Eve we all went to the village hall and enjoyed singing carols, as well as the exchange of gifts from ole St. Nick. Allakaket's St. Nick wasn't your usual jovial, friendly type. He frightened the children as they came forth to get their gifts. I was glad Zach was content to sit on my lap.

The following days were active with dog races, regardless of the temperature. It ranged from minus twenty to minus fifty. There were also snowshoe and coaster races, followed up in the evening with dances. Local fiddlers and guitarists, along with an occasional caller for square dancing, added to the fanfare. At night the temperature continued to drop. After a lovely Christmas dinner with Mo, Marie, Dan, Genie, plus their children, we all made it to the hall for another dance. As we walked home the temperature reached minus forty-eight degrees and the Northern Lights staged a stunning display of brilliant colors. They danced across the sky in varying grays and flickers of color in the night darkness. For some reason I felt the colder the temperature the more intense the color. Maybe my brain and thinking were just frozen.

The beauty of the Northern Lights night made us linger and want to stay outside, but the need to get inside was crucial. Intense cold temperatures played with your mind and lead to frostbite in five minutes. Body temperature decreases as blood moves into the core to keep your heart and lungs warm to prevent hypothermia. When circulation slows down, the blood in your extremities can start to freeze. Jed moved us along and back into the warmth of the apartment.

Potlucks were held before the dances at the hall and gave Jed's parents an opportunity to meet local families. I shared with Peggy that it was considered bad luck for women to eat bear meat. I wanted to be respectful of cultural traditions. It was said if women ate bear meat their hunter wouldn't get a bear the next time he hunted. Alaska Native people watched and listened to the environment. It was different than the non-Native hunter's frame of mind. Tracking and obtaining an animal was an honor for the Native hunter, which was contrary to the dominant non-Native mindset when they hunted. Alaska Native people said, "I am going out," not "I am going to bag a moose or bear." It was similar to the animal sharing itself, more than dominating the animal with superior powers. I saw it as a demonstration of humbleness toward nature and what it provided.

When Harold spilled his tea at the potluck, it froze to the floor. The wood stove hadn't been on long so the building was cold. Everyone kept their coats on and kids ran around in the hall to keep warm. Harold had moose head soup for the third time and decided it was an acquired taste. Jed's parents found it interesting Zach loved dry fish and ate it like candy. He was introduced to it in Holy Cross when he was teething. Mary taught me that chewing on it would soothe his gums. What a mess he was after he finished! He received nourishment as he pacified the teeth breaking through the gums. The Native elders thought he was cute when he toddled over to greet them with his fishy fingers.

The day after Christmas the 'real' dog races took place. Each team had ten or fewer dogs. The temperature dropped to minus fifty-five degrees so we figured the races would be called off. We were wrong. After the races, one of the mushers gave Harold and Peggy a short ride in his sled, which was quite exhilarating for them. They were bundled up tight with extra layers because it was so cold. I was proud they seized the spirit of the moment—carpe diem!

They found it interesting to see the dogs from inside the sled. As each dog was harnessed to the center rope they barked and jumped with enthusiasm. When the musher added the lead dog at the front it was crazy with noise and animal excitement. Then the break was released and the dogs were off. The dogs lunged forward at full speed and then magically settled into a trot, listening for their musher's commands, quietly panting as they moved along the trail.

Sunday was departure day for Harold and Peggy. They talked with Gary when they flew into Allakaket and explained they were headed to Hawaii. Western and Alaska Airlines had joined forces to provide this holiday opportunity. Peggy's brother and family lived in Hawaii so they were off to see them for the New Year's weekend before returning to LA.

The morning for their travel was beautiful with a clear sky. The temperature hovered at minus forty-three, not bad. We chatted about the warmth they would enjoy in Hawaii and reminded them to give

Part II: Teaching and Learning

hugs to everyone. Jed checked the weather in Fairbanks and found it only had a quarter of mile visibility due to ice fog. No flying happened that day so the sleeping bags were rolled back out on the twin beds and dinner planned for another night.

Gary was able to fly in Tuesday morning. Two days of thick ice fog squelched Hawaii out of their plans. We all headed out to the airport to bid them farewell. Peggy and Harold were intrigued with Zach wrapped on my back nestled into my kuspuk parka. After being there for a week, they felt confident he was toasty warm in the subzero temperatures. A fur hat and gloves protected his skin if he peered out, but he wasn't that crazy with below zero temperatures.

Early in January one of the houses in town caught on fire. It was between the school and our living quarters. Sparks from a wood stove landed on the floor, starting the fire. Many of us, including the people who owned the house, were at the hall watching a movie. A couple of guys who saw the fire broke into the school to grab the fire extinguishers. They should have gone to the hall and announced, "Fire." The 'fire fighters' were drunk and didn't make a good decision. The home was destroyed, all the fire extinguishers were exhausted, and two of the three doors at the school were broken and not easily repairable. At least no one had died and the fire hadn't spread.

The week before a young man had snow machined to the next village. He was drinking when the decision was made. No one stopped him. The temperature was minus thirty degrees and dropping. His snow machine gave out and he wasn't prepared. A trapper from the other village who was checking his trap line found him the next day.

Jed hauling water in Allakaket
December 1974

The house fire was the second fire experienced in Allakaket. The first fire was in the fall shortly after school started. Fires were never a pleasant experience, under the best of circumstances. With no running water they easily escalated into at 'out of control' fire. The fall fire started because kids had seen a movie at the hall in which burning arrows were shot at a building. Shortly after the movie ended, several kids in the village started shooting burning arrows at the village hall, resulting in a fire. Luckily people were mingling around outside, saw the fire, and stopped it before it built momentum. We didn't know about it until the next day.

The recent fire meant the school and teacher apartments were without fire extinguishers. Jed immediately reported this to the regional superintendent. It was January with extreme cold in several villages. We were told it could take a month before replacements would arrive. This thought was not reassuring. The temperature continued to drop to at least minus twenty to twenty-five degrees at night with little warmth during the day. Hauling water always required extra time to break the ice. Seconds and minutes were important in emergencies and we were hopeful there wouldn't be any fires, at least until the replacement fire extinguishers arrived.

So much for hope—two weeks after the house fire Jed noticed one of the Allis Chalmers generators was not functioning. The needed part was ordered. With only one working generator and the thought of no electricity he was anxious. The next day he noticed the working generator was burning oil heavily, so he increased his checkups. On Friday afternoon he smelled smoke as he walked into the building. When he looked up he saw the ceiling was on fire throwing sparks in the direction of the day fuel tank. The inspection cap had vibrated off which created an easier point of entry for a spark to land. Jed was fully aware now there was a direct and open link between this tank and the twenty thousand gallons of fuel in the bulk tank close by. His first thought was, "Where is the best place to run?" His second thought was, "Where would it be safe to run with that much fuel exploding?"

Deciding the best choice was to replace the inspection cap and gracefully announce to everyone the generator building was on fire, he returned to the school. He was aware there were no fire extinguishers, no running water, and the river had four feet of ice covering it! What miracle was going to save us all from being blown to who knew where and how long would it take before anyone would know the entire village of Allakaket was gone.

When Jed arrived back at the school and made the announcement about the fire, a couple of older students jumped up and said they would find people hauling water. Usually someone was at the water hole. Jed then directed a few students to get the water from the school's kitchen and teachers' quarters. Genie and I stood there for a moment not sure how we could be helpful. The remaining students wanted to see what was really happening. Knowing we needed to keep out of the way, we gathered the remaining students together. We explained they were to stay close to us. Everyone headed to the boiler/generator building.

Just as Jed and the students exhausted the last drop of water from the school and teachers' homes, several snow machines arrived. A casual bystander would have thought this scenario had been practiced in advance. The adults started a second bucket brigade from the barrels on the sleds to the students close to the ladder. Jed was at the top of the ladder emptying the buckets. He was wet because buckets had to be thrown upwards toward the ceiling. *Not a good thing when at twenty below zero, but he was standing in front of a fire.* After what seemed like forever, the fire was out. The whole scene about the fire, knowing the reality of no fire extinguishers, lack of hoses and running water, and watching Jed be the person to deal with the fire was more than I could handle. I was concerned about him getting hurt or burned. Jed told people later, I celebrated the event by passing out on the steps of the generator building. My job was to stay out of the way, but I failed.

With everyone feeling confident the fire was out, Jed released everyone to go home. He wanted to fully check the building to be sure no fires would start any time soon, if ever. A couple of men from the community who knew a little about generators assisted in the inspection. They agreed a defective valve worked loose and took up residence in the muffler, which was mounted near the ceiling. The leaked fuel became hot enough to ignite the muffler and the ceiling. We were lucky Jed was checking the generators regularly. Jed and I were thankful everyone was sober and worked as a team. Allakaket had a strong community spirit when no one was drinking. It was hard to really relax and sleep that night. My mind still raced with different *what if? thoughts*. I was glad Jed was safe, but knew he was worried about next steps.

The entire village was now without electricity. Both Allis Chalmers were down and the Witte still didn't work. The good news was the oil heaters for both of the teacher apartments still worked and Jed was able to stabilize the school at fifty degrees. After securing the generator building and closing the school he came home. Not knowing when electricity would be regained a decision about continuing school was on the table. We knew if school was closed the days missed were added to the end of the year. When the last day of school rolled around everyone—students, parents, and staff—was ready to be out. Alaska village schools were normally out by early to mid-May because families went to fish camps.

The three of us agreed—keep logging days. We decided our approach would be to hold individual and group conferences with students in our homes. We would provide homework for them to do. The only way to get the word out was to visit each family. We created a schedule and divided the families into two lists. Jed had the furnace to deal with, so Genie and I handled the visits to each home. Families agreed and students showed up on time.

Marie took Zach to her house since our living room was now a classroom. During the individual conferences students received work, which they returned the next day. If they had problems they were to ask for help, either from an older student or us. At night we reviewed their work, as well as prepared assignments for the next day. To our amazement the plan worked well. Students completed the work and seemed proud of their daily completion sheets. We found they helped each other. The bottom line was school continued. We were encouraged at how students and families understood the seriousness of the situation and pitched in to make it work. The comic book reading series helped. Students read stories to younger students and to their parents.

All three of us were busy, with Genie and I teaching and Jed with the generator problems. He kept learning on the job about the different maintenance issues. Sometimes someone in the village had experience that helped him. With limited resources on hand, his tactic was to rob useable parts from one generator to make the other one operable. I was impressed with his resourcefulness. I knew he enjoyed building things and was good at it when he tackled a project. Within five days we were back to full electricity, the school was thawed out, and students returned to a normal schedule in the school building.

At the next staff meeting we evaluated the emergency, including the strengths of how it had been handled. Most of the part-time staff members were parents so they had the perspective of seeing their children do work at home individually and with friends. Everyone agreed students accomplished as much at home as they did at school. Jed explained, "Despite the success of what we did, the state wouldn't have approved it." Our jaws hung open and one staff-parent asked the question we were all thinking, "Why?" Jed said, "Using Coleman lanterns was illegal and students weren't in school for full days, plus they were taught in private homes." We were all quiet, looked at each other, unsure of what to say. The thoughts running through my mind were: we were alive, students learned, and everyone was engaged, including parents and community members. That sounded like solid education to me.

Part II: Teaching and Learning

Now that the school was functioning and we returned to normalcy with electricity, the weather dropped. This time it stayed locked firmly at sixty-five degrees below zero. Maybe it was colder but the thermometer outside the apartment's lowest point was sixty-five below. The gauge was stuck there for three long weeks. I became crazed watching it and was sure it was broken because it never moved. Growing up in warm weather I never imagined living in a harsh, icy, deep-freezer environment. Still, there was beauty in the starkness I saw through the windows or when I bundled up to gather the clothes hanging outside. When I walked from the apartment to the school I made an effort to look around, but my face was covered. When Jed came in from hauling water or being outside for chores his beard was frozen. Beards froze and whiskers broke off if touched too soon. It was important to drip dry while thawing out or loose a piece of your beard. I saw it happen twice.

Water became even more priceless to me after the fires. I became obsessed with saving water in every way possible. When I cooked and needed to drain water from potatoes I saved it for cooking vegetables or rice. Sometimes I used it for sourdough starter or for baking tasks. I saved rinse water from dishes and baths to use again to wash the floor or for the first soak of Zach's diapers. Bathing in the big galvanized tub in the kitchen was planned with no interruptions or the bath was cold. Zach was first, then Jed or me, depending on what was happening. It certainly wasn't a relaxing bath with a lit candle, soft music, and glass of wine.

I had a wringer washing machine in the large room next to our apartment. It was always full of water for diapers, a three-cycle process requiring water each time. First I soaked them using recycled water (step 1), then drained that water and washed them with clean water (step 2), and then rinsed them with clean water (step 3). His diapers required a lot of hauled water. No matter the temperature I hung the diapers outside to dry. When it was minus twenty to minus sixty-five the air was extremely dry resulting in the moisture disappearing. After being outside for five to six hours I brought the clothes inside to finish drying. Diapers were part of each day. How many clean ones do I have? Marie was wonderful to help me during the week. When I bundled up to go outside to retrieve the diapers they were stiff as a board. I hung them everywhere in the apartment. I had never seen cloth rigid. They didn't take long to dry because oil heaters dried the air, and my skin, too.

The second week of February arrived and we began to notice a little more light at both ends of the day. The temperature seemed to be closer to minus twenty than fifty below zero. Allakaket taught me my temperature limits. After twenty-five degrees below zero I was unable to tell if it was colder. I couldn't breathe without a scarf around my face. When I saw Jed go outside in short sleeves when the weather jumped up from sixty-five degrees below to twenty degrees below I realized, "Wow! We, as humans, can and do acclimate to where we live." I had never been a person who could handle over one hundred degrees. Watching Jed go outside made me wonder if I could adjust to heat, as he had to cold.

The fun about more light and a degree of warmer temperatures was we could be outside more. We were anxious to work with our dog team. The original plan was to have thirteen dogs by late winter, but the litter of pups we were to get died before we received them. Our team remained small—six dogs: three Siberian huskies, two Aurora huskies, and one trusty Labrador retriever, Hidalgo, the lead dog by default. Jed drove the team as Zach and I sat in the sled. Zach was quite verbal helping his dad with the commands. I felt sorry for the dogs since they had two voices to distinguish. It was a highlight of Zach's day so what could I say? The dogs adapted, better than I thought they would. It was tremendous fun and by the end of the season we were looking forward to having more dogs the following winter.

In March, Dan left the village for ten days. Dan and Genie traveled to Russia to visit primary schools in the late '60s before coming to Alaska. Dan had a Ford Fellowship that provided travel funds for his family. They accompanied him in visiting Russian schools and bringing information back to the United States. He spoke Russian fluently and occasionally worked as a Russian interpreter. The Russians contacted Alaska to purchase a small herd of musk ox. The hope was to reestablish a herd in Siberia by transporting a healthy herd from Alaska. Dan was asked to travel with the state representatives and Russian visitors as the interpreter. The trip was to the community of Mekoryuk on Nunivak Island to see the herd and make arrangements for the musk oxen to be shipped to Russia. When he returned, it was dinner at their house with his famous *piroshkis*, meat-filled pastries sold on the sidewalks in Russia. They were amazing and so were his stories of his big adventure with the Russians.

We gave Dan money to purchase a mask. The masks from Mekoryuk we saw in *Alaska* magazine and at the museum in Fairbanks were captivating. Nunivak Island was strongly rooted in ancient times, a characteristic of each mask. Mask makers were committed to the tradition of designing each mask in a one-of-a-kind design. The artists ensured there was a strong connection to the animals in their environment. Bones or horns were part of each mask that told a story about the circle of life for a particular animal.

March meant it was time for the Iditarod. We were especially excited this year because we sort of knew two people entering the race. One of the racers was a former teacher from Allakaket and the other was a

Resting dogs before returning home
February 1975

person from Hughes, a village downriver. The Great Race to Nome was always unpredictable and entering the race didn't mean a person would finish. Like us, the big event was in its third year. Each year it became more sophisticated with rules and support systems. The grueling one thousand-plus miles race had such unforeseeable weather ranging from forty degrees below zero (or colder) to thirty degrees above. There was always open water somewhere along the way and the chance a person might be lost because of a blizzard.

The former teacher had to scratch when he made it to Nulato. His dogs' feet were having issues and were cut up. Dogs wore booties, but sometimes they came off. Mushers generally didn't know or see when it happened until it was too late. Dog paws needed time to heal. Henry from Hughes was sixth overall, which was great. I felt anyone who entered was a winner. The big deal about Henry placing in the top ten spots was his lead dog was from Allakaket. Lead dogs were trained differently and cost more than the other dogs. Even though we weren't in a village the race traveled through, we felt a part of the big event. I saw in Jed's eyes the desire to enter the race at some point.

During the last week of March the entire staff, part-time and full-time, attended a meeting in Tanana, where the regional office was located. Tanana, a small community established by the US Bureau of Indian Affairs, was ninety-nine miles south of Allakaket and approximately 140 miles west of Fairbanks. Most of the two hundred people that lived in Tanana were Koyukon Athabaskan Indians. Two rivers, the Tanana and the great Yukon, joined together creating a logical trading post. In the 1930s. a small four-bed regional hospital was established there to serve people throughout most of the northern regions of Alaska. It had limited services, and was a triage stop for anyone with serious problems.

Schools throughout the Tanana region sent teachers, staff members, school board members, bilingual instructors, and Indian Education representatives, as well as preschool, special education, and Title I aides to the meeting. The purpose of the workshop was to hear how the schools were doing in meeting educational goals established by the communities. Staff and school board members were to offer suggestions about how to improve student outcomes. Questions and conversations like this were new to many of the people attending.

Rural villages hired local people for teacher aides and part-time staff positions, but the majority of teachers came from the lower 48. Most of the teacher aides and maintenance positions were parents who never attended meetings or became involved in making decisions because they had never been asked. This meeting was a first for creating opportunities for new exchanges. People from villages were unsure how to respond.

During the conversations about village schools we began to question the progress of our students academically. The Allakaket School staff and school board members agreed students weren't doing as well as they should. While in Allakaket we heard elders share information about how long ago each member of the family had duties and tasks to complete, including children. Currently, the old traditional work responsibilities and discipline system wasn't being implemented. Children had limited structural boundaries and too much free time.

We felt frustrated, confused, and unsure of our abilities as teachers. The idea of working under the guidance of an active school board had been simple in June when we took the jobs and again in the fall during the first couple of meetings. All the drinking and violence associated with it stressed us to the point of unclear direction. We knew the school board had questions about student progress too. Rural Native villages were at a peak of historical, social, and economic turning points. The issues seemed like the proverbial elephant in the room that no one talked about. It was too new and raw.

Suddenly, I knew I needed to leave. Shortly after we arrived in Tanana, Zach started vomiting. At first I thought it was the flying, although the time in the air was barely twenty minutes and it was very smooth. After being on the ground a few hours I realized Zach's behavior was more than airsickness. Jed walked us over to the Tanana Public Health Hospital.

The hospital wanted to watch him for the night as they monitored his continual bouts of vomiting. I sat in a chair or stood next to his crib at the hospital. By morning the doctor on duty felt strongly Zach either had a brain tumor or spinal meningitis, neither one a good prognosis. I was in shock when Jed arrived to check on us early in the morning.

The doctor booked Zach and I on a flight into Fairbanks to see a specialist for further testing. The nurses reinforced the doctor's advice to encourage him to drink water so he didn't become dehydrated. Someone handed me large paper-towel like bandages, in case Zach was sick on the flight, as she placed the address where I was going in my hand. Another person said the temperature in Fairbanks was right at zero degrees, the norm for that time of year. Feeling foggy and barely able to speak, I said goodbye to Jed as he handed me my daypack and loaded us on the plane. Once again I was handling this by myself. I was scared and just felt like crying. I couldn't even remember if I had slept the night before.

No messes occurred on the plane ride to Fairbanks and I easily found a taxi. As I sat down in the taxi he asked, "Where to?" For a moment my mind went blank and then I remembered the note in my pocket. I fished out the address and off we headed for the clinic. The ride was bumpy because of the icy streets. The thawing and refreezing of the snow caused layers of ice to form potholes.

We just sat down in the waiting room, when Zach had diarrhea everywhere. The blanket keeping him warm saved my clothes. What a mess! I felt someone close and saw a doctor walking toward us. He smiled and said, "Mrs. Reagle, I presume. This is wonderful news." I looked up at him as if he was crazy. My expression told him I needed an explanation. He continued, "Vomiting is related to head issues and diarrhea is a sign of a strong case of the flu." I should have remembered the differences between vomiting and diarrhea. I felt relieved, but still stressed. The nurses helped clean Zach up, put all of the soiled clothes in a plastic bag, and found a donated blanket from one of the many angels that provide such items to clinics and hospitals.

The doctor advised us to stay in Fairbanks until the next morning just to confirm Zach didn't have any other issues. I called some friends we knew from our first year in Alaska. They now lived in Fairbanks. We stayed in contact and saw them whenever we were in Fairbanks. They graciously welcomed us into their home for the night, a common trait of people who knew people in the bush. After a conversation with the doctor we were on the morning flight to Tanana to participate in the last couple of hours of the meeting. Zach was back to his normal playful, toddler self. I was exhausted from the emotional and physical toll a scare like that has on a person. I just wanted to curl up and sleep. No time allowed for that luxury. The meeting ended that afternoon and everyone loaded onto charters to different villages. Back to life as usual.

April arrived proclaiming the start of spring carnivals in all the villages around us and in Allakaket. The festive events were celebrations of longer days and confirmation we made it through another long, winter. Dog races, snowshoeing, potlatches, tasty food, fiddling and dances, visitors from other villages, and whiskey runs. Not everyone drank until the whiskey ran out like we saw during the winter, but it was heavy.

We thought it would be fun to see how other villages celebrated spring, so the three of us jumped on a charter headed downriver to Husila. In Tanana, Jed chatted with teachers in different villages so he knew we could sleep on the floor in a school while visiting. In Husila we were lucky and stayed with a teaching couple in their quarters. Their running water made taking a shower easy. I washed my hair and stood an extra minute under the showerhead letting the hot water run down my back.

It was a fun, stress-free weekend where we made new friends. Another teaching couple traveled to Husila via their dog team consisted of giant malamutes. Jed was quite impressed. We saw George Attla[12], known as the *Husila Hustler*, in a dog team race place first in the men's division. What a treat it was to see him in person.

The spontaneous trip was a fun break and a breath of fresh air from the drinking exploits in Allakaket. The weekend before we left for Husila, Jed helped rescue a kid, Jimmy, who was caught in a snow machine track. His dad had been drinking heavily and driving too fast for the turn he made as he came up the bank in front of our window. Jed was standing at the window drinking coffee when he saw the machine stop and the awkward figure of the kid hanging from the side of the machine. His dad stumbled around to the side as Jed put his coffee down and ran outside. He used his pocketknife to cut the rubber track of the snow machine freeing the young boy's leg.

His leg had a strange diagonal type of cut that kept it from bleeding profusely. A couple of other people showed up. Jed told someone to run ahead and tell Agnes, the health aide and mother of Jimmy, to call for a medevac out of Allakaket. Jed cautioned them to wait to tell her it was Jimmy until after the call was made. Thankfully she wasn't drinking and was able to wrap his leg to control the bleeding. Jimmy hadn't grabbed his coat when he ran outside with his dad. The spring Arctic temperature was ten degrees above zero, which was still cold no matter how acclimated. He started shivering, a combination of cold and shock. Jed offered a couple of blankets to keep Jimmy warm during the flight to the hospital.

The April weekly weekend spring carnivals resulted in some issues including low attendance at school and more village drinking. Our class size dropped to 50 percent because families went to different villages for races and other activities. Village carnivals weren't like city events with rides and Ferris wheels. There were no trucks bringing in equipment and setting up ring toss games. There were dog races, snowshoeing, and two-leg gunnysack contests, with occasional snow machine competitions and potlatches in the evenings.

We changed the school schedule to start school at noon and end at 6:00 p.m. The previous teachers had started the alternative arrangement when the days became longer. Students were outside late in the evening and showed up late to school. It helped a bit, but attendance continued to be low. People in the village believed nothing could be done to get kids to school. We felt responsible for not having the critical component—kids—to do our jobs.

Jed heard over the winter that April was when logging projects started. Frank, one of his friends, asked him if he wanted to help 'knock down some logs.' The following Friday Jed left after school with three fellows. Two snow machines with two sleds traveled up the Koyukuk to the Henshaw River where they set up a wall tent in the snow. The tent was heated using a Yukon stove, with a pipe extended up through the tent. Wood was burned in the stove providing heat at night and a place to cook. By Sunday afternoon forty logs were felled, limbed, and ready to be floated after breakup.

Although it was hard work, there was fun, camaraderie, and a few challenges. One tree became lodged before it hit the ground. Three trees were felled on top of it and still it didn't shake loose. A decision was made to try an old trick seldom used. Albert explained the strategy to Jed and gave him the opportunity for the first shot. The goal was to shoot the branch of the tree supporting the four logs with a .30-30 and make them all fall. Was he perfect with the shot? Did the tree need the vibration from the bullet? It didn't matter; it worked and they were done.

There were a couple of groups in the area logging, but Jed needed to get back for school Monday morning. A couple of boats stopped by their camp over the weekend and informed them there was a BIG party in Allakaket. Frank considered staying to help one of the other logging groups, but decided to head home. He should have kept logging.

The next morning Frank was found dead in his bed. His throat was slit and he was stabbed multiple times. The knife was found in his wife's bed. There was much confusion over the details because no one was sober. The troopers arrived and took Elma, his wife, to jail in Fairbanks. She had never been out of the village. Her whole life was along the river, not even a trip to Bettles. Three sons watched at the airport as the troopers loaded their mom, two of whom were my students. They were now without their dad and mom.

The drinking became worse after Elma was taken with her husband's body. We continued with school because that was our job. It was difficult and some days even painful. Frank's body was returned for the funeral, but that couldn't happen until a hole was dug. For three days, three men (one of them Jed) worked with axes to dig a grave five and a half feet deep and six and a half feet long. The boys were shuffled amongst relatives, depending on who wasn't drinking. Elma still hadn't returned. It was decided the service needed to happen during a semi-lag in the drinking and before the body became more bloated.

After Frank's death I watched his two sons in my class carefully. I was surprised they even showed up, but in some way I think school was comforting to them. School had a routine and there was no normalcy anywhere in the village. Every day something crazy seemed to happen. One afternoon, right after lunch, Jed came into my class and said, "Fred's in the school yard with a loaded gun." He was forewarned from Ernie earlier that morning that Fred had gone berserk from drinking too much and was wandering around the village waving a gun. Jed told me to alert Genie. We were to keep students down and away from the windows while he went out to talk to Fred and get the gun. He had already locked the school doors. Once again I was to act normal (and hopefully, not faint this time) while he was in a life and death situation.

He walked cautiously outside and talked with Fred. Whatever was said between them worked. The gun was handed to Jed and they walked off together. Genie and I carried on as if things were normal or routine with the students. The older ones kept quiet even though they were fully aware something serious had happened with Fred. If Jed told me later what was said I don't remember.

Part II: Teaching and Learning

Two weeks after Frank was killed his oldest son shot himself in the head, while one of his brothers watched. The one that watched was in my class and even showed up for school the next day. I hardly knew what to say. "Sorry for your loss," just didn't seem appropriate or even enough. The younger brother also attended school that day. At least the day ended with me knowing both boys had eaten something.

When Jed came to see if I was ready to go home that day, he found me sitting on the floor of the small reading room, rocking back and forth in a trance. I was shaken to my core and not sure what we as teachers were doing that helped. Why was this village having such a rough year? All the changes in Alaska hadn't improved this village, at least not right now. Were there too many changes too fast? Alaska Natives were strong and proud people. One thing I knew for certain: what we were experiencing was never covered in any teacher education program or in the Alaska orientation training we participated in the first summer.

April was the longest month of our lives—so much drinking and too many deaths. May was a fresh start. The midnight sun stretched the daylight of the days. I still wasn't accustomed to going to sleep in daylight, waking in the middle of the night to daylight, and then getting up a few hours later to daylight. The river broke up on May 10, which meant people in the village were headed to spring camp. Genie and the students reminded us we were to send schoolwork to spring camp. Our plan was to visit each family during the week in our canoe. We figured we could visit two families per day, which was perfect.

Change of plans—another fire! *What?* Faulty wiring or malfunctioning heat tapes wrapped around pipes to keep them from freezing started a subfloor fire under Dan and Genie's apartment. The two teacher apartments were connected with a large room between them.

Under the floor of both apartments were distribution boxes used to carry septic and oil lines to the quarters. The fire was located along the route to the oil tank. It took Jed six chain saw cuts into the floor before he located the exact spot where a raging fire was headed full speed toward the last of the full five-hundred-gallon container oil tanks.

Everyone was asked to leave both apartments in case the fire blew up the building. The powerful flames seemed unbeatable. Lucky for us not everyone had left for spring camp. The community pulled together and helped extinguish the fire. A couple of fellows who worked at the school even attempted to empty the tank when they heard Jed mention it. Their plan was quickly derailed, because of course, the transfer pump didn't work and there was no place to rent another one.

While those who were left helped put the fire out, the health aide sent a garbled satellite radio message to the hospital in Tanana. The communication received was that the teachers' quarters were on fire next to the bulk storage tank. Interestingly, when the message reached the regional superintendent and was relayed to Fairbanks it had changed to, "Both teacher quarters in Allakaket were burned to the ground and a bulk tank had exploded." The Bureau of Land Management (BLM) smoke jumpers arrived just as Jed confirmed the fire was out. Although it was unnecessary for them to be there, it was good to have extra sets of eyes to validate the fire was out. The BLM lead told Jed he had done a great job. Jed confided to him there were a few moments that seemed to go on for hours where he wasn't sure everything was going to work out.

After everyone returned from spring camp we planned a village picnic at the airfield. It was fun. We cooked hamburgers, hot dogs, potato chips, and played baseball. Ice cream was to be the big surprise, but was eaten after the fire. All those that helped with the fire, including the smoke jumpers, enjoyed that special treat. The electrical wiring destroyed in the fire meant there was no refrigerator or freezer. The ice cream would have melted so it was eaten. Jed had no reason to work on the electricity since it was light all the time and the temperatures were now in the sixties to seventies during the day and fifties at night.

The year in Allakaket had drained both teaching couples. The various situations and emotions were packed with extremes, both high and low. When the village was engaged and everyone was sober, it was culturally rich and traditionally in harmony with the environment. When the alcohol took over it was scary to watch. I saw moms drinking while carrying their babies in barely a t-shirt and diaper, as they went from house to house during subzero weather. It broke my heart because I knew they were good moms. People struggled with all the change and influences the new cash economy created.

Some people in the village suggested I give Zach to Marie and Mo. Shocked at first, I maintained enough sense to quietly listen while they explained. Marie couldn't have children and I was a young woman so I could have more. Catherine, their daughter was really their niece. Zach could still visit me, but would live and be raised by Mo and Marie. Instead of seeing this through a lens of western cultural arrogance, I understood the honor they bestowed on me. I said I understood their cultural traditions, but my culture and family had different beliefs. My family would be upset with me if I gave Zach away.

Allakaket had taken a toll on Jed. He had saved the community with decisions and actions related to dangerous and life-threatening fires, and the gun incident at the school. The exciting and incredible weekend of logging with a good friend he highly respected was followed by his violent death. Children were left without a father, a confused mother, and another death of one of the sons. In this culturally vulnerable village, there were prejudicial comments where a few individuals lashed out at Jed, repeatedly calling him honky. Many villagers were more verbal about prejudices and misunderstandings when whiskey was involved. All the changes in Alaska affected Alaska Native men more than women. The frustrations from the cultural conflicts were often targeted at white men. There were gaps in understanding for Alaska Native men concerning their place within the new ways of living. Everyone was still adjusting and no one was sure of the answers.

While doubting our decision to leave, another death occurred, which reinforced our reasons. We remained hopeful Allakaket would return to its strong community roots. Seven deaths in less than a year was seven too many. None were from natural aging or because someone was ill. All deaths were preventable. They didn't need to happen and shouldn't have happened. Joe understood why new teachers were needed in Allakaket. Dan and Genie were headed to their cabin in Fairbanks and we were told to send our boxes to Nulato.

Part II: Teaching and Learning

"*Many times the stories about me and my loved ones are not flattering, but in order to begin healing through storytelling I must speak truthfully without intentionally dishonoring anyone.*"

—Velma Wallis, *Raising Ourselves*

"As I look back, I cannot get over the fact that our own people were so excluded from the workings of the classroom. In my entire eight years in grade school, I cannot recall a single Iñupiaq school activity. When we were in the classroom, it was as if our people did not exist."

—William L. Iġġiaġruk Hensley,
Fifty Miles from Tomorrow[13]

Part II: Teaching and Learning

Nulato

June 14, 1975

Departure from Allakaket was a month after school ended. The fire and disruptions slowed our packing and in many ways it was hard to leave. We wished Allakaket the best in mending the internal turmoil.

The flight from Allakaket to Nulato on June 14 was an adventure. When the plane, a Cherokee Six, arrived, we were surprised. We requested a Cessna 207 plane with only two seats besides the pilot's. *What's the big deal, you ask?* Nothing was ever simple—it was best to be flexible and creative when dealing with challenges in the bush.

The purpose for the 'almost' empty plane was the extra passengers—five sled dogs and their mighty leader. Alaska sled dogs traveled in planes buckled to a place in the plane, where seats were attached. The original plan was to load a primarily empty plane with the six dogs, our luggage, and us. The pilot would fly us to Nulato. From there we planned to jump on a scheduled mail plane en route to Anchorage. Most of our boxes were mailed and the rest would be loaded on the barge with our canoe to Nulato.

The red and white Cherokee Six had five seats with an optional sixth seat in the back. It was a popular plane for charters and mail runs. The unique feature of the Cherokee Six was the compartments in the nose between the cockpit and the engine and the large double door in the back for easy cargo loading. The plane arrived with all its seats, including the extra seat. The unnecessary seats made a big difference. The pilot couldn't leave the seats, so loading the plane became a jigsaw puzzle.

Finally, everything was loaded. The pilot, despite his long legs, lucked out with the most comfort. The dogs were packed on top of each other with their collars and short chains attached to each other and two screws in the plane. Good thing they liked each other. The extra seats were tied down somewhere. Jed held the mighty eighty-five pound Hidalgo and I held the mighty twenty-five pound Zacharia. Take off was to the engine roar, as well as barking of sled dogs and their powerful leader.

The three adults took a deep breath as the barking subsided. The dogs and Zach instantly fell asleep for the hour and a half flight. The vistas were spectacular, and captured stunning sights of Alaska's magnificence. The sky was an intense blue that sparkled in contrast to the various hues of the water in the rivers and streams, as well as the greens and browns of the tundra and trees. Even in the middle of June and throughout the summer constant patches of snow peeked out. The white carpets surrounded the trees or rested in shady spots in the mountains and valleys depending on the elevation level.

Neither Jed nor I had a solid contract to teach in Nulato. The good news was that the regional superintendent, Joe, had assured Jed he would have a job. The grade level was unclear. Knowing he wouldn't be the principal was a huge relief. The responsibilities and added stress of running a school was in someone else's hands.

The community of Nulato and the school were bigger than the first three villages we had worked in. The school had twelve teachers with a new high school program. A full high school required the principal have an administrator license. Our friends from Togiak, John and Mary, transferred there to help establish the high school program. We were thrilled to have friends in the village. They had a little boy, Nathan, who was three months younger than Zach. I offered to not work and be the stay at home mom and babysitter for the two-year-olds. Jed thought I was crazy. He believed a teaching contract was easier than two toddlers. I reassured him my sanity would survive.

When we boarded the plane out of Allakaket, I looked at Jed and saw relief in his eyes. The strain and pressure of the year had taken a toll on him. We laughed realizing Nulato would be his first big school. His educational career started in Marshall. All three years in Alaska were in three-teacher schools, with classrooms of small populations. I taught five years in California before moving to Marshall, so my adjustment was the other way around. California classrooms ranged from thirty to thirty-five students. Alaska had multigrade classrooms of ten to fifteen students.

The dogs began moving around as the pilot descended onto the Nulato airfield. Trucks arrived as the plane taxied to a stop. One of the trucks had an empty bed and offered to take us to the school. Jed threw our bags in the back of the truck and put Zach and I in the cab. Somehow, he secured all five of the sled dogs in the bed of the truck before he and Hidalgo jumped in.

It was a pleasant sixty-five to seventy degrees with a gentle breeze as we drove into town. Located on the west bank of the Yukon River, Nulato was thirty-three miles west of Galena, north of Anchorage, and

310 air miles west of Fairbanks. For a strange reason it felt good to be back on the Yukon. Maybe Robert Service knew what he was talking about when he wrote "The Spell of the Yukon" and how it captures you. We heard from other teachers that Nulato had cold temperatures that dropped to fifty below zero, similar to Allakaket. We just hoped it wouldn't stay locked at the extreme below zero cold for three solid weeks. The good news was dog mushing in Nulato was alive and winters typically had plenty of snow.

The truck drove past a small cemetery with Russian crosses and little roofs above many of the graves. The miniature dwellings gave the appearance of small dollhouses. I wondered what they represented. Nulato was home to approximately four hundred Koyukon Athabaskan Indians. The Koyukon people lived along the Koyukuk and Yukon rivers. For thousands of years their lives were based on subsistence hunting and trapping.

Even though Nulato was bigger in size compared to the other communities we lived in, everything was still close. The airport was a few miles from the school. We were told the community recently received a grant to build a water treatment building. There was a spigot open to the community for hauling water. In one of the conversations with teachers during the meeting in Tanana, Jed heard there were two stores. All of these details, helpful and necessary to our day-to-day living, would be investigated when we returned from our summer break.

We were anxious to get tasks completed and on to our summer fun. The Nulato principal said we could stay in the school for a couple of nights. Alaska's bush motto was to carry a sleeping bag since friendly floors were generally available. One of the teachers still in Nulato helped us find a place to stake our dogs close to the river and away from the village. Another teacher told us Tom, an elderly man, often fed dogs for teachers while they were gone in the summer. Jed found Tom, who said he would be happy to help us out with the dogs. Tom directed us to a woman, Ester, who sold fish used to feed dogs. Normally we would mix the fish with dry dog food. Knowing they wouldn't be exercised we figured they would be fine on just fish while we were gone. It was not the ideal arrangement but it would work since we would be back to Nulato in shy of two months.

It was disappointing not to see our living quarters but we understood. With a new high school program added to the kindergarten through eighth grade school, housing options for teachers were still being figured out. We were able to gather our boxes into one of the classrooms. Several boxes arrived over the last couple of weeks and were scattered all over the building. We collected them into one spot, did a final check-in with Tom and Ester about the dogs, and bid them goodbye. Hidalgo gave us a look that melted my heart, but my hands were full with an active, almost two-year-old.

While in Anchorage we shared a dorm room with our friends, John and Mary and their two-year-old. After five days we were all happy to leave for the No See Um Lodge, owned and operated by Jack and Nancy Holman. The Holmans were another of the teaching couples we met the first summer. They had recently bought a five-acre homestead from an old Russian trapper along the Kvichak River. The *Kvichak River* started in Lake Iliamna and was fifty miles long. Jack and Nancy taught in the community of Levelock, a small Yup'ik Eskimo village along the *river*. Jack's dream was to turn the homestead into a fly-fishing lodge. The first 'real' guests were coming in August. Jed and John offered to help Jack with remodeling projects to change the main cabin into the lodge area and the old scow into sleeping quarters for guest fishermen.

The day we arrived was Zach's birthday, so of course there was a party. Amongst the three families there were three two-year-olds, one five-year-old, one six-year-old, and a three-month-old baby. It was a rambunctious, demanding, chaotic week full of fun and laughter. After we fed everyone breakfast it was time to prepare lunch. Washing clothes was a constant chore. With the long daylight hours and walks in the afternoon, dinner always crept up on us. There were evening tasks, such as cleanup, and getting kids to bed. Camping lifestyle didn't include dishwashers or the latest washing machines. I adapted to wringer washers and hanging clothes outside to dry.

The Kvichak River was known for its salmon and trophy-size rainbow trout. The remodeling tasks were interspersed with fishing, which was so appreciated. I truly believed a person couldn't live in Alaska unless they liked fish. The Kvichak River was along an arm of Bristol Bay on the southwestern Alaska Peninsula. The No See Um Lodge was twenty-three miles from Levelock. On July 1 it was time to leave and continue to Los Angeles. I was anxious to see my mom and sister. It had been two long years since my last visit to California. Without a 'real' home base in Alaska, I referred to California as home, even though I felt less and less like I would ever live there again. I didn't know where I felt home was anymore.

Jack radioed Levelock and said he was bringing two and a half passengers to catch the mail plane into King Salmon and then on to Anchorage. He asked if they would check availability for seats on the next flight to Los Angeles. In the '70s travel in Alaska was so simple even though it involved many connections and miles.

Jed and I gathered our packs and climbed into the sixteen foot aluminum fishing boat. John tagged along so he could assist Jack with shopping before returning to the Lodge. There were four adults and Zach in the small fishing vessel. Off we went.

The morning we decided to leave was the day the 'red salmon' started their yearly spawning adventure up the Kvichak River to Lake Iliamna. Salmon return to the same spawning grounds each year. The constant spinning of their bodies as they flung themselves against the current was physically exhausting. During the ritual their bodies turned a crimson red color reflected in the water. The color was distinctive in contrast to the normal blues and greens of the water seen by observers. The eagles and bears waited eagerly for the annual event.

We knew salmon made the journey in June and July to spawn. Here we were actually experiencing this act of nature, not reading about it in *Alaska* or *National Geographic* magazines. We were in awe as we motored through the brilliant red wave of fish so valuable in the food chain for birds, animals, and humans. In preparation for the long trek they spent months fattening themselves by eating lots of plankton from the ocean. When they reached the river there was little for them to eat and they were ready to spawn.

Observing the salmon and other animals was breathtaking and exhilarating. Two eagles flew by, returning to their nest. I tried to call out the different animals for Zach—swans, cranes, ducks, and geese. Something moved in the bushes and I spotted two moose grazing along the riverbank. A couple of furry friends, probably beavers, dropped into the water before I could distinguish what they were. Jack laughed as he looked around the boat at the three of us. The water from the kicker soaked John, Jed, and me. The spray from the propellers while traveling the river drenched us, yet no one noticed or really cared. We were electrified from the experience. When Zach heard us laughing he pushed his head out of his raincoat and looked around. Up until now he had stayed pretty dry by peeking out as I pointed at things for him to see.

Suddenly the boat slowed down and stopped just as Jack said, "fuck." Zach was trying to repeat the word, as most two-year-olds do. I distracted him by saying "duck." We were stuck on a sandbar right out of Levelock. Looking up I could see the boat landing, our destination point to catch the plane to King Salmon. John and Jed quickly jumped out and began working to free the boat. They pushed and pulled the boat releasing it from the sandbar. The mail plane was circling while I prayed it would wait for us. We all laughed and agreed it was a trip we would always remember even if we missed the plane.

Luckily for us, the plane waited. We ran into the air service office, paid for the tickets, gave them our weight, adding pounds for the water dripping off of Jed. There was no time for him to change his clothes. We thanked them for the information about connections from King Salmon on to Los Angeles. The plane lifted as we took a deep breath to exhale the excess adrenaline we felt. About halfway to King Salmon the pilot spotted and circled over an enormous Alaska grizzly bear busy fishing. He obviously had received the memo about the red salmon running.

We made the connection out of King Salmon to Anchorage on a F-27 with barely thirty minutes before the flight from Anchorage to Los Angeles left. The layover in Seattle gave us an opportunity to call our parents and tell them we were arriving three days early. They were surprised but happy to pick us up. After three days of hugs, kisses, cooing over Zach, washing our clothes, and catching up on everyone's lives, we borrowed a car and headed north.

Part II: Teaching and Learning

After the difficult year in Allakaket I wanted to return to California. The visit to Northern California was a glimpse of what our lives would be like if we had never left for Alaska. We saw friends I taught with who had recently bought an old house in the Los Gatos hills. The house had been a speakeasy back in the day. They were busy remodeling the house. It was a real home, not a rented teacher's apartment. It didn't have furniture pieced together from whatever was ordered in the Sears catalog by different people over the years. We visited Jed's cousin and a few other friends, but ran out of time to visit everyone we had planned to see.

I felt like my body and head were in a massive tug of war—pulling in two different directions. Seeing life in Northern California made me want to stay and yet, the unbelievable experiences on the Kvichak, dog mushing, and the cultural, authentic life we were living in Alaska pulled in another direction. I felt confused. *How does anyone explain the events and incidents we had experienced? No one I saw understood.* Everyone just kept asking when we were coming back to California. I was disappointed no one talked about visiting us.

It was time to head back to Southern California and on to Mexico. We were grateful our parents' houses were next to each other on the Baja coast between Rosarita and Ensenada. Our plans were to relax in one location and have people come to us, which was exactly what we did.

The first couple of days we woke to cloudy skies, but finally the sun understood my need for warmth. I was extremely tired, which I chalked up to nerves from running around. My mom, sister Nancy, and her two boys came from Pomona. We laughed and watched the boys play together. The family gave Zach another birthday party where he mastered blowing out candles. Jed's grandparents came, along with his uncle, from Pennsylvania.

All good vacations come to an end. We had a great time, but it was time to return to reality. After a farewell dinner at Knott's Berry Farm we packed our bags, boarded an airplane, and headed north to Fairbanks. The few days flew by as we finished shopping for groceries and completing tasks before flying to Nulato. I headed to the doctor to confirm my suspicions and was told to plan for a March 24 delivery.

Before leaving for Nulato, we visited our friends Dan and Genie. After the turbulent year in Allakaket they had decided to stay in Fairbanks. We loved where they lived and told them if they ever heard of land for sale to let us know. When we showed up they told us about a dog musher who had five acres for sale. The parcel of land was a mile from their cabin on the Old Nenena Highway, two miles from the University of Alaska–Fairbanks campus. It was a beautiful area with birch and spruce trees and had an open spot, perfect for a garden.

The property included a small cabin easily rented to university students for practically the monthly payment. We were excited but knew the offer we made was low compared to his asking price. We looked at each other and decided, *why not?* Much to our surprise he accepted. We talked with the renter who planned to stay through May. Perfect! We finally had a place to go that was ours in the summers. No more camping out in friends' spare bedrooms and sneaking into dorm rooms.

We accomplished a lot while in Fairbanks. On August 7 we boarded a Cherokee Six for Nulato. The plane was chock-full of passengers—John, Mary, Nathan, Jenny (Nathan's nanny for the summer), their dog, Osa, Jed, Zach, and me. The cargo areas were full to capacity with luggage, sleeping bags, and a couple of boxes of food items to get us by for a few days. We had no idea where we would be living. The flight was pleasant, but a long two and a half hours. It certainly gave me time to think about the summer and our new purchase. A decision was made—Alaska was home. Before Alaska entered our lives we had discussed Oregon as a possible destination. We wanted to be further north and I fell in love with the Oregon Coast on a camping trip. My mind was racing. I felt a little uneasy, since it was unclear when we would ever live at the cabin. It was small, fine for summers, but wouldn't work for a Fairbanks[14] winter. I took a deep breath and felt confident it would work out.

The plane circled Nulato and brought me back to the present. The most important task was to find out about housing. Non-Native people couldn't buy land or build houses in Alaskan villages. Rural Alaska teachers were always stuck with whatever housing a district had for them. Bigger hub communities like Bethel, Dillingham, Nome, Kotzebue, or Barrow had places to rent, but not to buy. Occasionally, a teacher from out-of-Alaska married a local person and they could possess land. Not being able to own land and have a stable home created an empty feeling of not fully belonging to a community.

Over the summer the regional office had told us that with the addition of the high school there wasn't enough housing for all the teachers. Since we were the only teachers in town, the school maintenance operator gave us keys to a two-bedroom teacher apartment to camp in for a couple of nights.

Housing for teachers in a large school was based on seniority of years in Alaska. John, Mary, and Jed were new teachers so housing options were limited. Having been hired to help start the new high school was an advantage. The district office wanted to keep them happy. We understood housing politics. The trailers were desired housing despite the issues they had in cold weather. Running water was also a nice perk.

With only one teaching contract between the two of us we were on the bottom of the list.

Shortly after arriving in Nulato, Jed was anxious to check on the dogs, especially Hidalgo. We had never left him for more than a few days. After dumping our luggage in the apartment he and John went to check on them. When Jed returned with Hidalgo he was very upset. Tom, the elderly man, who offered to take care of our dogs had become ill and was sent to the hospital in Tanana. His adult sons agreed to take care of his tasks, but didn't follow through. The dogs were skinny and spooked at everything and everybody. Jed felt horrible about it. To make matters worse Hidalgo was shot in the hip. The dogs hadn't been loose or by anyone's house. We were both upset and agreed the dogs would never be left again. The whole plan to leave them wasn't what we wanted, but there didn't seem to be another choice. Conversations with many teachers assured us it usually worked out fine, but not this time. I was so happy to see Hidalgo. He received lots of hugs and plenty of treats.

Knowing our housing status, Jed investigated possible community options instead of waiting. He heard from one of the maintenance fellows a 30-by-30-foot log structure was available to rent. In the past it served as the Head Start center until they received a better building. It never had been a home. The building, owned by the city of Nulato, was away from the school compound area, closer to the center of town. When Jed told me about it I was pleased it had electricity. I was disappointed there was no running water or sewage system, especially caring for two toddlers still in diapers and with a new baby coming. I thought, *I have lived without running water and can do it again.* I knew we would have a workable system for hauling and storing water. The idea of no electricity was my bottom line. I needed and required electric lights in order to be comfortable. As much as I enjoyed running water I could keep everyone hydrated and clean with water from barrels.

Part II: Teaching and Learning

It amused me I felt wealthy when there were two thirty-gallon barrels of clean water. Before Alaska I took water for granted. I bathed and drank water as often as I wanted without thinking about it. Now I calculated the amount of water needed for the family. How much did we need for drinking? Preparing food, cleaning the house, mopping the floors, cleaning our bodies, and washing clothes? I was focused on reusing water.

Jed took me to see our new home. I was shell-shocked at first. There were no interior walls, no furniture, and only one useable shelf. The two doors to go outside were on opposite walls of the house and didn't have Arctic entrances. Arctic openings were critical in extreme cold. The covered porches created a barrier to the cold and provided a place to hang extra clothing and keep items, such as extra food. The doors to this building were on sides of the house with one-way paths for trucks, snow machines, and dogs to travel. Understanding the building couldn't have Arctic entrances made me realize it would be a cold year.

The principal heard Jed found housing. He helped locate kitchen appliances, a mattress (clean with no stains), couch, and kitchen table with chairs. I wondered where the items came from. It was not like there was a store to purchase them. Some schools had an abundance of appliances and furniture while others had hardly anything.

The bentwood rocker purchased in California shortly after we were married was in a box. Jed managed to keep the rocker together each year. It was left in storage while we were in Marshall, but was needed when Zach was born. It was dismantled each year and moved as part of the family. Being unscrewed and re-screwed wasn't the best situation, plus the extreme cold and dryness wore on the cane back and seat of the chair.

Jed rummaged around the school buildings for wood to build bed frames, a kitchen counter, and shelves for dishes and pans. Finding useable, salvageable wood at the school was helpful. When we purchased groceries in Fairbanks plywood was added to the order. We knew it would be useful, but the order was coming on the barge. Barge orders didn't arrive until September and this was early August.

Before teaching contracts began the third week in August, Jed and John had a trip out of Nulato. With Mary and I 'settled' into our housing, they left with Jenny to get her on a flight to Oklahoma. The morning of the departure Jed woke with a massive, uncontrollable headache. He still boarded the plane with John, Jenny, and Hidalgo for Fairbanks. After touch down Jed was rushed to the Fairbanks Memorial Hospital where he was admitted for spinal meningitis. While Jed recovered, John got Jenny on the plane to Oklahoma and Hidalgo to the vet. The vet gave Hidalgo medicine and explained the bullet had worked its way out. The vet said because he was a young dog the stiffness would disappear. After three days Jed was released and told to take it easy. Easier said, than done, with one more task to complete.

The three musketeers, John, Jed, and mighty Hidalgo, boarded a flight to Dillingham where they picked up a Piper Cub PA-12. John had his pilot's license and the two were now partners in ownership of the plane. They double-checked the plane and took off for Aniak, where they spent the night. The next day the journey back to Nulato began. They followed the Yukon, a route halfway across Alaska. Not knowing about the hospital setback, Mary and I were concerned, when they were not home when expected.

When they finally arrived we were extremely happy to see all three tired, smiling faces and Hidalgo's rebounded energy. A plane was now available for short trips. It was small and didn't hold everyone. Mary and I understood the plane was more for them than us. I was happy for a vehicle in case of emergencies.

We wanted fish for the dogs and ourselves. Our canoe was stuck in Allakaket because the barge didn't make it that far. We had hoped to get fish with it and even do some seining for fish to feed the dogs. I asked and found someone who set a net for the fall salmon and someone with a fish wheel. With fish purchased, I kept busy cleaning and preparing packages to store in the freezer for the dogs and us. Mary and I wanted to go berry picking but found it quite challenging. Nulato had an abundance of berries. The problem was the competition—the berries were located where the brown bears liked to graze and stuff themselves. With a couple of two-year-olds in tow, berry picking was limited.

Jed settled into his new teaching duties with a larger staff. The elementary school was in the older building. The new building was for high school students. The high school facility was equipped with a large shop, science lab, regulation size gym, and a large, open-space room. The same basic building plan was used around the state.

Everyone—parents, teachers, and students were adjusting to students attending high school in their home village. Nulato usually sent several kids to attend high school in other locations. The small village high schools were popping up around Alaska to provide equitable educational opportunities for students in rural villages. The basic building blueprint allowed for local options in selecting instructional areas for students in the program. Nulato decided four classrooms was a good use of the large open area.

Hauling water in Nulato wasn't easy. We were spoiled in Allakaket with our water source straight down the bank from the house. It was good water to drink and wash. The water sources in Nulato were difficult. The easy water from the Yukon was out. It was muddy and not for drinking. The water treatment center located behind the high school building was very busy. It had a couple of showers, washers, dryers, and even a sauna area. The public spigot was the easiest to reach but hauling from it was hard. When we first arrived one of the teachers let us use his car, which certainly saved a tired back. After the barge arrived we had John's Land Cruiser until it became too cold for it to run.

The water treatment center had opened the week before we arrived. After the first month of getting water from the treatment plant everyone was told the chlorine level was so high the water was undrinkable. At least it was good for bathing and to wash clothes. Jed heard from the men in the village the Nulato River had good drinking water. Hauling water from there was five miles round trip each week to bring the twenty-five to thirty gallons of water for drinking and food preparation. Gathering water was a huge time drain and kept Jed very busy.

During the winter, our dog team was the most reliable means of transportation when it was thirty to forty degrees below zero. Hidalgo and two of other dogs hauled 180 gallons of water each week, which included a trip to the Nulato River for the drinking water. I wondered, "Were there other places in the lower 48 states and Hawaii that people didn't have running water?" Maybe I was naïve about easy access to flowing water.

The size of Nulato increased the traffic of people who traveled in and out of the community, such as dentists, doctors, and other dignitaries. The visitors kept us informed about news concerning state and national business, weather, wildlife movement, and status of the barge. The Yutana Barge Lines was headquartered in Nenana, Alaska, approximately fifty-five miles south of Fairbanks. Nenana was located on the south bank of the Tanana River, a river that moved northwest into the Yukon. The barge made several trips to the villages in the summer delivering items difficult to fly in and was a cheaper means of transportation.

The final barge for the season arrived September 18. What an exciting affair it was! John came by at lunchtime and told me the big news. Everyone in Nulato talked about it. Once in a great while the barge even had travelers[15] on it. Villagers along the Yukon and adjoining rivers journeyed back and forth so news about the barge traveled fast.

Nulato had two stores, a K–12 school, a water treatment center, and city maintenance offices, all of which had supplies on the barge. We knew there were several vehicles on the barge too. John's Land Cruiser was the one we were looking forward to seeing. A few Nulato residents and teachers had trucks on board, as well as snow machines. There were endless pallets of food, paper goods, disposable diapers (something new to village moms), plywood, and infinite other supplies. All of this had to be sorted out and delivered.

After school, Mary and I took the boys down to see the organized chaos. We quickly realized the best place for us was back at the houses and out of the way. Mary and I gathered the boys and returned home to fix dinner at my house. We knew Jed and John would be hungry and need to eat at some point. They were in and out as they delivered items. They stopped to eat during one of the lulls in unloading the barge. Besides our two families' supplies, they helped with the stuff for the school and other places. Each time they stopped with supplies, the boxes in the house grew. Boxes were piled everywhere, with small walking pathways between them. Jed told me not to worry about putting things away. He said we would sort through things later.

One of the times when Jed stopped to drop off our boxes, he mentioned seeing numerous pallets of Budweiser, which made me groan a bit. We wondered what that meant in Nulato. Our experience in Allakaket left us weary of alcohol consumption. Nulato was larger so we were hopeful the drinking wouldn't consume the whole community and affect every family.

John took Mary and Nathan home during one of the trips and returned with Jed around 11:30 p.m. Having John's Land Cruiser to unload the barge made it faster and easier but it still had been a long night. Although exhausted, they needed to be to work at the regular time in the morning. Jed had a relaxing shot of Jack Daniels before climbing into bed. It was going to be an even shorter night for him because he had dogs to feed before going to work in the morning.

With two toddlers life was never dull. Jed set up a swing in the house, which the boys enjoyed and I appreciated. Zach had a toddler size trike and ATV he shared for them to ride. The wooden plywood floor was an easy riding surface for the miniature vehicles and the second-hand furniture kept me from worrying about damage. The floor slanted toward the center of the room, which was comical in some ways. We tied the wringer washing machine to a post so it wouldn't gyrate and twist into the center of the room sloshing water. Zach loved the inclined surface because he was able to ride his trike with his feet up in the air as he coasted toward the center of the room.

Barge arriving in Nulato
September 1975

When the weather was agreeable I took Zach and Nathan out for short walks and adventures in the village. We visited the river, walked to our dog yard, talked to people, saw the cemetery, investigated the boats along the river, and chattered about things we saw. The boys loved going to the dog yard. They were sure the dogs were saying *Hi* to them when they jumped on top of their doghouses and barked.

After the colder temperatures and snow set in, I pulled them on a plastic toboggan or pushed them in a small sled. Our outings were fewer and usually to the post office and store. The intense cold invigorated our bodies, created rosy-red cheeks, and provided a reason for us to get outside, for at least a short time most days. My spirit and sanity needed a bit of daylight and fresh air. Inside the boys burned energy when they chased each other around the table, rode their vehicles, played with toys, and listened to stories.

My enjoyment of social activities led me to agree to organize two Christmas parties, one for children and one for adults. The children's party was for kids under the age of six and, of course, included a visit from Santa Claus. I thought I had everything under control until the night before the event. The person who agreed to be Santa backed out! I twisted Jed's arm to fill the role. We worried Zach might recognize him, but he was too busy hiding his head in my shoulder and peeing down my leg. Oh, well, the challenges of motherhood and still taking on adult responsibilities. The adult party was a faculty-staff dinner party held at the school and was well attended. I made arrangements with the high school students to babysit the children so the adults could enjoy themselves. The evening went well and no one peed on me.

Our quality of life was much better in Nulato. Jed wasn't constantly checking on generators and buildings. Most of the teachers and their families left during the winter break. Our families couldn't come this year and we decided to stay in Nulato. Back to a single salary and purchasing the land in Fairbanks made us more cautious with our money.

The winter holiday break gave us two weeks to ourselves, which we enjoyed and needed. Jed and Zach bundled up in the morning to get firewood and water with the dog team. With the limited daylight they couldn't leave until 10:00 a.m. Zach was excited he was helping his dad. When they came in for lunch he was full of stories and had lots to tell me about the dogs. Once again our house was heated by oil, but firewood was necessary to cook for the dogs. Most outdoor chores were completed by 3:00 p.m., close to when the sun was setting for the day. Life was easier for Jed during the holiday break. He wasn't balancing teaching with the chores necessary in hauling water and tending to a growing dog team.

Zach helped decorate the house for Christmas. The three of us ventured out in the cold to get the tree. Zach and I sat in the sled gently holding the tree while Jed drove the team. The dogs seem to know this was an important mission. Their heads were high in their harnesses as they trotted, panting in the crisp air. The quiet and stillness were enthralling. In the light of the midday sun the dogs' breath exhaled like wispy clouds as we moved along the snow. While we were out getting the tree, I saw a ptarmigan and pointed it out to Zach. In the winter their feathers were white like snow. This ptarmigan moved in the low scrubs allowing for a quick glimpse before it was absorbed into the surrounding landscape. We were fortunate to see it. I had seen them in Holy Cross in the fall when their color was gray and brown feathers.

January and February were cold months. Jed was up early cooking a hot meal in a big pot for the dogs before going to work and in the dark

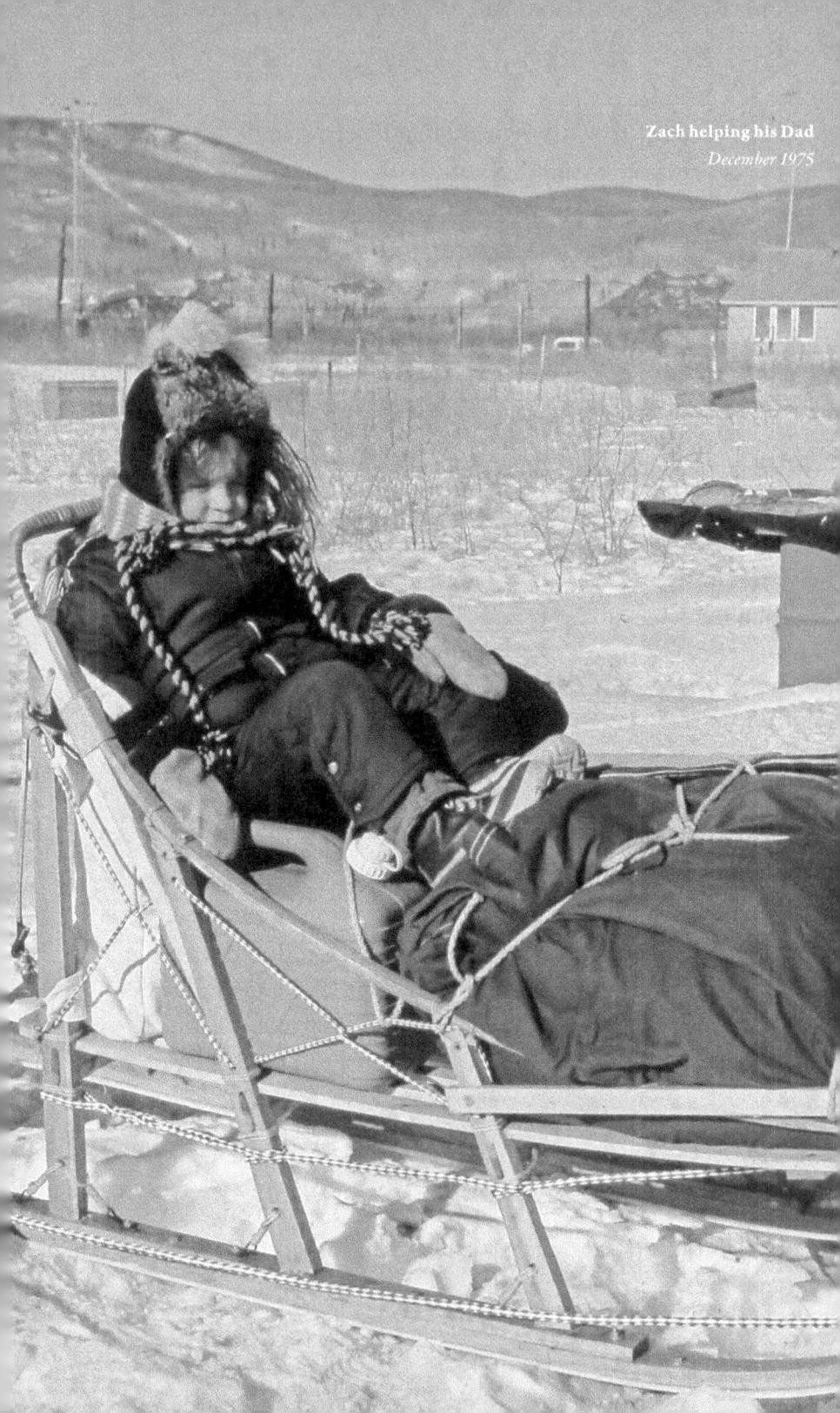

Zach helping his Dad
December 1975

after his school day was done. Dogs were individually staked with a short chain allowing them to get on top of their box or snuggle inside, but not tangle with each other. Our dogs were fortunate to have small, flat plywood houses with grass inside. Dogs without protection curled up on the snow and nuzzled their noses into their bodies for heat. When these furry workers were fed warm meals twice a day and given dry grass during the cold temperatures, a stronger attachment to their musher developed. I found it interesting they didn't have bowls. The food cooled quickly when poured on the hard snow. They lapped it up before it froze to the ground. Pouring food on the snow saved their tongues from sticking to a metal bowl or being cut by plastic dishes broken in the cold.

My prior experience with dogs was as pets. Alaska taught me about 'working animals.' Jed asked if I would make dog booties for their paws. These were small cloth fabric 'mini shoes' to protect their feet. Canine workers were only as good as their paws. The small cloth booties were secured to each paw with Velcro. This important item protected them from ice balls forming between their toes, as well as the sharp ice crystals found along the trail. The cloth surface allowed them to still feel the ground, nonetheless many dogs found them awkward to wear. Sometimes when a musher stopped to check a trap or take a break a dog pulled at the booties until they came off.

In winter when sled dogs worked harder, it was important the right types of protein were added to their dry food. Alaska Native mushers fed their dogs mostly fish, but that changed a bit over time. Dry fish was a main source, but other items, such as horsemeat or beaver meat, were common supplements to food cooked for them. One of the mushers Jed spent time with recommended horsemeat ordered from the Midwest. It arrived in buckets and was scooped out with an ice cream scooper. Dogs loved it. I was still in a state of shock that horsemeat was fed to our furry workers. It was just one of many things I learned living in rural Alaska. I added our food scraps to the dog pot, but discovered they wouldn't eat orange peels, not that we had them very often. They would spit them out. The cost involved in having a dog team grew as the number of dogs continued to grow.

Jed added more dogs to the team and spent considerable time on the weekends exercising them. He occasionally entered an event or helped friends with their dogs. When it was really cold Zach and I didn't always join to watch or help harness the dogs. I felt a little guilty until I heard about one of the other 'dog mushing' teachers. Larry told Jed that once when he finished running his dogs he was so cold he thought he had frozen his private parts. He secured his dogs with his snow hook and rushed inside to insert part of his body in a bath of warm water. When he was confident his body was intact, he bundled back up and took his dogs to the dog yard to unharness and feed them. I didn't feel guilty any longer about staying inside.

March was Iditarod Race time. Now in its fourth year (1976), the Iditarod was growing. It gathered interest and entries from other parts of the world. What started as an effort to support dog mushing and ensure snow machines didn't replace the sport had occurred! Joe Redington, Father of the Iditarod, reminded everyone that dog mushing was the reason for the race. In 1972, when the Iditarod Race was in the planning stages, dog mushing was selected as the official sport for Alaska. There were few rules the first couple of years. New requirements added each year focused on safety and protections for the animals and mushers. The four-legged athletes were treated with care and valued. Redington knew when sled dogs were respected and treated well they never broke down, and got their musher to the destination.

Part II: Teaching and Learning

In addition to the Iditarod, March signified two other big events in our lives: the birth of our second child and the Nulato Stick Dance. Several of the older women in Nulato were concerned the baby might arrive early. They looked me over, talked together in their Native language, and gave me their opinion of due dates. I was huge and uncomfortable. During my first pregnancy I just spread out, which helped me fly close to my due date. I didn't know commercial airlines had a rule about not flying after a certain date until someone told me. Women in Alaska didn't have a choice but to fly somewhere to have their babies. There were individuals in a village that could deliver a baby, but that wasn't the recommended method. Alaska Native women knew the risks all too well. Over the years babies died when there was an emergency and no back up was available.

I knew the recommendation about getting out of the village in time to deliver at the hospital in Tanana. One of the Tanana doctors visited Nulato during his regular village schedule. He checked on me and said everything was fine. To me that meant I could remain in Nulato until after the week of Stick Dance festivities. He didn't disagree, but wasn't thrilled either. He spoke with two of the women in the village who he knew delivered babies. I promised to monitor for contractions and be on the mail plane to Tanana on March 14 right after the final ceremonies on Sunday. That was still ten days before the March 24 due date.

Stick Dance, an Athabaskan Indian tradition, dates back thousands of years. The custom started when a family lost several people in a tragic accident. Friends and family members in the community and nearby villages supported them in their grief. Over the years Stick Dance ceremonies stopped in many Athabaskan communities, but not in Nulato and Kaltag, another village thirty-three miles down the Yukon. They took turns holding the weeklong event.

Stick Dance honored the dead and those who helped family members of the deceased person. Maybe they prepared the body for burial, helped dig the grave, assisted with the funeral, or cared for the loved ones left behind. For a period of time, the Catholic Missions had stopped the ceremony, but saw the importance of the event and reinstated it. Stick Dance activities demonstrated appreciation for the people that helped the grieving family by hosting potlatches and giving gifts. We were told many books were written about Stick Dance. I wanted to see and participate in it first hand.

People started arriving Sunday and continued through the week. The formal start was Monday morning. People sang and chanted every night after the evening potlatches. Friends visited from Holy Cross and along the Yukon, as well as Bettles, to participate in the festivities. Hosting families distributed gifts they made or purchased for every person who attended. It was the customary way of showing appreciation for the friendship and support. Friday night was the biggest night. People sang sacred songs and danced the official Stick Dance. The decorated sacred stick was secured in the center of the room while people chanted and danced around it. During the week food was put in the little houses above the graves, another way to reach out to the people who died. Saturday night was the conclusion. People chanted all night and into the next day when they finally broke the sacred stick and threw the pieces on the frozen Yukon. Being so close to my delivery kept me from staying up all night. I was nonetheless glad I remained for the event. This significant and poignant ceremonial week was an inspiring occasion, one I would remember.

On March 14 Zach and I boarded the mail plane for Tanana. It was two airplane rides with a quick stop in Galena. Tanana was a stopover for aircraft en route to Russia during World War II. The Tanana and

Part II: Teaching and Learning

Yukon Rivers converged there, making it a perfect spot for a trading settlement for Koyukon and Tanana Athabaskans. In 1949, a small military hospital facility was established and sometime in the '50s the hospital administration was reassigned to the US Public Health Service.

As we flew to Galena I remembered reading about a machine called an ultrasound. I didn't understand how a procedure told a pregnant mom about the gender of the baby, but it sounded interesting. The examination didn't exist in rural Alaska so I would just be surprised. Besides I was sure I was having a girl and what seemed like a long pregnancy would be finished.

Bobby and Sue, another couple we had met during the summer orientation, offered us a place to stay—typical bush hospitality. Their son was in elementary school and older than Zach, so their playing together was sporadic. During the days everyone was gone so we walked around Tanana. I read and reread books to Zach who loved hearing stories. The longer days wore on as we waited for the baby. Spring was in the air so it was important to be careful on the icy spots.

Bobby and Sue's single-wide trailer grew smaller each day. The long wait was hard on all of us. Our friends were going through a rough spell and my arrival wasn't timely. We were all getting on each other's nerves. I was tired of sleeping on the floor and moving the immense body I lived in. Finally on March 31, I woke up at 6:00 a.m. with a horrible low backache. The good news was that contractions coupled with back pain meant I was in labor.

Finally, this baby, who by now I knew was a boy, was about to arrive. I always imagined having a son and a daughter. Maybe it was because I wished I had a big brother. During the beginning of my pregnancy

I kept focused on a daughter to live out that dream. While staying in Tanana awaiting the birth two things happened to break that notion. I saw the movie *Jeremiah Johnson*,[16] about a strong, independent man and immediately knew my baby was a boy.

The second thing that happened occurred during Zach's stay in the Bethel PHS Hospital. I remembered a young woman whose baby was born without an anus. The mom had arrived from one of the forty-plus villages out of Bethel. She had no prenatal care during her pregnancy so problems weren't discovered. The baby died. It was a horrible to watch the young mother sobbing as she held her dead baby. I wanted to hold the young mom, but I had no right to disturb her privacy. I knew then having a healthy baby was the greatest gift any mother could receive.

It took every bit of my energy to get myself off the floor. I woke Zach, dressed us and fed him. We walked to the Tanana Public Health Hospital and they confirmed I was in labor. The hospital radioed Nulato and someone told Jed. The plan was he would jump on the mail plane and be there before the birth. It was a long day of labor while caring for my toddler. No day care options were available. I wished my mother or sister were there to help. He looked up at me and asked questions I couldn't answer. Finally, Jed arrived about the same time Sue came to take Zach to their house for dinner. It was hard to let him go. Jed assured him he would see him later.

The hours kept ticking. The nurses were great. When the doctor arrived to check on me he was the same one that came to Nulato. This time I didn't feel like a total stranger delivered my baby. I was tired, with little sleep from the night before. They asked if I wanted drugs and I said, "No." At the same moment everyone told me to push; I felt like punching them all! Finally, I heard a cry and a voice said, "What a big, beautiful baby boy." Jeremia Levi was born at 9:43 p.m. (*yippee, no April Fool's baby*). His dad beamed and I was exhausted. I heard Jed say to the doctor, "Born along the Yukon will undoubtedly provide this kid with the stamina needed to survive life." I was glad to be done with the physical work of giving birth. Jeremia was placed in my arms and my heart melted. Once again I was amazed at the whole process of birth.

Jed returned to Bobby and Sue's for the night. In the morning Jed brought Zach to see his new brother and visit me. On Jed's birthday, April 3, they both flew home to Nulato. As I gave Zach a big hug, I realized this was the first time I would be away from him since right after he was born. Saying goodbye to him brought back memories I never wanted to revisit. Living in rural Alaska was so different. The Tanana hospital kept us for a full week, which gave Jeremia and I time to bond and for me to rest. The nurses positioned his crib next to my bed. What a difference this was from the big hospital experience in California.

Jeremia's birth was stress free. I fed him when he was hungry and his routine was in my hands. He was quiet and easily soothed. When Zach was born his first week was rough and disjointed. The hospital kept him after they released me. They fed him despite knowing I was breast-feeding so his body was confused. I was frustrated with the hospital and felt out of control.

On Tuesday, April 6, Jeremia and I were able to leave. The three weeks and one day in Tanana had been lengthy. I was ready to be home. Rural Alaska deliveries necessitated longer hospital stays. It was cheaper to remain in a hospital facility for a few extra days than risk a medevac from the village. Infections, hemorrhaging, or endless issues had occurred in the past, so the rule was to keep a new mom and baby for a week. I wanted to be home, but understood the importance of being sure my body was ready. Jeremia was a solid baby, very content as he took in the world around him.

I packed the small bag Jed had brought to the hospital. Jeremia fit snuggling in the tummy carrier. My mind remembered the ice I saw dripping from the eaves of the buildings around the hospital. I didn't want anything to happen to my precious cargo. I felt rested and relaxed with renewed energy.

The sun welcomed us as we stepped outside of the hospital. The two flights were smooth and the views continued to say 'spring has arrived.' Jed and Zach were happy to see us. It felt good to have the family together and adjust to the peaceful new member. Mary, who was also pregnant, had left for Anchorage a week before I arrived back in Nulato. Nathan was born in Anchorage, so she wanted the same doctor to deliver her second baby. John and Nathan took off to join her about the time Jeremia and I arrived home.

One of my friends in Nulato had told me about Athabaskan baby cradles. There were two types: traditional Athabaskan infant cradleboards made from birch bark and hanging bassinets made of fur.[17] Learning to weave with birch bark was something I couldn't replicate. It was a craft that took years to learn. The thought of a hanging bassinet intrigued me. The outer surface was traditionally made from fur but I used a thick denim fabric and then lined the inside with calico. Before sewing the inside and outside together I appliqued little children on both sides of the denim. There was a blanket folded for a small mattress inside. It was hung with a large hook. It was sturdy and easily moved from by the bed and into the kitchen. Jeremia was happy sleeping or sitting in his infant seat that sat inside of the cradle until he started to be more active.

Part II: Teaching and Learning

The school year wound down even though there were six more weeks until the end of the year. Carnivals and dog races happened in Nulato and in the villages close by in April. Everyone in Nulato was excited with the plans for a high school graduation ceremony for two students. These two teens attended high school out of the village prior to when the new high school program started in Nulato. When they heard about the high school teachers in their home village, they wanted to graduate at home. The new Nulato program had worked with them individually to complete their requirements.

The 1976 Alaska legislative session finally abolished the Alaska Unorganized Borough School District. Twenty-one Rural Education Attendance Areas (REAAs) were established that included village advisory boards and an elected district-wide school board. This legislation was a huge change for rural Alaska education. Only a few rural Alaskan Native communities understood the regulations and the opportunities they had to affect school policy and governance. A few superintendents stepped up and provided education, advocacy, and support to the advisory groups to assist them in understanding their role.

The educational changes happening matched our personal philosophy in promoting local involvement. We were excited to see how Nulato would accept the opportunity. Our little home was comfortable even without running water. Life was difficult on one salary, but we felt we could tighten our belts for another year.

Three weeks before school ended Jed came home and announced we were leaving. I was surprised until he explained. Edith, a local Native woman, finished her teaching credential and applied to teach in Nulato. There were no openings in the elementary grades where she was qualified. She substituted for Jed a couple of times and he knew her methods of teaching. He offered to resign if she was hired. We discussed how important it was to have qualified Native teachers in the villages. Jed felt it was a win-win for the students, the village, and her, and I agreed. She was an excellent role model for students and good teacher. We hoped she would lead others to consider education as a career.

The village of Nulato was now part of the Yukon Koyukuk School District (YKSD) to be headquartered in Nenana. Jed's current boss, Joe, accepted an offer to be the superintendent in Nenana to launch the new district. During the discussion about Jed's resignation Joe asked him if he would be interested in one of the two correspondence teacher positions for the district. The new program was to provide education for families in the district's geographic area, but that didn't live close enough to a school for the children to attend. The new program sounded interesting so he agreed. Jed had a contract and we were to be in Nenana by August 15.

We were on the move again. My head started the packing process before I located boxes. At least we had a home for the summer—our cabin in Fairbanks. I knew there were two options to get stuff to Nenana—plane or barge. I hoped the charter plane would have enough room for the growing dog team and family we now had.

Part II: Teaching and Learning

Life at Fifty Below Zero

An Alaskan Memoir on Teaching and Learning

PART III

Back and Forth

Ridgepole for Log House
Summer 1978

Life at Fifty Below Zero

Part III: Back and Forth

Summer 1976

Packing boxes in Nulato was simple. In other villages, decisions about what to take and what to give away were constantly made. With a move to Nenana the transportation cost was minimal since it was the last stop for the Yutana Barge Lines.

The charter flight out of Nulato was jam-packed. *How can two small, little individuals have so much essential stuff?* Naturally, the dogs accompanied us, adding to the craziness. The boys watched, their four little eyes, entertained by their dad working with the pilot to arrange boxes, bags, dogs and us. It was similar to packing a car—only a big net held everything in case of turbulence. I was glad the net didn't cover us.

My job was easy—holding a baby and a three-year-old. Zach was concerned his dog friends might not fit in the plane. I assured him no dogs would be left behind. The thought occurred to me I might be left before a dog. As the plane took off, so did the barking. The pleasant sound of the engine humming stopped the barking and put Jeremia and the dogs to sleep, followed soon by Zach. It was a sunny seventy degree day in late May as we left Nulato.

The plane lifted and I thought, *Did leaving Nulato mean we were leaving the bush?* Life was changing again. Neither one of us knew much about Nenana, fifty-five miles south of Fairbanks. I read somewhere

Alaska was divided into four divisions: rural bush villages; cities (Fairbanks, Anchorage, Juneau, Ketchikan); road communities; and hub centers, such as Nome, Bethel, Kotzebue, Barrow, and Dillingham. The highway between Fairbanks and Anchorage was 360 miles with small road communities including Nenana.

In the lower 48, fifty miles was considered a normal commuter drive, but not in Alaska. When the weather dipped to thirty degrees below zero or colder tires squared and had problems. No one commuted between Fairbanks and Nenana. Alaska was a large state traveled primarily by air—even the capitol, Juneau, was accessed only by plane or boat.

Our car, stored for the winter, was near the Fairbanks airport. Jed contacted the storage provider so the car was ready when we arrived. Somehow everything including the dogs was stuffed into the Toyota Land Cruiser. I had both boys in my lap so I couldn't look in the back. I knew by the barks and whining all the dogs were there, and felt confident Jed hadn't left any baggage behind. We drove to our property, two miles south of the University.

We couldn't remember what the inside of the small dwelling looked like. When we purchased the five acres a student was settled in the cabin, so a quick glance inside was all we had. Our renter left the cabin clean. It was small, but adequate for the four of us. We had Jeremia's hanging cradle so he was set. There was a piece of plywood the size of a double bed with a mattress on it, a makeshift wooden counter, and a small refrigerator. The outhouse was in good condition. Our list for town was a cot for Zach, groceries, and water.

The cabin had electricity, but we needed a place for good water. Our friends Dan and Genie were a mile down the road, so we stopped to say "Hi" and check on water sources. They explained the easiest spot for water was at the University close to the showers. This information fit nicely with our plans to sign up to use the pool and showers for the summer.

While we visited, Dan mentioned they were joining with another couple in cutting and hauling house logs. He knew there was room for us to join because the permit secured was for three houses. The logging location was convenient, only ten miles down the highway from our places toward Nenana. We were stunned by the opportunity and knew it was a once in a lifetime chance. The plans for a quiet summer in Fairbanks were just altered.

The five acres we bought were thickly wooded with birch and spruce trees. There were a couple of spots on the property less woody. The cabin was close to the entrance of the road. With the new opportunity to build a second, bigger place we could rent the cabin year round. Jed surveyed the property for the best spot for the future house and a dog yard.

We introduced ourselves to the neighbors, a dog musher family. They had close to fifty dogs. The rumor around the neighborhood was he had a wolf he bred with his bitches. Dog mushers were known to seek out dogs with a wolf somewhere in their pedigree. Rumors aside, they were great neighbors with children close to the boys' ages.

Anxious to become acquainted with their second grandson and see Zach, Jed's parents came to visit. They purchased an Airstream trailer for retirement knowing the first trip was 3,608 miles to Fairbanks for the summer. When they arrived Jed helped his dad arrange the Airstream approximately one hundred feet from the little cabin for the summer. After they were settled Jed filled them in on the logging adventure. Harold was excited and eager to be involved. The hard, intense work started the next morning.

Felling and hauling logs was hard work. It required hours of time and food to keep them sustained. They selected the logs and worked as a team to fell them without anyone getting hurt. With the long sixteen to eighteen hour days, we sent food with them, delivered food to the site, and occasionally cooked food at the logging site. It was helpful they were so close.

I preferred to have dinners at our campsite. The logging site was near streams and stagnant water where mosquitoes were thick. All the movement in the area stirred the little devils up and made them blood thirsty. One day I took both boys out to the site, Jed warned me it was thick with the little critters. He suggested I bring one of the full body nets we had from boating on the Yukon. The winged creatures were bad around the cabin on certain days, but nothing prepared me for the amount encountered when we stepped out of the Land Cruiser. Just the intense sound of their wings vibrating was enough to let me know there were tens of thousands or maybe millions of them.

Learning that mosquitoes can travel up to three hundred miles to find food made me concerned they would follow the car back to our property. We disturbed their home; was it their turn to disturb ours? I hated that they ruled summers in Alaska. Once we took Zach camping in the canoe and both his hands received massive little bites. That night the sandbar protected us from the bears, but not the mosquitoes. One of my friends told me putting toothpaste on children's bites kept them from scratching, which I did. During the night I worried about the bears smelling the toothpaste but not Zach scratching himself. Jeez!

There were many cookouts by the fire pit Jed had built before his parents arrived. Everyone brought something to share. The smoke from the fire kept the mosquitoes in control. Mosquitoes in Alaska arrive as soon as the weather begins to warm up, usually in mid June, and continue munching on folks into August.

Felling and hauling logs was hard work
July 1976

At the end of the logging work, 250 house logs were harvested. Most of the work was performed by hand. The men from the three families worked together to get the selected logs felled, stacked, and ready for the logging truck. When a family's logs were ready, a truck and crew of additional men and machines helped load and unload the logs at the designated site. Each family was responsible for peeling their own logs, which was done at the house site. Sometimes there were ten guys helping when it was time to load a truck to take logs to the families' properties. There were evening gatherings with good food, fun, laughter, and stories about a log coming down, the struggles and triumphs.

The other two families were building their houses before the snow fell so their logs were gathered first. Jed and his dad carefully selected the logs for our 25-by-30-foot house. When they finished, eighty-five logs were stacked on our property to season over the winter. The average log was twelve inches across at the butt. The ridgepole selected had a butt end of twenty-two inches across. It was exciting to see the logs and know this portion of the hard work was done. I contributed by peeling a few logs. If the logs had been purchased it would have cost $10,000. The logging took three solid weeks of long hours. Everyone slept solid those nights, except maybe the mosquitoes.

Before we headed down the road to Nenana, we decided a relaxing break was well earned. We packed the vehicles and drove to the Kenai Peninsula for rest and fishing. The fresh seafood in Homer was scrumptious. The camping was peaceful and enjoyable. The night we camped on the Russian River included a visit by a black bear. Harold and Peggy saw it early in the evening when they were walking. After we settled in for the night we heard clanging around outside. Harold looked out the window and was face to face with his new friend, the black bear. As the bear ran off into the woods, it knocked over a garbage can. The next morning we learned it tore up a tent in a neighboring site. Lucky for them they decided to sleep in their car. I was glad we were in the Airstream and not in a tent.

Part III: Back and Forth

Fairbanks and Nenana

August 6, 1976

The fun week of camping and fishing was what we all needed. Zach slept through the bear visit but told everyone about it. The bear got bigger and bigger each time he shared the story. Jeremia sat in the comfort of his infant seat listening to his big brother's every word.

We rented the cabin to a university student and headed to Nenana to check out our new home. Jed's contract started in ten days. Nenana was close so we knew we would return to Fairbanks in the fall to store belongings before winter.

Peggy and Harold helped us settle into our home at the Yukon Koyukuk School District (YKSD) area. The new school district was given an old Federal Aviation Administration (FAA) site two miles south of Nenana. It hadn't been inhabited for several years. FAA sites were set up throughout Alaska while airport systems were developed. They were built with the same configuration: four two-story houses, an apartment building, and several outbuildings for storage spread out in a large oval area with a common green space in the center.

The apartment building had five apartments. The building was ten to fifteen years old with modern conveniences (electricity and running water). I learned to never assume those services were part of any housing until I saw the lights go on and water running. There were two one-bedroom and two two-bedroom apartments, plus an attic efficiency apartment in the structure. We were given one of the two-bedroom apartments.

The four large double-story houses were homes for the superintendent, assistant superintendent, and offices. One house was for clerical and business tasks and the second house accommodated the itinerant positions, such as a district maintenance supervisor, vocational teacher, business education teacher, special education coordinator, and correspondence teachers. Student files barged and flown in from the district's ten schools were stored some place. What a mess! There was no plan, so everything was chaotic.

When Jed picked up the keys to our apartment he heard new carpeting was being installed the following week. I was excited! Whoa—running water and carpeting. We called the barge lines and found our boxes were waiting for us. I contacted the storage unit in California and gave them the word to ship everything to Nenana, Alaska. After five years we were about to have all of our belongings in one place.

As we entered the building Zach asked when Nathan would arrive. John, our friend from Nulato, was hired as the itinerant vocational teacher. Mary and I called the Nenana City School District before leaving Nulato to inquire about jobs. We were told—no openings. Although happy I would be home with my children, money would be tight with one paycheck. Living in Alaska was expensive.

The apartment building needed a fresh coat of paint inside and out. It was obvious the building had been empty for a few years. Stairs went down to a daylight basement where there was a laundry room and storage rooms. Walking into our apartment, the air was noticeably musty and stale. We opened windows to encourage fresh ventilation and energy. Screens were missing. It was obvious no one had been hired to clean the building. The biggest shock was the iron-stained kitchen and bathroom fixtures with horrible reddish stains that were difficult to remove. I saw similar discolorations in other places in Alaska, but these were the worst.

Alaska's hard water problem was from the iron in the soil. There was a sulfuric odor and it wasn't a reliable source for drinking unless it was filtered. When I turned on the water Zach said, "What is that smell?" Cleaning the stains required a substance called Iron Out, similar to Ajax, only stronger. It required covering my face when I cleaned because it was so toxic. Bleach wasn't useful. I knew keeping clothes looking clean and white was going to require constant attention. Someone told Jed that the district was working to find solutions to the water conditions. With babies in diapers and active three-year-olds, laundry was a daily chore.

With the apartment in a state of neglect, we spent another couple of nights in the Airstream. Soon Peggy and Harold would head east to visit family in Pennsylvania. We benefited from their help until they departed. The extra hands were put to work.

Peggy and I cleaned and painted the apartment, as well as hung wallpaper in the boys' bedroom. I continued to clean the Iron Out spots in the house daily and slowly made progress. It was fun to finally do things for my children's room. I knew this wasn't a home we owned but felt we might be here for a few years. Windows needed curtains and drapes, so much to do. When things arrived from Santa Cruz it was like Christmas. After five years I had forgotten about many of the items, but seeing them made me eager to use them.

A dog yard was constructed for the growing sled dog team that now required eight doghouses. Jed was approved to use an area two hundred feet from the apartment. The dogs were easily seen and heard from the bedroom windows. It was good we weren't the only family with dogs, because they barked. When sled dogs were fed or harnessed to run they jumped straight up and down and barked. It was fun and annoying at the same time. Both the superintendent and assistant superintendent had small dog teams. The three dog yards were conveniently placed close to trails that traveled directly to a larger wilderness area used by other mushers.

Our dog pack included a puppy, Bingo, a female Labrador retriever purchased to be a mistress for Hidalgo, but also a pet for the boys. She was often in the house or in the puppy pen built in the center of the dog yard. It was fun to observe her as she ran around the pen watching the activity. Lady, our lead dog, was pregnant so the pen would be utilized beyond Bingo. Dogs, dogs, and more dogs!

A couple of days before Harold and Peggy left John and Mary arrived with Nathan and Melissa. The fun of two babies and the chatter of two toddlers playing was a great way for them to end the summer. As the Airstream pulled away I am sure the quiet was a little strange for them. The day before Harold and Peggy left, a meeting of the district principals and administrators was held, followed by a barbeque. The assistant superintendent fished in Bristol Bay a month each summer so he contributed seven large, fresh salmon to the feast. He knew well how to cook the salmon to retain the moisture and tenderness. Each bite melted in my mouth, reminding me the fresher the salmon, the better it tasted. Bread, fresh vegetables, rice, and dessert rounded off a delicious dinner and made for a lovely send off for Harold and Peggy and the principals as they headed to their villages.

Part III: Back and Forth

Located southwest of Fairbanks, at Milepost #412 along the George Parks Highway, Nenana was east of the mouth of the Nenana River and on the south bank of the Tanana River. The building of the railroad in the 1920s helped Nenana become an active community. The population swelled to five thousand residents, but when it was finished an economic slump occurred. Currently, the population was less than five hundred. The new George Parks Highway, completed a few years earlier in 1971, was projected to be a valuable route in Alaska bringing more traffic through Nenana. Mt. McKinley, sixty-seven miles south of Nenana, was in the process of enlarging into a National Park. Other communities along the highway hoped a dependable highway between Anchorage and Fairbanks would provide better access to goods and services. The state promised to keep it open through the extreme cold.

I drove into town, found one grocery store, and the same number of churches as bars. Buildings in town included a post office, grocery store, railroad station, Native community hall, and an office for the famous Nenana Ice Classic. We heard about the annual event when traveling up the ALCAN. When we had stopped for coffee in a small restaurant, the waitress heard we were headed to Alaska. She brought out a book with Ice Classic guesses for each year.

The Ice Classic started in 1906 when six individuals wagered a bet on the time the ice on the Tanana River would break. It started as a fundraising event. People purchased a ticket guessing the exact time the Tanana River ice broke, pushing the Yukon River to break up. When ice moved in these two rivers it was the tipping of the first domino in a long line. Moving ice signified summer was close.

The Ice Classic tickets sold each year starting February 1 through April 5 in Alaska, the Yukon territories, and beyond. The recent Ice

Classic group registered as a nonprofit charitable gaming organization. Proceeds benefited the volunteers, selected nonprofit organizations, and the winners.

Fall weather made travel to Fairbanks for food and other items easy. We continued to settle into Nenana as Jed started his new job. Shelves were built in the downstairs storage unit and rooms painted. When in Fairbanks we covered and protected items left at the property. We peeled a few more logs and took measurements for the house foundation. After the first frost, the mosquitoes and no-see-ums were gone. The boys and I went berry picking with Genie for high bush cranberries. The pungent smell made my nose tickle and the flavor on my tongue tasted tart. The berries made a great applesauce when mixed with dried apples. Mixing the berries with spices created a savory meat sauce, which tasted delicious with moose meat.

Two of the families we had gathered logs with over the summer completed their houses. We attended one of the open houses. The hard work done over the summer was celebrated as everyone examined the detailed craftsmanship in the finished houses. Food from home gardens and kitchens provided a delicious potluck.

Jed and Tom were hired to develop the district's new correspondence program. The students for the program lived on homesteads within the forty thousand square miles of the Yukon Koyukuk School District (YKSD), but had no school. Non-Native people couldn't own land in a village or close by, so they opted for homestead land. There were no Alaska Native families living on homesteads.

Part III: Back and Forth

The State ran the correspondence program from Juneau before the new school district system was established. It made more sense for the program to be close to the different geographic areas. Jed and Tom had no clue how it was going to work, but were determined to figure it out and do a good job. The program required the district have one elementary teacher (Jed) and one high school teacher (Tom). Between the two of them, they had fifty students. Sometimes a family had five or six kids all in different grades.

Weather was the wild card and led to decisions on how to travel. Extreme weather made it physically hard to reach all of the students. It took a combination of four-wheel vehicles, snow machines, dogsleds, and planes, sometimes on floats and other times on skis. Some families lived off the railroad line so the train and hiking in was another method. The majority of the families came from the lower 48. They lived as much off the land as they could in environments most people would consider primitive, radical, and harsh.

Students were excited to see their teachers and families came to rely on them showing up each month for reasons far beyond education. They brought mail, and if the family was able to get a message to the district office, Jed and Tom would bring other requested items. In the winter they always tried to take fresh produce as a treat.

Many families had several children so Tom and Jed often traveled together. The district contracted with Calvert Education, a company in Iowa, for grade level education boxes. Calvert Education had worked with families for decades to provide home schooling to students in grades 3–12. After parents registered their students with the Yukon-Koyukuk SD, grade level boxes were ordered and visits were arranged. Without telephones, the communication wasn't fast or specific.

Tom and Jed learned to tell a family they planned to visit during a week, not on a specific day. Sometimes they stayed the night.

Each grade box included structured curriculum lessons in all content areas. Parents were the primary instructional teachers and the itinerant correspondence teachers were facilitators. The visits helped parents as much as the students. Parents were busy teaching their children, as well as handling homestead tasks. Besides bringing supplementary enrichment materials, Jed and Tom assessed the students during the monthly visits and returned assignments.

Occasionally, a husband commuted into Anchorage or Fairbanks part of the year to work for money, leaving the wife alone. Children were responsible and helped with younger siblings. The boys and I accompanied Jed a couple of times in the early fall. It was fascinating to learn how people ended up on the homesteads, as well as the challenges and obstacles they faced. Homestead families worked hard and long days. They were resourceful and self sufficient beyond what many of us could imagine. I admired their spirit and determination.

In the fall, Mary and I took long walks with the babies in carriers and the boys running ahead to keep up with Bingo. John and Jed tried not to be gone at the same time, but it happened. Mary helped me by watching the kids while I fed the dogs. If John was home, Mary came downstairs or I took the boys up to their house while I completed the dog-feeding task. Eight dogs meant the five-gallon feeding bucket mixture was half to two thirds full. The food and water was in the basement. As the weather got colder, I made sure no liquid spilled because it instantly froze and made things slippery as I carried the bucket upstairs and outside.

Part III: Back and Forth

During the winter the dogs water froze almost instantly so I watered them a couple of times a day. They learned to drink it up quickly or ate snow when it was fresh. At first my arms were sore carrying five-gallon buckets of dog food and water, but I became stronger. I tried to keep them half full.

Going to the post office became a treat. The postmistress, Della, was a delightful woman from Noatak, an Inupiat village close to Kotzebue. I wondered how she wound up in Nenana, but the topic never came up. She quickly learned my name; "Good morning, Christina. How are you and your boys?" Her vibrant personality and good humor made a mundane trip to the post office cheerful. She always had candy at the counter so the boys wanted to go with me.

On December 2 the family Christmas presents were ready to be mailed. I was concerned about their arrival for the big day. Our families adjusted to the length of time it took for letters and packages to and from Alaska. The slippery parking area at the post office made carrying boxes challenging. I heard Della laughing as someone came out holding the door. As usual I was trying to multitask by carrying all the boxes in one trip so they towered over my head. She came around the counter just in time to catch the top two as they fell. Her belly laugh made me smile. I didn't feel stressed anymore when I saw her face. It seemed like her eyes and mouth were individually smiling.

As I finished the package information and paid my bill, we chatted. I told her how much I liked her earrings. They were a unique beaded design I had never seen. Many beaded earrings dangled and this pair was an octagon shape. She took them off and handed them to me. I was speechless and unsure of what to say. After a moment I said, "Thank you, but I can't take these from you." She said, "Yes, it is our custom."

In her culture when someone admired something it was given to the person. I felt so honored and hoped I would find a gift to give her.

The oil heater for the apartment building stopped. It was cold outside, around zero. Jed and John were gone, as well as the maintenance supervisor for the district. Mary watched the kids while I ran over to the main building to find someone to help. The assistant superintendent knew a little about the oil heaters from having a similar one in a previous school. Within a few hours it was working, which was good since the temperature was dropping. We added 'check oil heater' to our daily responsibilities. The funny thing was that we could have called the office. After four years of not having a phone, neither one of us thought of calling.

Jed and Tom were stuck in the office for two weeks because of thirty degrees below zero weather. When it warmed up to zero, they needed to catch up with visits. A typewriter arrived for one of Tom's students, Dorothy, who needed it for a business class. Typing lessons were in the Calvert box, but not a typewriter. Dorothy wanted to finish requirements to graduate. Tom suggested Jed take the typewriter to her since he needed to visit the younger siblings. This arrangement allowed Tom to travel to another family and helped them both from getting further behind.

A typewriter had never been delivered in a sled behind a snow machine. Knowing there were bumps and curves along the trail they were concerned. Sleds were less apt to turn over with a standing rider on the footboards. Jed asked if I wanted to go. With the limited daylight he knew we would need to spend the night. Dorothy's dad Bill was working in Anchorage, so having me along was more comfortable for him. The weather was cold so we felt the boys needed to remain behind.

Mary and John offered to watch them for the night. The typewriter was carefully bundled with school materials, the mail, and a box of food that Bill wanted us to deliver to his family.

Jed told me about the trail so I felt prepared. Guiding the sled while riding on footboards required concentration to see the bumps and be ready for the turns. I knew it was important to keep my knees relaxed. The ride to the house included a cold breeze, but we were well covered and dressed for the occasion. While Jed helped Dorothy get acquainted with the typewriter, I worked with the younger students. Before dinner, Jed helped with outdoor chores while I visited with Betty, the amazing mom who kept things organized. No easy feat at twenty below zero and colder. Dorothy and Betty were excited she would officially graduate in a few months. It was obvious her mom would miss the help and companionship.

It was my nature to investigate communities. I was curious. At the Nenana store I asked Sue, the checker, if she had always lived in Nenana. I was one of two people in the store so I didn't think I was keeping her from any pending task. She said, "Yes, she was born in Fairbanks and raised in Nenana." She was pleased I asked about her hometown. In Athabaskan, Nenana meant 'a good place to camp between two rivers.' She was surprised to learn we lived in three Athabaskan villages before arriving in Nenana.

After a cold winter, the days began warming up. The definition of cold and warm became funny to me. The temperatures seemed extreme on the cold side. I grew up never knowing about zero degrees, let alone fifty below zero. Jed checked the temperature regularly, either at the airport or through the radio at the district office. The district itinerants needed the information to plan their weeks. Jed often relayed the current and predicted weather to me. I needed to know because the layers of clothing I put on the boys and myself were based on the degrees of cold. I wanted to be ready and prepared, whatever that meant.

Zach, Jeremia, and me playing outside
January 1977

April 9, 1977 was the special day. The sounds of my restless one-year-old and thinking about the day made me smile. Longer days and more sun gave me a warm glow of contentment. I was becoming aware of how important sun was to me. I often felt guilty for being a little grouchy, uneasy, and uncomfortable without understanding my need for at least some sun. Maybe I had the condition known as Seasonal Affective Disorder (SAD).

After a week of dreary, overcast weather the temperature was eighteen degrees above zero and predicted to get warmer as the day progressed. Jed called the pilot to check about our flight and confirmed the departure time. The pilot said, "This is the kind of day pilots live for—clear, crisp, and still." It was the beginning of spring in the interior of Alaska and was a special day for a young woman who worked hard to make it happen.

The Cessna 206, a six-seat plane was perfect for the five passengers and pilot. Tom and Jed had to attend, but the extra seats allowed for the boys and I to participate in the first high school graduation of the Yukon Koyukuk School District (YKSD) Correspondence Program. Today was Saturday and five of us were headed to Wilderness Lake on a chartered flight for the festive event. As we flew out of Nenana, we headed northwest toward Tanana where Jeremia was born. Wilderness Lake was seventy-five miles, approximately the midpoint and accessible only by airplane, floats when the lake ice was melted, and skis or snow machine when it was frozen. Spring thaws hadn't happened so the plane was still on skis. The homestead we visited was 160 acres in size and owned by Betty and Bill. They were one of many families who came to Alaska in the '60s and '70s to fulfill their dream of living simply with little influence of the 'lower 48' world.

Wilderness Lake was a lovely site, surrounded by alder, birch, and spruce trees; however, it had its share of the harsh, extreme weather conditions. The need to be totally self-sufficient was a basic requirement and this family understood this fact well. As the plane taxied to the main cabin, we saw nine smiling faces anxious to share the happiness of the occasion. The biggest smile of the day was on Dorothy's face. It was her initiative that made the day happen. Dorothy was the first student to graduate from the Correspondence Study Program.

Dorothy planned and orchestrated all the details. The materials for each student's studies came in a box from Iowa. When a student graduated, the normal procedure was to fulfill the requirements and receive a diploma in the mail. Dorothy decided that wasn't enough. She wanted more to remember and experience than opening an envelope whenever it arrived on the lake. She artistically created her own announcements to send out and, with the help of a family friend, designed a high school ring and pennant with 'Class of 1977' on it. This all happened via mail, which was complicated on a lake in the middle of a wilderness area with no mail service.

The announcement stated the graduation ceremonies would start at high noon. After arriving and visiting for a short time, we wondered if all the guests were here? "How naïve of us!" Just because we were seventy-five miles from the nearest village, town, or city didn't mean we were the only guests. A little before noon, two people walked up the path from the other cabin close by. Still no sign it was time to begin, so we waited. Soon we heard the familiar buzz of bush Alaska beckoning through the treetops. Two small planes arrived with families from surrounding lakes, Becky Lake and Shultz Lake, anxious to be part of this celebration. The group was now composed of twenty-four adults and children contently packed into the small, two-room 12′ by 32′ cabin, as well as three dogs, two puppies, and twenty-six newly arrived chicks eager to assist and share in the special festivities.

The atmosphere was full of gaiety and laughter, no one at all awed by the fact they came by airplane or foot, instead of by car to a graduation ceremony out in the middle of nowhere. Even Dorothy's father flew in late Thursday with the chicks. Currently, he worked in Anchorage, but tried to come home as often as possible. In Alaska the weather dictated people's abilities to travel. April's weather was more predictable.

Part III: Back and Forth

After a simple ceremony of words and accolades about the extra tasks Dorothy had performed as part of her high school experience, a delicious lunch was served that included a special cake decorated with a scroll and cap to mark the momentous day. Dorothy's mom went all out with food and many of us brought simple dishes to add to the potluck, a norm in Alaska. Nothing was ever assigned; people brought what they had to share. The younger siblings made little paper Easter baskets with goodies for each of the smaller guests who attended the graduation.

As people ate and chatted, the visiting families were impressed with the activities Dorothy had in her last semester. The month before graduation, the district flew her to a ski meet and a vocational education shadow experience. I thought about what a change it was for Dorothy, who seldom interacted with young people her age, to be suddenly immersed with a large group of her peers. She and three other students represented the Correspondence Studies Program by competing in the Yukon-Koyukuk School District Ski Meet preliminaries in Kaltag[18] and then in the finals two weeks later in Ruby[19].

During the end of March and first few days of April, she traveled to Fairbanks to attend the Rural Schools Vocational Program (RSVP). This program was designed for high school students in rural settings throughout Alaska. It provided students a chance to choose a vocational area they were considering for life after high school. Government offices and businesses in Fairbanks, Anchorage, or Juneau provided two-week experiences in work positions. These opportunities gave students a snapshot of what jobs were like, as well as what was needed to be prepared.

Dorothy enjoyed a two-week session at the Fairbanks North Star Borough School District (FNSBSD) office. Her training involved learning about different business machines including keypunch and

10-key calculators, as well as knowledge of business office protocols. Her last day there was celebrated with a cake provided by her new office friends who celebrated her approaching graduation. This experience aligned well with Dorothy's plans to attend Alaska Business College in the coming fall.

As I watched Dorothy unwrap her presents I looked over at her mother. How bittersweet this moment must have been for Mom! Her eldest daughter worked hard for this moment and yet, how would she cope without her? Alaska homesteads weren't for the meek. Betty, Dorothy's mom, would be busy keeping up with the six children ranging from seven to fifteen. Dorothy was her right hand in overseeing the children and the schoolwork, as well as the endless tasks. Cindy, the second child, learned from helping her sister and, hopefully, was ready to take over.

Before people left, Dorothy gathered everyone together for a picture. Friends, family and teachers were included so she could look back and remember the exhilarating occasion. Everyone was reluctant to depart. The day was full of energy and electricity. People expressed their enjoyment. This rite of passage was difficult to see come to a close.

Our pilot arrived promptly at 3:00 p.m. for the return to Nenana. As we taxied off the frozen lake, the traffic was light and courteous. Dorothy beamed and appreciated the time we had taken to help give her a strong send off to a bright future. As our little plane winged its way back to the bigger world of Nenana, I wondered if other 1977 graduates would savor and revere their graduation as much as Dorothy. Larger communities had several events—baccalaureate evenings, various award ceremonies, different school affairs, and the graduation 'walk across the stage' highlight, as well as all-night parties with friends to experience. I knew I would always remember the special Graduation at Wilderness Lake.

Part III: Back and Forth

Springtime meant we were outside more. Jed exercised the dogs as much as possible throughout the long, dark winter, even when it was really cold. The extreme temperatures kept the boys and I cooped up inside more than what I needed to be happy. April meant added daylight and warmer temperatures. Jed was home more and I was able to get out for an occasional short morning run before he left for work. I returned smiling and relieved we had made it through the coldest part of the year.

In May, John and Mary told us they were moving. The lack of a job for Mary and constant travel for John was more than they wanted, so they investigated work in the Kenai Soldotna Peninsula. I didn't blame them. I really understood, but was crushed. The friendship and companionship was enjoyable and made the long days manageable. My life would be different without Mary. We promised to come their way for Thanksgiving.

The superintendent and assistant superintendent wives were both teachers in Nenana City School District. Their time was filled with teaching, managing their homes, and each had a small child. I saw them at social gatherings for the district and talked briefly if we saw each other outside. I somewhat understood, but dreaded next winter. I embraced my Scarlett O'Hara attitude, "I will worry about this in the fall."

The snow melted, fully announcing that summer was coming. Little seeds sprouted in the window for the garden I planned on in Fairbanks. During one of our late winter shopping trips into Fairbanks we visited the Extension Office on the University of Alaska–Fairbanks campus. While mapping out the property last summer, we chose a spot for a garden with southern exposure and sloped land. One of our neighbors mentioned raised beds on a slope heated the plants and increased their production during the short season.

During a weekend trip the garden was prepared for the horse manure delivered from a Fairbanks neighbor. The earth looked rich after it was plowed and turned. I loved the smell of fresh earth as I dug into it—the color and the texture told me it was anxious for things to grow! I had wanted a garden in California before coming to Alaska and now I was about to have one.

Jed's parents came for another Alaska visit to help with our numerous projects. They were invested in seeing their grandsons and experiencing Alaska, mosquitoes and all. Harold enjoyed the hard work. The involvement of building a log home wasn't a typical California experience. They knew how to 'rough it,' as their friends called it. Many fun weekends were spent on their five acres in Twentynine Palms, California during college. Their rustic cabin didn't have running water either.

With the cabin rented year-round (helpful to our budget) a place to sleep was top priority. Jed had two months off, a typical teacher contract. I checked the Nenana City School District for openings in the fall and found none were expected. Building the log house with no bank loan and no second income increased our vigilance in making decisions.

We investigated semi-permanent tents and decided an 8-by-10-foot wall tent was the best option. Wall tents were made of a lightweight sturdy canvas and provided more headroom than typical camping tents. Hunters used them often, which seemed like a perfect recommendation. Zach had a cot and Jed built a platform for us to put a mattress on. I wanted Jeremia to sleep in his playpen. He started walking at nine months and was hard to contain after he woke up. I had nightmares he would innocently wander away to investigate his new world. He was physically curious and constantly on the move. Jed drew a diagram of the inside of the tent to show me how tight everything would be. The drawing helped us to organize every nook and cranny.

Wall tents were advertised as easy to set up with either an internal or external frame. We knew they were all season tents but we never planned to stay in it in the winter. The question we didn't have an answer to was how many summers it would take to build the house. A wooden floor was constructed to keep the tent off the ground. An electric line was strung to the tent for electricity. With constant daylight our one light in the tent was seldom used.

With two small children we didn't put a wood stove in the wall tent, rather we opted for an electric heater to use at night or early in the morning to take the chill off. I used a two-burner electric hot plate on a daily basis for coffee and simple cooking. I called our summer home my 'all electric' tent. Outside the wall tent was a refrigerator and Jed built a large picnic table. He used logs. It was sanded and covered with a thick protective resin to handle different weather conditions. Many meals were eaten at the table with family and friends.

The rock fire ring used the first summer was expanded, making it easier to cook and grill. The light smoke from the fire ring kept the mosquitoes under control. At their most active time in the summer, we lit green curlicue mosquito punks in the tent and around the fire ring area. The punks had an overpowering smell but allowed for restful sleep at night and kept the biting madness limited. I felt like a mama bear protecting her cubs from the whining, agitating, mosquitoes. Jeremia's hands were covered with toothpaste easing the irritation from the bites. Zach swatted them, but Jeremia was still innocent of mosquito abuse.

Me peeling logs
Summer 1977

It was hard to believe it was barely a year since the log house project had started. The learning curve continued straight up. Select, fell, and stack logs—done! Now prepare building site, construct a foundation, peel logs, raise the logs, erect a roof, and much more. Wow! Our limited financial resources and time led the decisions. The prior summer we hauled water in containers knowing we would figure something out this year. Wells were difficult in Fairbanks, so many people created water systems, such as tanks under ground or holding containers inside a heated mudroom. With twelve dogs, a garden, a growing family, and friends stopping by we knew we needed a summer water system.

Three water stations were constructed. In both the dog yard and garden area Jed built structures that held six fifty gallon barrels positioned in two rows of three each, plumbed together with a spout coming out of the lower central barrel. The slightly sloped surface the property sat on provided a natural gravity flow. We made good use of Mother Nature when selecting the watering posts. In the garden, a hose was attached that included a way to turn it on and off similar to a city water spigot. I was pleased I didn't have to lug buckets. The water pressure from the slopped terrain was outstanding. The third watering trough, as we called it, was a single water barrel for washing dishes and hands. We used separate containers for drinking water. Since the university was so close to the property we drove there and showered in the late afternoon or evening. We found it to be the best place for drinking water.

Harold and Peggy arrived and started pitching in with the infinite tasks on the to-do list. The Airstream was parked in a different location this year to give our tenant privacy. Zach loved the freedom of walking to the Airstream to visit Granddad and Dodo (a family name for grandmother). Peggy watched Jeremia while Zach and I slipped away to a community education class called, *Creepy, Crawly Things* at the

Fairbanks Library. It was perfect for a four-year-old and his mother who benefitted from learning about strange creatures that moved in weird ways.

The yellow and zucchini squash seeds Harold had sent, along with peas, beans, carrots, celery, and broccoli were all planted. I started them as small starts in Nenana. One of the neighbors told me about a wild weed that was really good if picked when it was only about four inches tall. Cooked with garlic and onions it tasted amazing. This interesting weed had several names. A friend called it pigweed and told me I would hate it by the end of the summer. When I checked with the Extension office they told me the biological name was Chenopodium, more frequently called lamb's quarter. I thought it was wonderful. It was from the spinach family so when steamed it was great. I even froze some for winter. Whenever I did my runs to Nenana to check mail and do laundry I took any I had frozen to put in the freezer in Nenana. The pigweed season was short, late May to mid June.

The plants were in the garden when Peggy and Harold arrived. I demonstrated the water system, showing them the hose and water pressure. The pressure was similar to running water in a city. Jeremia tagged along in the garden. He wanted to stomp on the little hills (raised beds), but I told him those were off limits. I was excited to see how quickly the plants grew especially after we got into mid June. The daylight was twenty-four hours a day. I worried I wasn't watering enough since Fairbanks had little rain. Water was delivered every other week or as needed by truck with a trailer that held a five hundred gallon tank. The extreme cold of Fairbanks and limited city infrastructure meant many families didn't have running water. Water Wagons were common and a booming business year round in Fairbanks. We wondered what type of water system would be best for the log house. That concern was far away at this point.

Summer of 1977 was busy and moved fast. Jed's first task was building an outhouse. It was almost finished when his parents arrived. He and his dad completed the final details except for the stained glass window. That artistic element would come later. A wire fence was erected around the garden to keep critters from eating the produce. They changed a dirt path into a driveway leading to the log house site. Although a fairly clear spot on the property was chosen for the house there was still brush and small trees to clear. All of these tasks took time but were important. Each chore helped establish a footprint for the house. It was fun to imagine where the rooms would be.

The garden vegetables started to provide us with eating pleasure except for the zucchini and yellow squash. The squash plants were huge with no flowers, thus no fruit. Harold didn't understand and I had no experience growing anything. One afternoon I stopped at the Extension office and explained my problem. The person in the office asked about the seeds I used. I told her my father-in-law sent them from California. She chuckled explaining the constant light in Alaska required seeds that don't need darkness to germinate. With no darkness the seeds Harold sent grew into large, healthy green plants, but couldn't germinate. As I left her office I made a note to myself, next year use Alaska seeds.

We were all sad to see summer end. Peggy and Harold enjoyed their grandsons and the boys reveled in being spoiled with the attention. It was hard to see the Airstream pull out and head back down the ALCAN. For us it was time to readjust to a school year routine. We loaded the dogs and headed back down the road. The drive back and forth between Fairbanks and Nenana was so easy in the summer.

In the winter there were a couple of spots in the highway that buckled, breaking through the asphalt. These ruts happened when winter temperatures severely dropped and stayed low for days.

They became further complicated if an odd warm spell occurred, followed by another fifty degrees below zero drop. The results were hazardous potholes difficult to avoid until repairs were completed.

We continued to visit the property for another month. I finished gathering produce and cleaned the garden beds. We covered things up and secured the wall tent for winter. The reality of our friends' move hit me when Zach asked about Nathan. We reminded him they moved to Kenai and we would see them at Thanksgiving. I started thinking about how different our lives were going to be and wondered what I would do. I knew the days were getting shorter. I mentally began the count down to the shortest day of the year. My mind struggled with frustration about the property in Fairbanks and the reality of Nenana, back and forth. I was perplexed. What was I going to do? Again the darkness was coming and again, *I was not prepared.*

I was committed to getting the boys out as much as possible before it was too dark or too cold led to many small walks. I wasn't sure who needed the walks most—the boys or me. The district compound included a small airport used by private planes and a couple of charter services, but most of the time it was quiet. Bingo tagged along with us on our walks and occasionally our silly cat thought she was a walker. She started out but after about ten minutes scurried home. I knew she was back to the safety of the building when I heard the dogs bark. She found a spot close enough to the dog yard to wait for us and tease them into a barking frenzy.

Zach and I searched for willow ptarmigans and then pointed them out to Jeremia. We told him about their speckled brown feathers that turned white to shield them from predators once the snow came.

During the summer we visited the Fairbanks library to learn about them; they were sometimes referred to as Arctic grouse. This beautiful bird was referred to as the state bird in 1955, four years before Alaska became a state. The boys loved the outings as much as I did. Fall time was too short, with the first snow arriving in early October.

Life was different with Mary gone. The district secretary moved back to Tanana to be with her family, leaving me as the lone female in the building. Everyone in the building served in an itinerant position, so they traveled. During the week, many evenings the boys and I were the only ones there. The life of itinerants in rural school districts required travel, which was hard on families. Zach helped me remember to check the oil heater. It became a task the three of us did together. As soon as we were in the basement, Zach would tell me it was on or off. He knew the sound as much as I did and Jeremia loved pushing the big red button to restart the system.

I was a social person, but now my world was narrow. Talking and reading with my children was rewarding, but I missed interaction with other adults. With limited opportunities for the boys and worried about money, I asked Jed what he thought about a childcare business in our home. He thought it was worth considering. Our small apartment would only accommodate a few children, which I felt was workable. I put the word out within the district office and two families were immediately interested. One family had a baby six months younger than Jeremia and the other had two little girls, five and three.

A redheaded five-year-old, named Susan, attended kindergarten, so she was gone part of the day. Her mother worked at the district office. Her little sister, Jane, had penetrating blue eyes and was close to Jeremia's age. They instantly hit it off. Both were curious about how things worked, which made me aware they could easily get into mischief. The baby, Jonathon, was an only child and still catching up from being born a little early. He loved all the excitement of the other children, and crawled around after the chatter and laughter. When the younger ones slept Zach and I still did some preschool activities.

Mealtime was interesting. I felt it was important for children to learn to help, so I let them fill their glasses with milk. They felt grown up as they poured from the small container I provided. I put my finger at the halfway point on the glass, knowing they would fill all the way to the top. I always had two towels ready to clean up excess milk as they developed their small motor skills. We made no-bake cookies and some days were focused on letters in the alphabet. The challenges of getting everyone down for a nap required strategizing and bargaining techniques. I knew parents wanted them rested when they picked them up, but not too rested because then they wouldn't be ready for bedtime. I did my best and we had fun.

My mom came to visit in January. We worked around the day care responsibilities. She took the triangle flight from LA to Hawaii with a stop in Alaska before returning to LA. When she arrived it was forty degrees below zero, not easy for someone who was not a cold weather person. Her motivation was to see Jeremia and get caught up with Zach. I warned her about the cold but she tackled it anyway. When the temperature warmed up to zero we bundled up and drove into Fairbanks for an Alaskan winter picnic on our property. As she left, we agreed her next trip would be in summer. I promised the boys and I would come south.

My mind continued to be restless and needed stimulation. I considered joining a church. I wasn't sure if I was looking for a spiritual connection or people contact. I dragged the boys with me as I checked out churches in Nenana, searching for like-minded people. All of the churches were very conservative and didn't appeal to my more liberal beliefs. One evening I attended a private home function where I participated in a Pentecostal 'laying on of hands.' After that evening I was done attending church and spiritual groups. I learned a great deal over those several months but the need I was looking for wasn't fulfilled.

There were no neighbors around the district compound, which made me feel isolated. When I was in Nenana I realized the Native community and the non-Natives weren't as interactive as in the villages. After living in Native villages for four years, it felt strange not to see and talk with Native people. During the railroad era, several Caucasian families moved into the Nenana area and stayed after the railroad heyday passed. Alaska was a young state and many decisions were made about Native people by non-Native people who were more interested in changing Native values to fit the modern, Western world. At least Alaska Natives were past the segregated water fountains and bathrooms they experienced in the '50s and '60s.

Mitch Demientieff was one of several young Alaska Native men who worked to build alliances between Native ways and Western influences. Mitch was a leader in the Nenana Native Council, connected to Doyon, one of the thirteen corporations established by the Alaska Native Land Claims Settlement Act[20] (ANCSA). He strongly connected to his Native beliefs and demonstrated it by his respect for elders and their wisdom. One of his strengths was his ability to facilitate conversations amongst Native and non-Native groups. Mitch had leadership roles with the Tanana Chiefs Conference[21] (TCC) and the Alaska Federation of Natives[22] (AFN). Both of these groups were crucial to assisting the Alaska Native Claims Settlement Act, an act dedicated to the protection of traditional values for all Alaska Natives. This interested me, so I inquired whether I could attend a meeting or any scheduled event.

When I called the Nenana Native Council office Mitch answered the phone. I was startled, thinking he would have a secretary, but then remembered that was my Western thinking. He told me everyone was welcome and mentioned a couple of events. When he told me Emil Notti would be speaking about the Alaska Native Claims Settlement Act I was sold. I didn't know who Mr. Notti was but the topic was of major interest to me. I checked with Jed to be sure he was available to watch the boys and not at a dog mushers' meeting.

Emil Notti, a Koyukon Athabaskan, was an indigenous activist and politician. He was a quiet, soft-spoken man and obviously well respected by the people who attended. He shook hands and talked with the Native elders before starting. His manner and approach was characteristic of a village meeting. He stated his name and history of his Native family roots (a typical introduction) before beginning his presentation. People felt at ease as he welcomed questions along the way. I learned he was a vital leader in the development of the Alaska Native Claims Settlement Act signed into law by President Nixon in December 1971[23]. His current role was president of the Alaska Federation of Natives (AFN), an organization focused on ensuring the human rights and economic stability of Alaska Natives. I left the event energized, encouraged, and pleased Native people had skillful and capable leaders. I understood at a different level the critical importance of the Alaska Native Claims Settlement Act and its effects on Alaska Natives. I was glad I stepped out of the YKSD compound and into the Nenana Native community.

Part III: Back and Forth

Spring arrived! Once again the darkness and cold lifted. It felt like a huge weight was taken off my chest. The temperatures stayed closer to zero at night and at least twenty degrees above during the day. The severe cold and dark walls of winter created claustrophobic feelings that started to dissipate. During the shorter days, I struggled not to become crabby. The day care provided two grown-ups to talk to each day, even if it was to share information about a child's new tooth, status of potty training, and if a daily poop had occurred.

With longer days and better weather, Jed was home more. This allowed me to escape early in the morning for a thirty-minute run before he left for work. I loved the opportunity to be outside when it was quiet and still. The spring birds sang as I ran along my route close to the airport. I stepped into a mental space of mindfulness of my surroundings. It was almost hypnotic. One day, looking down the airport, I saw something move. I didn't think it was a moose and we never saw bear in the area. *And yet, I knew there could be a first time.* The image gave the impression of tall grass moved by the wind, but there was no wind. As I approached I realized there was a group of birds almost as tall as me. At five feet, one and a half inches, that seemed tall for birds. They flew away when I was less than a one hundred feet from them. It was such a treat to be close as they took flight. I arrived home exhilarated and chattering like a magpie asking Jed what type of bird he thought they might be.

They were sandhill cranes just stopping in Nenana on their migratory route to Fairbanks. I found a picture of them in a bird book that depicted the gray color, red forehead, and pointed bills of the cranes I saw. They were found in grasslands, abundant by the airport. Although solitary during most of the year, when migrating they congregated in groups. I felt privileged they became accustomed to me running by them. I was quiet and respectful, delighted by the peaceful company.

May 1978 arrived and the weekend trips to Fairbanks started. I closed the day care business June 1. Being gone for two months meant parents needed to adjust their children to a new day care arrangement. I knew they wouldn't return in August. There were only so many transitions that were healthy for anyone. Constant back and forth changes were difficult.

Harold and Peggy arrived the end of May. The ALCAN was considered questionable through the month of May with the possibility of serious unexpected storms. Harold was an experienced driver by now and knew how to be prepared. They warned us the Airstream was packed with house supplies. The previous summer they had brought six different Mexican tiles for us to consider. Log homes were dark, especially in the winter months. I wanted color in the house and thought the kitchen counter and back splash would be great with Mexican tiles. There were numerous items stuffed in the trailer, such as wiring and electrical supplies.

During the Memorial Day weekend the foundational base logs were placed. The house was going up! Much of June was rainy, an unusual occurrence for a Fairbanks summer. Nevertheless, Jed and Harold continued to notch and move logs into place. The felled logs varied in sizes, which required careful decision-making with each log. July was an extremely busy month with family visiting from Pennsylvania, as well as the continued log work. On the final weekend in July, the ridgepole went up. It was an adrenaline-charged experience to watch. Friends assisted in hoisting the two purlins and ridgepole, a log four and a half feet in circumference at its fullest point. Many hands helped in the completion of this significant feat. My job was simple—keep all small people away from potentially dangerous locations.

After the ridgepole was completed, food and drinks appeared from everyone's cars or trucks—the Alaskan potluck style I loved. It seemed magical Ircinraq (Yup'ik for little people) planned the menu ensuring there was enough food for all. The 'ridgepole raising' party included toasts to Harold in appreciation of his continuous help for three solid summers. We were so grateful. Thank you Dad! What an incredible feeling of accomplishment came over the group as we looked up and saw the top logs set into place.

The hardest part of summer in Alaska was when it came to an end. Harold and Peggy started down the highway to California and we headed to Nenana. Jed resumed his itinerant teacher position, Zach started kindergarten, and Jeremia and I were on our own. Zach was very enthusiastic about school and already sounded out words. His teacher was excellent and he instantly fell in love with her. My heart was broken; my son had found a replacement for his first love, me.

Jeremia and I settled into a routine of being outdoors as much as possible. He needed the outdoors as much as I did. We heard the geese as they flew south and tried to count them. We threw balls back and forth, he played with his trucks, and we took short walks. While in Fairbanks he visited the dog yard with his dad and granddad, so his interest in the dogs increased. Now in Nenana he enjoyed saying their names as if I didn't know them. We talked about the snow coming and the shorter days. Even his little brain knew the days were numbered when the weather would insist we stay inside.

Over the summer I stopped at the University of Alaska Fairbanks (UAF) campus to inquire about the Master of Education (MEd) program in Cross-Cultural Studies. Each year the dark months increased my cabin fever. I believed a stimulated mind would distract me from another depressed winter. UAF was well respected for its cross-cultural studies programs and I was interested in different cultures. The master's program was a mixture of on-site time in Fairbanks and correspondence courses. I hoped my time in bush Alaska would be useful in completing the assignments. I was excited and ready for the challenge of balancing one class each semester with family responsibilities.

In the middle of September I received a phone call from a friend about a job opening. The position was halftime, as a coordinator for the University of Alaska, Rural Education–Nenana Valley Regional Center. I didn't know Nenana had a regional center connected to the University. No one mentioned it when I signed up for classes at UAF. After receiving more information Jed and I discussed the stress of living on one salary. I hadn't had a teaching job for three years. A decision was made I should complete the interview process. I wondered if they would fly me to Anchorage, but all I did was answer a few questions and the job was offered to me. Alaska was still at a point that finding qualified people wasn't easy.

The day care income hadn't helped much. I felt confident the halftime professional position would pay better. The University of Alaska (UA) system had three campuses: Anchorage, Fairbanks, and Juneau, and a fourth arm focused on rural areas. Alaska was geographically large, with a small population of four hundred thousand people. There were pockets of people scattered throughout the state interested in educational programs past high school, so the University established regional learning centers, similar to community colleges.

Each regional learning center developed classes based on student interest, available professors, and number of students. The Nenana Valley Regional Center served 110 miles along the highway from Nenana to Cantwell, plus two villages, Minto and Manley Hot Springs. My tasks as a half-time coordinator were to determine the type of classes adults in a community wanted and needed, find qualified instructors, locate places for classes, and register students. The courses varied from basic community education; emergency medical technician (EMT) and cardiopulmonary resuscitation (CPR) classes needed for certification or recertification; basic bookkeeping and business programs; as well as entry-level university classes for adults interested in general business and teacher education.

There was no office to work from and no one helped with paperwork. The person who previously had the position lasted six weeks. He delivered a box to the front door and declined my offer to discuss the job. I looked through the box and was unclear of how to start. Much of the first couple of weeks was spent on the phone with someone in the Anchorage office. Jeremia napped in the afternoon, so I was able to work from home. He was good about keeping himself busy when I was on the phone.

Life was busier with work and the class I was taking. I enjoyed the challenges and was fascinated with the process of finding students and instructors. When I met with students to discuss their interests they told me about people they knew had taught classes. The names they gave me led to other people. The paperwork in the file box wasn't much help.

I studied for the class I took when Jed was gone and after everyone was asleep. One class at a time was a slow way to complete a master's program, but I was determined. The boys were old enough to help prepare the dogs' food so they helped me when Jed was gone. I told them their job was to make sure I didn't forget to feed any of the dogs. They decided which dogs they would watch. I sloshed out to the dog yard as the huskies barked and jumped up and down. When I came in, they assured me I hadn't missed feeding or watering any dogs.

Nenana had two options for day care, Nenana City's day care or the wife of a new teacher. The first one was well respected, but had no openings. My job required I travel occasionally to communities to meet with students and set-up classes and into Fairbanks to meet with instructors. There were even a couple of meetings in Anchorage where all of the Regional Coordinators met with the dean of Rural Education. I needed part-time day care help.

I called Sue, the woman who had the small day care. There were two children at her home for full days, plus her children still at home. Jeremia was there two days a week, occasionally three. I wasn't comfortable with the situation, but felt stuck. I wished for Marie who had taken such good care of Zach.

My day travel was planned carefully and arranged around Jed's itinerary. Clear Air Force Base (AFB) was one of the communities served, so I scheduled a visit. When I arrived it felt as though I had stepped onto another planet. This facility looked sterile. I grew up around military bases as a child because my dad had been in the air force. Bases generally had family housing so signs of children, like toys in the yards and bicycles by the front door, were common. Clear AFB only had men stationed there with a few civilian employees. A lone woman secretary worked in the office where my appointment was. She and the other civilians lived in the bedroom community of Anderson, a mile away.

The few military enlisted men I talked with about potential classes spoke as if Clear AFB was an overseas assignment. They wanted assurance the classes were transferable to other colleges in the states. At first I was dumbfounded but learned they seldom left the base during their 'overseas assignment.' Fairbanks was less than three hours away. It seemed strange and disconcerting. The base officers were required to offer college classes for the enlisted men so they requested undergraduate business courses.

A call came from a man who asked me to arrange his yearly class held at the Mount McKinley Park office. He talked as if I knew all about the class. Finally, I broke into his chatter and asked a few questions. His class was on photographing wildlife. I took his name and told him I would call him back. When I called Mount McKinley National Park[24] they confirmed he was a regular instructor and had quite a following. Several Park Service employees and teachers in the valley filled his class annually.

I needed to make a trip to the Park office, so I arranged it when the photographer was there to teach his class. He sounded like a character on the phone so I wanted to meet him. He was as eccentric in person as he was on the phone, but very knowledgeable. He gave me a beautiful print of a bald eagle looking straight ahead with his wings out to each side. His course helped the rangers provide safety guidance to Park visitors as they took wildlife pictures. People weren't accustomed to the number and variety of wildlife in Mount McKinley. They often walked too close to the animals in order to get a better picture.

At the end of my long day to Mount McKinley and the Denali Borough School District, I stopped to pick up Jeremia. I was tired and looking forward to a full three-day weekend at home. When I knocked

Jeremia and I in front of wall tent

at the door, Sue said, "Come in." I walked in. Usually Jeremia came running when he heard my voice. I asked where Jeremia was and she pointed behind me. He sat alone and didn't jump up. I immediately went over to him and he whispered something to me. I leaned down for him to repeat what he said. "Mommy, I wet my pants. I am sorry," as he started to cry. I cradled him in my arms. He had never wet his pants and I envisioned his skin red and raw. His red hair made his complexion very sensitive.

As we left, Sue said see you tomorrow. I reminded her Jeremia wouldn't be there. I was perplexed and irritated. Why were her two kids eating ice cream while the day care kids were unsupervised in the bedroom with the door closed and my son sat on the couch alone in wet clothes? Cradling Jeremia's head I carried him to the car carefully maneuvering the icy spots. Thinking, I remembered his extra clothes at Sue's house and asked why he hadn't changed. He said he mentioned them to Sue, but she told him, "You'll be going home soon." We picked Zach up and headed home. I bathed Jeremia and put lotion on the skin irritated from his wet pants. Annoyed and frustrated this happened to my child, I felt guilty for being a working mom.

The next day was the monthly Friday afternoon movie at Nenana School. It was open to the community so it became a treat the boys and I shared. This month the movie was *Charlotte's Web*, a favorite book I read to them. Jeremia and I were able to sit with Zach. As the three of us walked to the car talking about the movie, Jeremia noticed his friend, Timmy, from day care. Timmy looked confused and scared standing on the sidewalk. I said, "Hi Timmy, are you looking for your mom or Sue?" He told me he was looking for Sue. We offered to take him back inside to find her as a car pulled up and Sue jumped out. She greeted me with nod and said, "Let's go Timmy." I reluctantly released his hand.

My mind was racing; *had she just left this child?* I knew at that moment there was no way Jeremia would return to her house. That afternoon I called the other day care provider. Without stating my reasons, I inquired if she might have an opening for Jeremia. She remembered me from the first call and said she would call back. Maybe it was the desperation in my voice or an opening really occurred. Either way, she called Saturday afternoon and said she had room for Jeremia. I was pleased and thanked her profusely.

The boys were excited the weather was warm enough for them to be included in the dog mushing excursions. As we entered the dog yard they became excited by all the noise and eagerness of the dogs. Even though they were young, they understood the importance of not goofing around when the dogs were being harnessed to a sled. Jed had two sleds ready when we brought out the lunch and extra gear. He laid out the gang line, while the boys and I brought harnesses over to the necklines. We checked each harness to be sure it wasn't tangled before it was attached to a dog. Dogs didn't run well in a tangled harness and developed sores. The harness crisscrossed over a dog's back and under the belly area. Good dog mushers carried extra equipment for 'just in case' situations. I made a canvas bag that hung beneath the handlebars of the larger sled to carry a few tools and extra gear. My team was three dogs and Jed generally had five. With both of us running a team, more dogs were exercised.

The weather in March 1979 was sunny and good for dog mushing every weekend. We felt the boys were old enough for two to three hour outings with the dogs. In February Jed and a friend, Brian, set up a wall tent with a stove out in the woods about an hour and a half from the compound. A small cast iron Yukon cook stove heated the tent up quickly and provided an area away from the wind if it kicked up.

Part III: Back and Forth

Sometimes ten or more of us gathered for hot dogs, s'mores, and cocoa or tea. Friends came by snow machine or dog team. A canvas blanket was spread out for people to sit on and children to play.

Driving three dogs was perfect for me because I felt in control while still watching my three-year-old bundled up in the sled. Our ride out to the wall tent was great, windy, but the trail was clear. Jeremia was anxious to be out of the sled so he could explore. Jed and Zach's sled was right behind us, as well as two other couples who arrived by snow machine. Someone got the stove going in the tent for people to warm up by. Everyone had rosy cheeks from the gentle breeze coming out on the trail.

As the day began to wind down, a few of us moved into the tent to visit before departing. I sensed Jeremia was getting restless. All bundled up made it difficult to play. I asked Jane if she would watch him while I prepared the dogs to leave. Jed and Zach helped me turn the dogs around when I heard Jeremia crying. I entered the tent, as Jane looked up at me, puzzled and unsure of what was wrong. I sat down next to Jeremia to ask why he was crying. He held his hands out so I started to gently rub them. He pulled them back, "No Mommy. The stove hurt my hands." I suddenly understood he placed his hands too close to the iron stove and burned them. In a snowsuit and mukluks he was always teetering on uneven ground.

As I examined his hands I saw tiny blisters forming on a few fingers. I jumped up and gathered our hats, gloves, and sled blanket. Jane asked how she could help as Jed came into the tent. While Jeremia cried and clung to me, I explained what I thought happened. We both knew he needed to go to the clinic. Everyone helped get my dog team hooked up. Jed said he would be right behind with Zach. Our friends offered to take care of the fire and close the tent up.

I explained to Jeremia he needed to keep his hands in his fur gloves and under the blanket. Luckily he understood and settled down. Hopefully, I could encourage the dogs to go home faster. After traveling for about fifteen minutes, I saw another team headed our way. It looked like it was a five-dog team. My biggest fear was a tangle, which would take time I didn't have. As the team approached I saw it was driven by, Jim, the local physician's assistant—just the person I wanted to see. I called out so he wouldn't just fly by me. We both were able to stop our dogs. I quickly told him the situation. He said he would turn his team around and meet me at the clinic. Before leaving, I alerted him to watch for another team following close behind me.

The dogs knew the way home and seemed to know it was important to get there quickly. I told Jeremia to stay in the sled as I unhitched the dogs and secured them at their doghouses. Jed came into the yard as I gathered Jeremia. Zach helped his dad unharness the dogs and attach them to their short chains. I started the car and off we went to the clinic. Jim arrived as we pulled up. Jed helped him attach his dogs along the back of the clinic trailer and we all went inside. Jeremia was being so good about not crying.

We took off his fur gloves. The blisters hadn't gotten worse, which pleased us all. Jim examined him and said the burns were minor, but could burst and become infected. To keep the blisters from getting infected he put ointment on them and then wrapped them into mummy hands. He told me to give Jeremia baby aspirin to help him sleep. We left with bandage supplies and were told to come back in three days. I asked what activities he couldn't do. Dr. Jim said, "Jeremia will let you know what hurts and will most likely stay away from those activities." Within an hour from the time we got home he was an expert at playing with his toys using mummy hands to move his cars and trucks into the usual straight lines. I was once again amazed at children's ability not to focus on pain, but to relax and play. He wanted to take his bandages off but I said no, they needed to stay on.

In late May, shortly before we headed to the wall tent for the summer, I had a meeting in Anchorage. Twice a year all the regional coordinators congregated for two-day meetings with the dean of rural education, our arm of the university system. I missed the fall meeting since I was hired late. The original person hired for the job attended the fall meeting. He realized the job was more work than he wanted to do for a half-time salary.

It was a juggling act to make the two-day trip to Anchorage. I didn't realize all the things I did until I wrote them down for Jed. Jeremia's new day care was close to the school and convenient for Zach to walk to after school. Usually I picked Jeremia up after I picked Zach up from school. Over the eight months my job had gone well. Classes were already scheduled for fall and a couple planned for summer.

I was the newest and least educated person in the regional coordinators group. The other coordinators had master's or doctorates, which at first intimidated me. Everyone welcomed me to the group. Each center was so different and yet we had similar responsibilities. When I stopped at the business office to submit paperwork I had brought instead of mailing, Gail looked up from her desk and said, "You're the one the office has talked about." I was surprised and unsure of what she meant. She continued, "Student enrollment has doubled in the eight months you have had the job. And more classes have been offered than in other years." I was surprised, inwardly pleased, and smiled to myself as I returned to the meeting.

The next afternoon I met with the dean, Dr. Martha Sheen. This was her third year in the position. Our conversation was interactive with questions flowing back and forth. She asked what I liked about the job and how I found instructors so quickly to match the needs of the students. I explained that I asked questions of different people, agencies, and former students until I found an instructor. It was a good meeting. I felt confident I was doing a good job but was still surprised when Dr. Sheen offered me a full-time position starting August 1. I took a deep breath and said, "Yes. That would be wonderful." The thought ran through my head, should I discuss this with Jed?

I had never made an independent decision like this. Falling into the typical pattern of women of my era, decisions were based on the husband's needs. Jed and I met when I was sixteen. We made it through high school, college, and the big Alaska decision. Even though my life was enriched living and learning from Alaska Native people, everything was hard. The last couple of years I felt focused on what Jed wanted. Nenana hadn't been a healthy place for me.

Building the log home consumed our lives with no realistic timeline of when we might live in it. Between the house and the dogs, there was never any time for Jed and I. I loved my children dearly, but with nothing to do in Nenana, no friends, and no brain stimulation, I felt a part of me was dying. The thoughts of returning to the depressed state I was in before the job overwhelmed me. I was a better mother, wife, and person when I worked.

Understanding the details of running the house while working full-time required even more organization and planning, I knew I had a couple of months to figure it out. My biggest concern was whether Bonnie had room for Jeremia in her full-time day care in the fall. I called the day after I got home; she did. Hurdle number one overcome. He enjoyed being there. The parents of the children who attended appreciated the rich variety of toys available, a daily story time, a regular schedule, and the firm and loving discipline Bonnie provided. Children were treated equally and there was a mix of Native and non-Native children. Her peanut butter and honey sandwich on homemade bread, served with fresh apple slices and soup, was everyone's favorite. Jeremia was happy—he understood the expectations, which were consistent.

Memorial Day weekend the wall tent was cleaned out, the beds set up, and the kitchen area prepared. The next weekend we began our third summer of living in the wall tent. The cars were packed and the dogs moved to their summer doghouses. With all the doghouses Jed had built over the years he could practically build one in his sleep. Dog mushers shifted dogs around to keep areas dry and clean, healthier for their paws. The summer move to Fairbanks allowed the Nenana dog yard to dry out completely.

June 1, the official date for planting gardens in Interior Alaska arrived. I finished putting the garden starts in the ground before going to bed. The sky was clear when I stepped into the wall tent after my final walk to the outhouse. Everyone was fast asleep, so I just sat there for a moment pleased my garden was planted. The next morning I woke up feeling cool, so I turned on the electric heater. When I stepped out of the tent I was surprised to see a fresh dusting of snow. My heart sank, as I immediately thought of my little plants.

How could clouds move in after midnight, snow happen, and the sky be clear at 7:00 in the morning? I couldn't believe it, but my eyes reassured me it was true. The day warmed up and the dusting disappeared. I talked with my neighbors who said, "Don't worry, everything will be fine, just slower." Once again Mother Nature humbled me.

The goal for the summer was roof and windows, which were both accomplished. The extra income from my university job made it easier to purchase needed materials and rent equipment for the rafters. Harold and Peggy didn't come, but my mom joined us for two weeks. A second wall tent was set up for her, similar to ours. It had a wooden floor with a single cot. A Blazo box was added for a lamp and to keep personal items, plus a chair. It was sparse, but comfortable. I told her about the ruthless mosquitos and introduced her to the green punks to keep the menacing rascals away.

We took a short trip to the Kenai Peninsula so Mom could see another part of Alaska. I told her moose and bears were usually in ponds and grasslands along the highway. Just as I finished the statement we rounded a bend and there in the road was a large moose. He crossed in front of us as Zach pointed off to the left, saying, "Nana look over there." A black bear was moving through the bushes. I wondered if anyone would believe her when she told the story of seeing both animals within a few minutes. Her visit went quickly, but the boys were reacquainted with Nana by the time she left.

Small but important tasks were completed after my mom left. A wood stove was installed with a brick hearth behind it to protect the logs. It looked great, just waiting for us to use it. My garden yielded more than I had predicted, despite the snow dusting. I learned not to let zucchini get too large because it became all seeds. Zucchini tasted better when they were smaller. Someone gave me a recipe for a zucchini chocolate cake that was incredibly delicious. I made it as bread, cupcakes, and cake.

Early in the summer Jack, our friend on the Kvichak River, who we visited in 1974, contacted Jed about coming to assist him with a building project. The main building of the fishing lodge was remodeled, but the outhouse needed to be larger. Bringing fresh salmon and rainbow trout home for the winter was the prized carrot for us to say, "Yes."

When we found out Jack was getting remarried during our visit we decided to surprise him with spawning salmon stained glass inserts for the swinging saloon doors for the outhouse. Jack and Jed decided the saloon doors would add character to the outhouse. No one interrupted someone in the outhouse if they saw the person's trousers from below the swinging doors.

Zach caught his first fish
August 1979

The person who had made our fireweed stained glass window for our outhouse was contacted and completed them by departure date. The bride and groom were pleasantly surprised. The wedding celebration was fun and festive and the outhouse doors were unique. The big surprise of the week was that Zach caught his first fish, a twenty-four-inch long rainbow trout. He was delighted beyond words. He shared it with everyone.

Summer came to an end and the reality of working full-time intensified the pace at home. I was grateful for my car, a 1976 Volvo station wagon. Cold temperatures required plugging cars in.[25] I counted on it to drive Jeremia to Bonnie's house and drop Zach at school. There was wrestling for six- to eight-year-olds offered at the elementary school on Saturday mornings. Zach enjoyed it and Jeremia ran laps with the other young children. I was pleased the school had at least one extra curricular activity. The YKSD Correspondence program grew. Jed traveled to the Bettles area only, so he was home more. He was immersed in the dog-mushing world.

The dean funded a small office in Nenana for me, including a part-time person, Cindy, to help with the paperwork. I shared the office with a social worker, Diane, who traveled from Fairbanks to Nenana two to three days a week. Meeting the different needs of the regional center students and classes kept my mind active. One of the people in the Nenana city office asked if I could write a grant to help with community education funding. I had no idea what a grant was, but agreed to review the paperwork and process. The work seemed reasonable, so I completed the grant. The city reviewed it before submitting it to Juneau. The City of Nenana was awarded the grant and I now was a grant writer.

The different regional centers throughout the state helped people of different ages reach educational goals. Meeting with the other coordinators helped all of us to brainstorm ways to find instructors and determine needs. Alaska's vastness demanded we think creatively to assist individuals with certification and recertification. I worked closely with various groups in Nenana, including the Nenana Native Council to brainstorm instructors for classes and guests for community meetings. I met professors in several department offices at UAF. The challenges with the job were beyond my scope of experience and I loved it.

In January 1980 I took the boys to California to visit family. I was disappointed Jed wouldn't go with us. He didn't want to leave Alaska in the summer or really ever. It felt strange not traveling together as a family. Jeremia hadn't been out of the state. My sister and her boys took us to Disneyland. Zach and Jeremia thought it was incredible. We packed the week with visits to Sea World and Animal Kingdom. They saw their grandparents and played in the ocean while in Mexico. The trip was invigorating and the warm sunshine was magical for my spirit.

It was hard to return to Alaska. The darkness was there and immediately sapped part of the energized spirit from the California sunshine. I buried myself in keeping up with the boys, my work, house responsibilities, paying the bills, and the class scheduled to start in a week. While in Fairbanks to meet with a new professor I scheduled an appointment to see my doctor.

During our trip I was sick a couple of times in the morning, so I wanted to check if I was pregnant. The summer before I experienced a miscarriage, which surprised me. Both of my full-term pregnancies were healthy, without problems. The current timing of being pregnant wasn't perfect, but I was excited about a third child. Smiling with my good news I headed back to Nenana. I knew Jed wasn't enthusiastic about another child, but had agreed. It was important to me. I loved being a mother. I immediately thought *no more dog-mushing activities for the rest of the winter.*

The university class, Philosophy of Education, was held in Nenana at the YKSD office. All I did was walk across the snow-filled lawn to the district building, not drive to Fairbanks. It saved hours and tons of stress from driving on icy roads. I hadn't taken a philosophy class in my undergrad studies.

There were six students in the class. Two people drove with the instructor from Fairbanks. The class opened my eyes to how people think about values and different types of knowledge. I felt like a sponge soaking up diverse concepts, understanding how objective or subjective each of us can be. Jed listened, but appeared to not be interested. The class focused primarily on Western philosophy, touching briefly on Eastern thinking. The professor introduced the idea of 'Native ways of knowing[26].' I knew Indigenous Native cultures had different perspectives than the more dominant white culture, but the class helped me to understand why.

The pattern of taking one class per semester frustrated me. It was a difficult way to complete a degree. The experience made me admire my students even more. Most of them worked full-time, kept up with families, and completed their assignments toward AAs or BAs/BSs. I learned from them about the critical need to organize time as I planned each day. I was comforted Zach was pleased with school and Jeremia chattered about day care.

It was the first week in March 1980 and the weather was holding at ten below zero. I woke up knowing something wasn't right. Always feeling I needed to do what was expected of me I dropped the boys at school and day care and went to work. About noon I called Jed and told him I needed to go to the doctor and needed him to drive. The boys were surprised to see me when I picked them up. The plan was to see the doctor and head home before temperatures dropped. We didn't want to get stuck in Fairbanks if the ice fog returned. I hoped the weather would hold.

My suspicions were correct. I lost the baby. We hadn't told the boys so they had no idea what was going on. I walked out of the examination room and told Jed I needed to have a procedure done before we could leave. Fairbanks doctors and nurses were accustomed to rural patients who needed emergency work before returning home. The boys knew something was wrong and asked, "What's wrong Mommy?" I couldn't respond. I knew I would start crying and needed to be strong at the moment. I gave them each a kiss and returned to the nurse.

The doctor insisted I have a dilation and curettage procedure that cleaned out the contents of the uterus. I felt the machine sucked out the insides of my body, similar to a vacuum. The insistence for this process was based on women going home and hemorrhaging because they couldn't get back to a hospital. *What other choice did I have? Why wasn't I checked into the hospital?*

The nurse explained that I might experience cramping pain and bleeding after the miscarriage, similar to a period. We drove back to Nenana. I fed everyone, put the boys to bed, and cried myself to sleep. Jed went to a dog mushers' meeting. I wanted to be held and not feel alone. I was excited about the baby. *What had I done wrong?* Probably nothing, but the feeling lingered. After the miscarriage, something inside me changed. It was more than physical pain. I couldn't explain the emotional and mental feelings in my head. I felt a little numb.

Summer of 1980 came and it was time for the yearly transition to the wall tent. Now, with a full-time job, I only had a month off. The master's class I took over the summer was to write a handbook for rural students taking university classes. This assignment allowed me the flexibility to stay in Fairbanks for six weeks. It was a great assignment. I met with different professors on the UAF campus who taught classes for the regional center. I traveled to Nenana weekly to check in at the office and wash our clothes.

The outside structure of the house was mostly finished. Friends helped install the windows and Jed painted the trim a bright orange. A young man with a strong back was hired to help with the never-ending hours it took to sand the inside logs. Rounded edges were time consuming but added to the overall appearance. The logs were preserved both inside and out with a varnish that made them shine. Everything took time. We actually spent three weeks in the house before returning to Nenana. The kitchen and inside rooms needed walls and cupboards but that was a future summer. We talked about a water system. With no plan to live in the house year round, the decision didn't seem to be urgent. It was bittersweet seeing the house at this point and yet, living in it was undetermined. Each summer the illusion down an unknown road that seemed farther away grew fainter inside my heart.

In August I attended a meeting in Anchorage for the university regional coordinators. When I returned, we spent the weekend at the house. It was a lovely evening sitting by the fire. The nights were now dark longer. Returning from the outhouse I was stunned by the brilliance of the northern lights. I felt August sightings were a gift. Seeing the lights at that time wasn't as colorful as in Allakaket in the dead of winter at fifty degrees below zero. They still danced though the color was less brilliant, but there they were high above my head. The magic of them, the spectacular display of waves of color in the Arctic skies, was breathtaking. Alaska was mysterious in ways I could never explain. Sometimes I felt I could never leave, and other times, I wanted to drive to the airport and board a plane to anywhere.

The constant back and forth wore me down. I wanted a home that was ours, not a dream we talked about. We had become what we didn't like about bush teachers who went to a village for the school year to teach and then to their 'real home' in the summer. Our jobs weren't conducive for the house we spent five summers building. We knew the fifty-five mile drive in extreme weather made that unrealistic. After four years in the apartment we decided a place in Nenana might help. Housing structures in Alaska weren't easy to find. Choices in Nenana were limited. We opted for a new single-wide mobile home with an enclosed porch that included a place for a wood stove.

Thanksgiving weekend the mobile home was finally ready for us. The fall weather delayed the foundation work, the completion of the enclosed porch, and our move-in date. The decision to settle for a trailer was a hard one, based on hours of conversation. The back and forth frustration and the need for a stable home seemed more of my need than Jed's. The mobile home certainly wasn't the 'work of art' Jed built in Fairbanks. Somehow in the building process, we lost each other. It seemed we had two lives. *Why did everything continue to feel awkward and unstable?* The reality of 'us' on the same page was gone. It used to be easy, but not now.

Thanksgiving day was Jed's first race of the season. Despite the move, the race happened and we were all there to cheer him on. We now

Zach and Jeremia with puppies

had nineteen dogs in the yard. Compared to some of our friends who had sixty or more, our group seemed small. Jed was constantly occupied by the dogs, keeping them fed and trained while he learned which dogs worked better together. Zach was old enough for Junior Mushers and raced using one dog.

During lunch breaks Jed ran the dogs on a short loop. Occasionally, I joined him. With only an hour of time, it was tight to run home, change clothes, and jump on the sled. Today's run was the regular route with a couple of tricky corners. I left the dog yard first because Jed helped hook the dogs up. Returning the dogs to the yard was easier. After the run they were less high-strung. The dogs were excited and noisy as we took off. Jed shouted over the noise of the dogs, "Remember the ice and don't let go of the dogs." A real dog musher didn't let go of their dogs.

Off we went faster than normal, but I relaxed and the dogs fell into their normal pace. It was a beautiful sunny day of ten degrees above zero. I hoped for a relaxed run. Hearing the quiet panting of the dogs as we moved along was hypnotizing. Running three dogs was my comfort level. It was unclear to me if that was ever going to change. As much as I loved being outdoors and physically moving, I wasn't an adrenaline speed junkie. The loop corners challenged me. I knew to gently lean into a turn but the degree of the lean was the trick.

The first corner went well. I heard the slick sound of the ice under the rails. Approaching the second corner I attempted to slow down, but the dogs sped up as I leaned into the turn. The sled started to go down as I tried to bring it up and keep myself from falling. I fought hard but couldn't right the sled. As I yelled directions to the dogs I felt my body and right cheek hit the ice. I knew better than to let go of the dogs.

Fighting to stand up wasn't simple. The stinging on the right side of my face hurt, but the efforts to regain control of the sled paid off. I eased back into control of the dogs as I brought the sled up. We finished the ride. I unhooked the dogs, returned them to their boxes, gently washed and put lotion on my face, before returning to work. When I saw Jed later he asked what happened to my cheek. I explained the turn. My face was scraped, but no permanent damage was done. The good news was I didn't let go of the dogs.

December was a dark month. John Lennon's death on December 8 shook us both up. By Christmas, the windows in the mobile home were frozen. We added extra insulation hoping to keep them free of ice. I was back in a cave of darkness and it was an extra cold winter. Many days I walked the boys to school and Bonnie's, then to my office. It was a short distance of less than a half mile and helped save the motor on the car. We didn't have a garage, so starting a car in the severe cold, even when plugged in, was hard on vehicles. There were no streetlights so I carried a flashlight and tried to move quickly.

The thought of how dark it would be in that area of Nenana never entered our minds when we selected the land we purchased. I worried about animals. After twenty-five degrees below zero I was sure we would have frost bite in minutes. Zach understood the need to move quickly, but Jeremia was fascinated with the hoar frost on the shrubs. He didn't understand the harshness of weather. He saw the frost as magic ice crystals glistening in the moonlight. When the light from the flashlight hit the frost glimmers it ignited his curiosity. I struggled to keep us moving. I lost my ability to stay positive, constantly worrying about life and death in the blackness of winter. We had privacy but no light. No decisions we were making were right.

During my 1981 spring class I was presented an opportunity. The University of Alaska –Anchorage received a Title IX Women in Leadership federal grant to involve more women in school leadership. The Anchorage campus reached out to the schools of education in Fairbanks and Juneau, as well as the dean of rural education to submit names of women. My name was submitted and I was one of ten women selected. Each of us was involved with school districts or higher education. The chair of my master's committee coordinated with the superintendent of Yukon Koyukuk School District to design a plan for my internship funded by the grant. Hearing the leadership experiences of the different women was remarkable. I learned so much. I found my passion was in supportive leadership responsibilities.

The assignments and added travel further taxed our personal life. The balance of two professional careers and household duties was difficult. I was in charge of childcare, cooking, cleaning, and paying the bills. Plus, there was my job and the class I took.

In spring 1981, the Nenana's Business Association had a dog race Jed thought I should enter. Our time together to do things was limited and usually involved the dogs. Dog mushing was Jed's passion and I tried to be supportive. I dragged my feet, but both boys encouraged me, "Come on Mom, you will be great." I was a sucker for them, so I agreed, "I guess I better try."

I entered the race representing the University of Alaska, Rural Education-Nenana Valley Regional campus. I was always trying to get exposure for the center. On the Saturday of the big event, we loaded the boys, the dogs, and the sled to head to the race. I was nervous and didn't want another face-sliding experience. Five of us entered the race. It was a short, beginners' run. Racers had staggered starts. I was the third team, so I was concerned teams would pass me. I focused on holding the dogs firmly. I heard people behind me and worried about a tangle if I was passed. I held onto the handlebars and praised the dogs. When the race finished no one was more surprised than me to find out I came in second place. Zach and Jeremia jumped up and down! Jed smiled and I took a deep breath.

I couldn't figure out my feelings. Frustration, anger, detachment, and resentment—*what was going on with me?* I tried to talk to Jed but his attention seemed focused elsewhere. I felt like smashing the television and saying, "Read my lips, I am drowning." We met when we were teenagers, so in love. We were on the same track for a long time, but life and Alaska happened. I had an affair, which left me hating myself. I knew it took two people to make a marriage work and have it go wrong. So many wonderful and horrible experiences made me tougher and more sensitive at the same time. *What happened to us?*

The constant pressure of the severe cold wore me down followed by Jed's refusal to leave Alaska even for a short vacation. Nine years in the interior disturbed and confused my inner core. My mental and emotional cupboard was empty. I initiated a divorce; Jed suggested a separation. We tried counseling, confirming to me, we were headed in different directions. The communication gap had created 'a no fault' situation.

When we told the boys, they didn't understand. *Neither did I in many ways.* I just knew I wasn't where I needed to be, whatever that meant. Zach became very lethargic. His appetite diminished and I felt even worse. *What had I done?*

Part III: Back and Forth

After we called our parents to tell them, we discovered Zach had the mumps. I was relieved the mumps caused his listless and unresponsive behavior. Then felt badly that I was relieved. After Zach recovered and Jeremia didn't get ill, we decided to send them to California. Finishing the details of eighteen years of life together made everything hard and nothing felt right. Quitting the job that saved my soul wasn't what I wanted, but necessary.

When I picked up a magazine to distract me I discovered the three most stressful things a person can do—divorce, quit a job, and relocate. I just did all three. I had visited Juneau in the spring as part of the women's leadership program. The weather was rainy but averaged in the twenties to forties in the winter. I decided to move there. I wanted to stay in Alaska so the boys could visit their dad. I worried no decision I made was right.

I knew one thing for sure—I couldn't live in the interior for another winter. Juneau never saw fifty degrees below zero.

PART IV

Juneau, Anchorage, and Beyond

Zach, Jeremia, and me at Eagle Beach
1985

Part IV: Juneau, Anchorage, and Beyond

Arriving in Juneau

July 2, 1981

I walked off the ferry with my backpack and bicycle. Now, with no car, my confidence was shaken. Jed and I had agreed about sending the boys to California to visit our families. He was staying in Nenana and I was going to Juneau. He asked, "Is there another man?" I said, "No." The affair I had was out of character for me. *Was it to get attention?* I wasn't always good about letting my needs be known. I continued to beat myself up over it. *How stupid could I be?* I felt numb and my emotions continued to unravel. Nothing had made sense the last couple of years. I felt deeply we were no longer on the same path in life. The love for the log house we toiled over had disappeared. It seemed like a fairy tale, not reality.

When I arrived to sign the divorce papers in Fairbanks my car was packed with all of the strange items difficult to mail. After we were finished we each went to our cars. I started the drive to Haines. *How does anyone say goodbye to someone in a situation like this?* Eighteen years of our lives intertwined and two children. As I got into my car I took a deep breath.

The coordinator that ran the Tok Regional Center had contacted me about a job posting he read about in Juneau. Tok was two hundred miles out of Fairbanks on the highway to the ferry terminal in Haines. I told him I would stop and pick up the information as I headed south.

It seemed a good spot to take a break. When I arrived in Tok, Brian and his wife, Sue, insisted I stay for dinner and suggested I spend the night. Their invitation was tempting, but I wanted to be alone.

The constant emotional roller coaster of feelings had made sleep difficult over the last few months. With the long daylight hours at the end of June, I felt confident if I drove another couple of hours I would make it to the Alaska-Canada border. Maybe I might wear myself out enough to sleep and make the last leg of the drive shorter.

When I was ready to leave, Brian realized he left the job information at his office. He told me to follow him and go on from there. The dirt roads from their mobile home on the outskirts of Tok were heavily overgrown on both sides. The road was a well-used dirt path with two-way or four-way intersections. I followed Brian to the four-way stop. He stopped and crossed. I was right behind him. I stopped, looked at each of the four corners. The path to the right was difficult to see around because of the angle in the road. I took an extra moment to look a second time before I started out.

Bam! I was hit. A truck smashed into the passenger front corner of my 1976 Volvo station wagon. I stared through the window looking at the driver, not really knowing what happened. The truck hadn't stopped for the sign. My left arm throbbed with pain. I wanted out of my car but couldn't move. I don't know how long I sat there screaming or sobbing. I was in a trance, my mind foggy and disorganized.

Brian saw what happened. The next thing I knew he offered his hand and gently helped me out of the car. He asked where I hurt. The question helped me regain control of myself. I sensed someone else standing close asking, "Is she OK? Is she hurt? I am so sorry." Was I

OK? No, I was not. The car crash was the final blow. I had held myself together the last few months by little strings that had now unraveled.

I felt confident my body was intact, *but what about my car?* I couldn't think. Brian guided me somewhere, Sue was there, and then she helped me settle into bed. The next morning when I started to get out of bed I realized how sore my body was. I hurt all over but could move. Sue took me to a doctor to confirm nothing was broken. My left arm was badly bruised, but the rest of me was just tender and disoriented. The car was towed to a mechanic, carefully examined, and declared totaled. Despite the fact it only looked badly scratched, the frame was damaged to a point it couldn't be repaired. Volvos were known to fold around their passengers to keep them safe. This situation was a perfect ad for Volvo. I imagined myself saying, "This Volvo saved my life, but now I have no car, no job, and no place to live." The protection given by the Volvo didn't help my body and psyche feel better. I was completely drained. Now I had a bicycle, backpack, and odds and ends to maneuver down the dusty highway.

I sat with Brian and Sue dumbfounded and speechless, unsure of what to do next. I could barely talk. Brian knew a colleague we worked with was traveling to Haines with her husband to visit family in Ketchikan. He called her and asked if they had room in their car for the bike, my backpack, and me. They did. My spirits lifted a bit. He said they would pick me up the next day.

After the arrangement for a ride, plans started to fall together. I called the insurance company and went through the steps to get a check sent to me in Juneau. Sue helped me pack what could fit into boxes to mail. Brian and Sue were planning a trip to Juneau later in the summer and offered to bring the items that didn't fit in cartons. I was grateful and relieved. *How does a person thank such kindness?* All I did was cry. I hadn't cried during the last few months and now tears were flowing constantly.

The drive and ferry ride went well and I was able to get into my temporary place to live. In less than a week my mother would arrive from California with the boys. Zach turned eight days before they left for California and Jeremia was five. With all the recent changes, I felt we were all emotionally raw. Were they wondering what our new life would look like? I know I was. Patience, time, and careful steps was my daily mantras. I didn't want to make things worse.

A gentle mist fell as I sat listening to the water lap on the rocks. I hadn't even thought to call Jed when I had the car accident. This surprised me. I heard an eagle's high-pitched whistling sound above. The paper inside my rain jacket confirmed everything was final, my new reality. I was on my own for the first time in my life. I wasn't eighteen, freshly graduated from high school, off to college or my first job. I was to turn thirty-six in two months, with no job, no real place to live, no car, and few people I knew or trusted. With full responsibility for two little boys, I suddenly felt scared.

The people I met in Juneau told me, "It rains a lot here." I nodded my head and thought, *rain doesn't need to be shoveled and cars start even when it rains.* To keep myself optimistic I referred to Juneau as the Bahamas of Alaska. After letting my mom know about the divorce she said, "Come back to California." I thought about it, but hesitated. I wanted the boys to see their dad as often as possible, plus I wanted to be in Alaska.

Sitting on the rock I felt terrified. Nothing in Juneau was familiar, but felt right. I was in a new part of Alaska as different as each village I had lived in. Juneau was smaller than Fairbanks, but seemed bigger. There were stores similar to ones in Fairbanks. An influx of people over the past five years had increased the population to nineteen thousand. Many Alaskans in the interior didn't even consider Juneau part of Alaska.

The difference in daylight between Juneau and Fairbanks surprised me. Juneau had three to four hours of actual darkness in the summer nights. The Fourth of July fireworks started at midnight on July 3 when it became dark. When I looked at a map I realized how much farther south Juneau was. It was 640 driving miles from Fairbanks to Haines and then four and a half hours (approximately seventy-four water miles) on the ferry. I found comfort in having a few hours of darkness each night. I slept better since arriving in Juneau. I remembered people in Fairbanks had a 'we are the real Alaskans' attitude. Juneau was different, but felt refreshing.

The trees in Juneau and the surrounding mountains were soothing and seemed to embrace me. I felt safe and secure. It was as if they were whispering, "Everything will be fine, trust in yourself." On the ferry I read that Southeast Alaska was composed of many islands with a narrow coastline nestled in the Tongass National Forest. The variety of trees—birch, mountain ash, yellow cedar, western hemlock, and Sitka spruce—amazed and delighted me. The Alaska interior had trees, but not like the Tongass National Forest. It encompassed roughly seventeen million acres and stretched to the Alaska-Canada border. Five words described southeast Alaska—eagles, bears, whales, glaciers, and trees. I felt I could handle four out of five of them.

The clock was ticking—my mom would bug me to return to California with her if I didn't have a job by the time she arrived. I knew my money was running out. I called the lead Brian gave me and found it was filled internally. The local newspaper listed a couple of openings with the Juneau Borough School District. When I stopped at the office I found the teaching jobs were filled, but did apply for an advertised position. The district was seeking a project supervisor for the new Federal Indian Studies Program. Preference was for an Alaska Native person. I applied knowing it was a long shot. My time in rural Alaska *might* get me an interview. Another thing in my favor was the Master of Education, Cross-Cultural Studies I was close to finishing. I thought maybe the experiences in rural Alaska would get me in the door and my knowledge of cross-cultural studies would be valuable if they were desperate and hired me.

Housing was an issue in Juneau, because it was the capital. Our current living situation was good for a few months. From January through May, legislators lived in Juneau and leased out their places the other months. A friend in the adult education division of Alaska Department of Education (DOE) referred me to a legislator who agreed to sublet her place. The place was clean and safe, but not in the best condition. The building was on the city's short list to be torn down. I was grateful for a roof over my head and a place to land when I arrived.

I stopped at the Department of Education to thank my friend for the housing reference. I asked him about state jobs and he told me to talk to the person down the hall. As I was leaving he suggested I also stop by South East Regional Resource Center (SERRC). I asked what SERRC did and the jobs they had. He laughed and said everything you can think of related to education. SERRC staff wrote state and federal grants for smaller districts in Alaska and then helped the districts accomplish the work. I was confused but thanked him. It was almost 4:30 p.m. when all the state offices closed for the day. I would visit SERRC in the morning.

The little apartment I was staying in was in downtown Juneau, close to the state office buildings. Everything was in walking distance. Downtown included state office buildings; a dock area where ferries and cruise ships arrived, and a variety of homes on the hillside. Across the bridge on Douglas Island were Sandy Beach, various homes, and the Eagle Crest Ski area. Just ten to twenty miles out of the city was the only strip mall with five stores, the Mendenhall Glacier, and more homes and apartments. There was a final area referred to as 'out the road.' All together, Juneau had forty to fifty miles of drivable roads.

The next day I discovered SERRC's office was two blocks away from the apartment. The sun peeked out of the clouds as I walked to SERRC. A small sign let me know I was at the right place. When I entered, I heard people chattering quietly. A receptionist told me to take a seat while she checked to see if someone could talk with me. A few people walked by and smiled. The office had positive energy.

I talked an hour and a half with Mark, one of two associate directors. He knew about the grant I wrote for the Nenana Community Education program because he reviewed it. Wow! I was overwhelmed with my luck. We talked about my experiences as he scanned my resume.

Wrapping up the conversation, he told me about a two-week contract that started soon. The person hired would be responsible for getting fifteen students from Eight Fathom Bight, a logging camp in the Chatham Straits, to swimming lessons and one city experience each day for twelve days. The kids ranged in ages from six to sixteen. In the conversation he said they were staying at a motel close to where I lived. Mark mentioned the City of Juneau public swimming pool was next to the high school and close to their motel. Two chaperones were accompanying the students, so I wasn't responsible for feeding them. The work was funded through a migrant education contract SERRC had with Chatham School District.

The contract sounded great. He asked if I was interested, adding that there was a stipend for the coordinator in the budget. I told him I didn't have day care for my children. He said not to worry; they could go along. He needed to confirm no one else was assigned the work and asked me to call him the next morning. I was surprised he said the boys could be part of the group.

I called my friend at DOE to thank him for the lead. He filled me in on recent changes to the regional resource centers. Five of the six centers established by the Alaska State Legislature in 1976 to support Alaska's unique rural school districts had struggled and finally closed, except for SERRC. The resource centers hired specialized educators to do work for small districts. The itinerants traveled to schools providing services, such as speech, physical or occupational therapists, school psychologists, and even administrative assistance.

SERRC's leadership was effective in balancing people willing to constantly travel with the needs of the various districts. They added adult education, job training, English as a Second Language, and citizenship in 1980. In 1981, the Alaska State Board of Education approved SERRC's request to incorporate and provide services statewide. Funds were generated from contracts with school districts and the ADOE, as well as federal, state, and community agencies.

Mark was clear that one problem people new to SERRC had was the lack of guaranteed employment. SERRC was a soft-money agency with new grants and contracts written and negotiated yearly. I thanked him for the information. The rest of the day was spent filling out applications for every job I felt remotely capable of doing.

After a restless night's sleep, I called Mark to check on the job. He offered it to me. It was only for two weeks but it was a start. We discussed a few details and set up a time to meet the following week. I was relieved. Getting hired to be a tour guide when I knew nothing about the community felt a little daunting, but I knew I would figure it out. The stipend for my time was not large, but fair, especially since my children could be with me.

On Thursday I was making beds and preparing for my mom and the boys when the phone rang. The call was from Judy Franklet, Director of Federal Programs for the Juneau Borough School District. Franklet was one of the few Tlingit Indian women who had an administrative position in Alaska education. Her bachelor's was in bicultural education and her master's in educational administration. She interviewed me for the Indian studies project supervisor position. I enjoyed talking with her and felt honored to get an interview.

She told me she talked with my former boss. When she reiterated the Indian studies project supervisor was a Native-preferred hire, I heard the 'thank you for your time' coming. I was stunned when she offered me the job. She asked if I could come in to complete additional paperwork. I immediately said, "Yes, I would be happy to."

The past twenty-four hours had yielded me two jobs. Yippee! I felt my chest and shoulders lift and relax from the tension I carried. After the meeting with Judy, I went for a walk along the dock where the cruise ships and ferries arrived and offloaded passengers. There was a gentle mist falling. The fresh air I inhaled into my lungs tasted clean and fresh. Again there was the calling sound of an eagle. I found the high-pitched shrill comforting. It was not sharp or difficult on my ears. The sound was like no other I had ever heard. As I tried to locate the eagle, I saw the sun playing peekaboo with the clouds. Juneau was already beginning to feel like the right place to live. I wanted the boys first day in Juneau to be fun and welcoming.

On Friday I drove to the airport to welcome my mom and boys to Juneau. I rented a car since the check from the insurance company still hadn't arrived. Zach and Jeremia walked slowly off the plane. They were hesitant and quiet at first. I hugged everyone and kept chattering, hoping one of the boys would say something. Everything seemed awkward. As we waited for the luggage, Mom said flying into Juneau was a little unsettling with the mountains on either side. The boys perked up and agreed it was different from Fairbanks. I said 'yes' and explained the distance from Fairbanks. They asked how I got to Juneau and if I had any of the dogs. As we loaded bags into the strange rental car even more questions were asked. I took a deep breath and realized I had lots of explaining ahead of me.

As we drove to our temporary home I pointed out Juneau landmarks. The afternoon skies were full of clouds, but picturesque with no rain. We unloaded the car, climbed up the stairs, and entered our little home. The boys walked around checking the rooms out. I asked the boys if they would like pizza for dinner, hoping it would be a big deal. I wasn't disappointed. Their eyes lit up. The free popcorn increased their enthusiasm.

Part IV: Juneau, Anchorage, and Beyond

The pizza establishment was convenient, just two doors from our apartment. Bullwinkle's Pizza opened in the fall of 1973 with a moose logo. I personally found it funny because moose sightings in Juneau were very rare. My mom thought the cost was exorbitant compared to what she paid in California. I grinned, reminded her we were in Alaska, and that it was the only option. It seemed a repeat of the mother and daughter conversation I heard when shopping that first summer I was in Alaska.

The next day was clear and warm. When I arrived in Juneau late on July 2 it had rained. It felt so good on my dry, weathered, and exhausted skin. By the evening of July 3 the rain had stopped and on July 4 there were high clouds and no rain. As I watched the parade, I heard people laugh and talk about the 'good weather' (no rain) that always appeared on the Fourth. I thought the conversation about no rain on the Fourth of July was odd, but when I woke on July 5 it was raining again, I smiled.

Today was July 11, the skies were clear and it felt warm. I told the boys we were going to Sandy Beach. They were accustomed to California and Mexico beaches, so they asked if they could get in the water. I said sure, but reminded them we were in Alaska, the water would be cold, and there might be mosquitoes. I made sandwiches, stuck in water and Capri Suns drinks, grabbed extra towels, and put some vodka in a thermos with grapefruit juice. When we arrived at the small Douglas Island beach, Mom put her foot in the water. She shuddered and said it was way too cold for her. The boys, however, were happy frolicking in the water as she and I sat on the beach drinking 'salty dogs minus the salt.' We watched them splash around. This was the warmest summer day for Juneau that year. Seeing the boys laugh filled my heart with joy. It also gave Mom and I time to catch up.

When she departed two days later she was more at ease about my decision of living in Juneau. She knew I had work, the two-week gig, followed by the permanent job with the school district. We laughed and cried together. She told me the boys constantly asked questions when they were in California. No one had answers for them. But, everyone assured them they were loved. I felt guilty, but also knew sending them to California had been the right decision.

After Mom was gone, the boys and I investigated activities for kids. The logging camp chaperone wanted to see the schedule for the two weeks. The days began with swimming lessons, then lunch, followed by an afternoon outing. Juneau had a state museum located downtown, a roller-skating rink in the valley, a cruise ship tour, and a couple of playgrounds. The Mendenhall Glacier was twelve miles from downtown. There was space for kids to run around, a great picnic spot at the Glacier, as well as trails for kids that weren't lengthy. I rented a van and we took the bus to some of the places. Mark had children so he gave me a few suggestions. He reviewed the plan and sent it to Anne for approval. Anne was the wife of the logging camp manager.

The two weeks as a tour guide for the logging camp students went well. The weather cooperated and all the kids seem to enjoy the activities. We even went to Bullwinkle's for pizza. Most days were sunny, definitely, not the norm for Juneau. I learned quickly when the sun shined in Juneau it was one of the most beautiful places in the world.

There were a couple of weeks between the start of my job and school. I needed half-day childcare for Jeremia and a place Zach could join him after school. The local newspaper, the *Juneau Empire* listed downtown day care options. We visited a day care, which had structure and creative activities. They had room for Jeremia, but I was surprised at the cost. Children that attended half-day cost the same as a full-time child, plus the afterschool program expense for Zach. I was learning about costs in a city. Someone suggested I check into day care assistance.

It didn't seem possible I would be eligible, but I was. When I arrived in Juneau I applied for unemployment. A week later I contacted them and told them about the two jobs. They explained I was still entitled to two unemployment checks. I was grateful. The transition to being single with children was making me internally stronger. I had worked in some capacity since I was twelve. The divorce court awarded me $150 per child, which didn't cover half the day care cost, let alone food, rent, etc.

With the car insurance money I purchased an orange diesel Volvo station wagon. It was an automatic, which I wasn't fond of, but reliable used cars in Juneau were hard to find. The day care assistance program gave me a schedule for afterschool activities. The boys decided to try soccer, which we knew nothing about.

My job started. It was a new program and we were all 'newbies' at the school district. I was the last person hired because Judy had hoped to find an Alaskan Native with the required qualifications. Native people were limited in the field of education. I was the only non-Native on the four-person team. Our task was to blend Alaska Native culture into the K–12 curriculum for the Juneau Douglas Borough School District (JDSD). Judy also signed a contract with Mark at SERRC to assist with the JDSD Scope and Sequence Curriculum Plan.

The first staff meeting was tense, as I predicted. I asked everyone to explain previous positions prior to this job. I read their files, but was trying to build a foundation for our team. After I was hired, Judy and I discussed the fact I was non-Native in a Native-preferred position. She wanted to know how I would handle the issue when it came up. I told her I knew it would arise at some point and I was prepared. My plan was to learn about southeast Native groups and build a team approach with my staff. I knew from my university classes that experiences of Natives in the southeast part of the state were different from interior Eskimos and Indians.

Because Southeast Alaska Natives lived where the climate was milder and the geographic access to the lower 48 states was closer, there were increased opportunities for interactions with non-Native people. Over the years, those two factors made a difference in the issues they dealt with. Most southeast Natives were Tlingit or Haida Indians, with some Tsimshian. Judy asked if I knew about the Alaska Native Brotherhood[27] (ANB) and Alaska Native Sisterhood (ANS) Grand Camps. I recognized the names but didn't know much more. She told me about the Roberts' Rules of Order formalities they followed in meetings and organizational structure. ANB and ANS had a joint education committee she wanted me to attend and report about the Indian Studies program.

During my staff meeting, I purposely was the last one to share. I shared the Cliff Notes version of my years in villages and in Nenana, plus my time teaching in California before coming to Alaska. I mentioned the master's in cross-cultural studies at UAF and the fact that part of our course work was developing classes for rural Alaska schools. My final comment was that Judy, our boss, had asked me to attend the education committee for the ANB and ANS to share information about our new program. I explained how I wanted them involved in attending the meetings and presenting the information. I expressed how I felt it was important we were seen as a team and not 'some white woman' telling them about Alaska Native curriculum. I believed they were surprised and pleased I was blunt about the 'white woman' issue.

The apartment we lived in was available until December, but we weren't obligated to stay that long. Each box I unpacked reminded me the sooner we were settled the better. There were no places to rent in downtown Juneau so I checked Douglas Island and the valley. I found a small two-bedroom townhouse in the valley to lease with option to buy. There was no down payment and the owner was willing to give me six months to secure financing. I figured the Fairbanks property would be sold by then.

I received approval from the school district and day care to keep the boys in their downtown locations. Driving from downtown Juneau along Eagan Drive to the valley was only twenty minutes. It gave the boys and I time to discuss how their school day went. Our new home was off the Mendenhall Loop Road approximately two miles from the Mendenhall Glacier. The boys found other children their ages to play with in the cul-de-sac. There was a path close to the Mendenhall Loop Road going out to the Glacier used for running, walking, biking, and even roller-skating. I started running again. When we were in villages and Nenana I ran in spurts or when it was convenient to everyone's schedule and the weather wasn't fifty degrees below zero. Now I got up early for a short run before getting the boys up and ready for school.

I began to understand the inner strength and tranquility I derived from running. Even though it rained and rained, I looked forward to the time outside. The constant mist that fell most days was standard in Juneau. My skin soaked up the moisture and my cuticles didn't bleed during the winter months. Some days I walked outside and put my face up in the air just to feel the rain. During my runs I felt the drops the first mile, then I was OK, relaxing into the Zen feeling of running.

Playing soccer was a great way to meet kids and their parents. I met another single mom who asked if I was another divorcee as a result of the *Kramer vs. Kramer* movie. I knew nothing about the movie. Most of Alaska was always a couple of years behind in TV and movies. Anchorage and Juneau were a little more current. Nenana didn't have a movie theatre and TV was limited, so I hadn't seen the movie. I was intrigued by what she meant.

It was a while before I saw the movie. Watching Meryl Streep's respond to the questions about her marriage made me think. She graduated from Smith College with a degree in advertising and was prepared to work. Her efforts in college were as hard as her husband's, but after the marriage her work future was disregarded. She was to clean, cook, and care for the children. If she voiced her needs she was a 'women's liberator,' not an equal marriage partner. It was a confusing time for women and I related. Children were to be reared by women while men pursued their goals, both personal and professional. It didn't seem to matter that women worked as hard to be educated.

Attending the ANB and ANS meetings was time well spent. I learned a lot and gained respect from many Native people. I asked how I could help and wasn't discouraged when assigned tasks in the kitchen. Food preparation and serving was expected by everyone as part of the work during events. I quietly observed protocols and listened to my staff's advice.

The Federal Indian Studies program required board members to participate in quarterly meetings. Judy asked specific Alaska Natives in the Juneau community to be on the Board. Their task was to review and provide input to the Curriculum Scope and Sequence Plan to ensure it included cultural information about the different Indian groups. She attended the first meeting to welcome the board members and introduce the staff. A few people saw me at Alaska Native Brotherhood and Sisterhood functions, but the board president had never seen me. It was obvious he wasn't pleased I was the supervisor over the Native staff. He formally asked Judy for a complete report of the blood quantum of each of the staff members. At the next meeting Judy asked me to provide the report as the first piece of business. To everyone's surprise, including myself, I met the requirements of blood quantum. When Judy asked me privately if I had any Indian blood I told her my mother's family hailed from Arkansas and my great grandmother was part Cherokee. The board president's demeanor changed and I realized from here until eternity my blood quantum was noted in formal minutes of a federal meeting.

The year progressed with periods of depression from all the adjustments, stress from work, and mixed feelings of inadequacy. One particular evening on the way home, I was distracted by news I received. When refueling my car at the station I filled the tank with gas. As I drove out of the gas station the car spurted to a stop. I suddenly remembered the car was diesel. It was pouring buckets, the boys were bickering in the backseat, and I started crying when someone knocked on the window. I immediately pulled myself together as I rolled down the window. I explained what I had done and the attendant said he could drain the car and have it running in a few hours. I asked the price, handed him the keys, and said we would be back in two hours. What else could I do?

Struggling and feeling overwhelmed I called Jed and asked him to please call the boys each week. They missed him. I even suggested a planned visit to see him would be helpful. He didn't agree to shared custody and the courts hadn't required regular visits to see him. He thought about it, called back, and agreed to Thanksgiving weekend. They were very excited.

One evening I realized I had stopped buying red meat without even realizing it. My limited income shifted my choices at the market. I felt bad. The boys enjoyed red meat and were accustomed to moose and caribou. The next time Jed made his weekly call, I asked to talk with him. I asked if he was still hunting and whether he could share some meat with the boys. He offered to send a box home with them when they visited at Thanksgiving. It made the boys happy to have meat from their dad and it helped me financially. I thanked him. I was grateful—a large box of meat became a regular luggage item each Thanksgiving.

In April I spoke with Dr. Barnhardt, Chair of my master's program. He told me I needed to speed up completion of my master's program to meet the required timeframe. Since arriving in Juneau I had finished one class, but all the life changes interfered with completion of the second class. I had twelve credits to finish the program—two classes and my thesis. How was I going to manage the completion, work full-time, care for my children, and be sane?

After the conversation with Dr. Barnhardt I spent time thinking about restructuring my life. In June we moved to a small basement apartment on Douglas Island, close to Sandy Beach and several of the boys' friends. I had kept them on teams associated with downtown Juneau or Douglas Island. My office was even in an old school building on Douglas so everything was more convenient. I signed a year's lease.

Part IV: Juneau, Anchorage, and Beyond

In August I told Judy I needed to finish my master's program within the year. She understood the need to comply with a university timeframe or I would be under different requirements taking longer. She offered to be helpful in any way she could. I thanked her for the support. A month later Judy gave me a resume for a woman she said would be calling me. She was Alaska Native, had just completed her education, and was looking for work. Judy knew our program might have some contract work. Back in my office I reviewed her resume. I was impressed. She was qualified and would have been hired for my position if she had been in Juneau fourteen months earlier.

Finishing the master's was constantly on my mind. I was so close and felt strongly it would give me more career options. Dr. Barnhardt knew the past year and a half had been difficult. He suggested I consider doing an internship while I finished. It required I stop working, but would provide a small stipend. It seemed like my opportunity to finish the degree.

Monday morning I called Dr. Barnhardt and said I was interested in the internship. He called his friend at the ADOE. I talked with Judy about an idea I had. Knowing Juneau was small I wasn't going to leave her stranded. I told her I felt she now had a qualified Alaskan Native woman to hire as Indian Studies project supervisor. She agreed. We discussed how she needed to talk to her boss and make some calls before she offered the job to the interested person. I also needed to confirm the internship.

After Dr. Hazelton called from the ADOE, it seemed several puzzle pieces fell together. He asked when I could meet to discuss the internship. After talking with him I called Judy to tell her the internship was to start in January. She received approval to move forward with the job offer. Rosetta Thomas accepted the position. We announced the decision to the board and staff. I had six weeks to finish tasks and meet with Rosetta to share information about the program.

I called a family meeting with the boys to explain what I was doing. I told them things would be a tight with money. They didn't completely understand, especially when I sold the car. We walked or took the bus everywhere. Selling the car was hard but I knew I could get a cheaper car if necessary. I also felt confident the money from the property would come through sometime in the spring.

After Christmas break we all three boarded buses. To make life easier I transferred the boys from the downtown elementary school to Gastineau Elementary School on Douglas Island. Many of their friends attended school there. Upon my arrival at DOE, I met Dr. Hazelton's research team and was assigned some tasks.

The newly appointed first Alaska Native commissioner, Dr. William Demmert, heard I was coming and asked to meet with me. Word got around when masters' students needed projects. He offered me an opportunity to work with the commissioner's study group on Native achievement, a group he pulled together to focus on helping rural students think about life after high school. Now I saw the connection to Dr. Barnhardt, who continued to find ways to work with Alaska Natives on educational issues. The newly formed small rural high schools needed advice from Alaska Native leaders to help high school students understand why graduating from high school was important. Finishing high school was still new to rural students in Alaska because for years they only attended school through eighth grade.

I was thrilled. The commissioner's idea was to create a video for Alaska Native high school students. He wanted students to see the options available to them after high school graduation. Many rural students didn't know anything about training possibilities or college after high school. Many had never heard of Seward Vocational Center, a facility in their own state, where they could learn mechanics, building trades, or cooking skills. There were scholarships available for colleges in and out of Alaska. The video was to include interviews with students and Alaska Native leaders. The project had a budget and filming crew from the Northwest Arctic Instructional Television Center, located in Kotzebue.

Fingers crossed, I called Dr. Barnhardt to explain the proposed project to him. I asked if he felt my committee would approve it as a substitute to the earlier canceled project. He felt they would, but needed to talk to the committee members. He asked for a one-page summary. I mailed it to him the next day knowing I wouldn't receive formal approval for a month. It was winter in Alaska. I maintained a positive attitude it would work out.

I worked closely with Dr. Hazelton to develop a script and interview questions needed for the project. We discussed every detail including the sites to visit. Commissioner Demmert checked in with us. May was the best time for the travel. I was happy to have the travel dates to make arrangements for the boys. Finding babysitters was never easy. I wasn't able to focus unless I knew the boys were in good hands. Juggling the moving parts was demanding and challenging at times.

By May I had a babysitter arranged and a couple of friends as back up. It was time to head to Anchorage to join the film crew and confirm I had put all the details in place: van rental; housing while on the road;

location and meeting space at the schools; and arrangements for the interviews with people and the educational institutions. Our itinerary was Anchorage, Seward, Kenai, Fairbanks, Tok, Kotzebue, and Barrow. Everyone knew the schedule and was ready. I was the only female on the four-person team, nothing new for Alaska in 1983. Alaskans joked there were seven to ten men for every woman.

Being a producer was different than imagined, but here I was knee deep in the varying responsibilities. The director reviewed the script, said it was enough for a two-hour movie, not a twenty-five-minute video. I was stunned. He told me not to fret—stay focused on the message students would take home from the video. Cuts were easy, better to have too much, than not enough. We made a few revisions on questions for the students and adults.

The travels and interviews went well. A group of high school students in Tok worked with a road crew in town. We used it as a filming opportunity. The local mosquitoes saw it as an opportunity for dinner. Everyone swatted at the mosquitoes, but the swats didn't surface in the edits. Seasonal work in road maintenance was needed in Alaska, but required training, and many students didn't know about it. The one glitch in the trip was Barrow canceled. The village got a whale. A captured whale was a community event taking precedence to our visit. I respected the decision toward commitment of their strong cultural traditions.

When finished there was ten hours of film clips to cut to twenty-five minutes, requiring a trip to Kotzebue for me. The crew and I shared schedules and a date was established. The May babysitting arrangements hadn't gone as well as I expected. I didn't want a repeat so I checked with Jed to arrange the boys' summer visit while I was in Kotzebue.

Part IV: Juneau, Anchorage, and Beyond

The week in Kotzebue involved a lot of sitting with the film crew. The Northwest Arctic Instructional Television Center was located in the basement of an old building in Kotzebue. Ten to fourteen hours each day we made decisions about cutting and weaving the scenes together to finalize the video. We took short breaks for walks or to eat. Days and evenings were the same with the summer light that far north. It didn't seem to matter what time it was. One time as I left to get some sleep, one the editing crewmembers asked about music. I said whatever they thought would sound appropriate. He told me he would find a popular teen song and I responded, "Sounds good."

The crew selected a song from Michael Jackson's *Thriller* album. I knew nothing about popular teen songs in 1983 but I had heard it was big. It was used at the beginning and end of the video. Students in rural Alaska were beginning to listen to music because villages were now receiving satellite television and a few radio stations.

When I returned to DOE on August 9, I proudly shared the video. The commissioner was pleased, as well as Dr. Hazelton. The only question concerned the music. Someone said *Thriller* was selected as album of the year for 1982, so if I planned to use it I needed approval. I knew nothing about 'getting approval' to use a copyrighted song. Bob, another person in the research office suggested I go to the Alaska State Library and ask for help. A librarian brought me phone books to dig through to find a number for Michael Jackson's office in Los Angeles. I called and left a message about the video. They returned the call, told me to send a copy, and when to call back. It took a month. I was told Michael Jackson watched it and approved its use for 'education purposes only.'

The copy sent to the master's committee was approved. They suggested a small brochure be developed to accompany the video, which

ADOE liked. During the next year, one hundred copies of the video and brochure were distributed throughout the state. The best part for me was completing the Master of Education Degree (MEd) with an emphasis in Cross-Cultural Studies.

Zach, Jeremia, and I settled into our new home
1983

My ADOE internship officially ended June 30. The video project funded by ADOE, paid the travel and food costs for the film crew and myself while on the road and in Kotzebue. The small internship stipend and salary for a couple of classes I co-taught with another instructor for the University of Alaska Juneau were the only funds coming in for eight months. I felt broke and anxious to see a monthly check. Beginning in May, I had continuously checked the school district and SERRC for potential jobs. The Fairbanks property had sold, making it easier to purchase a small Honda Civic.

Mark told me SERRC usually knew about contracts by mid August. On August 14 I called for an appointment. He had part-time work in the Adult Education office and asked if I was willing to write grants. He couldn't give me a full-time contract that day but did a month later. In September 1983, I once again signed a contract with SERRC. I was uneasy because it was soft money, but I trusted in the system. It was one of the best decisions I ever made. Alan, Mark, and Twyla were honest about the grant world. Alan said, "Working at a Resource Center is only as successful as the people who trust in it and are willing to work long and hard." They told employees sometimes good, well-written grants weren't funded. When that happened it was time to find another one to write. The grant world wasn't for the faint of heart.

The boys and I settled into the small condo we bought on Douglas Island, very close to the rental we occupied for a year. Our condo was a two-story end-unit, which made it feel more spacious. It wasn't luxurious, but was affordable. The view was fantastic since it was up the hill overlooking the water. Seeing the cruise ships at night was spectacular. I called it my million-dollar view. There were usually two to three each week that sat during the day, allowing their passengers time to visit and left around midnight. The reflection of the lights as they departed was magical. The condo had three bedrooms, two average sized and a smaller one, plus a full-bath and a half bath with laundry. We were the second owners of the condo.

We barely had furniture but none of us complained. Happy to be in our space, we watched for garage sales. Furniture came when money was available. Our home felt safe and secure.

"The ability to look at events from different perspectives can be very helpful. Then, practicing this, one can use certain experiences, certain tragedies to develop a calmness of mind. One must realize that every phenomena, every event, has different aspects. Everything is of a relative nature."

—The Dalai Lama,
The Art of Happiness[28]

Part IV: Juneau, Anchorage, and Beyond

Working and Surviving

July 1983

Working for SERRC was creative and motivating, as well as challenging and grueling. I continued to learn about federal, state, and local funding for education. It wasn't the same as being a teacher or administrator in a school district. My attitude was—be resourceful and adapt.

The lack of assurance of a job made me a little crazy at times. I continued to teach one evening class at the university each semester. Being an adjunct professor didn't pay well but the extra money was always needed for something.

In November 1983 a change occurred in Alaska that was considered monumental. Alaska's four time zones were reduced to two, with ninety-eight percent of the state in one time zone. The larger of the two zones was called Alaska Time, formerly known as Yukon Time. Bering Sea Time was eliminated, forcing Nome, Kotzebue and several smaller villages to move forward an hour. Southeast Alaska was in Standard Alaska Time but shifted clocks back two hours to the new Alaska Time. The major adjustment gave everyone in the state greater accessibility to state offices in Juneau and Washington DC.

The boys were happy in Juneau. Days were focused on work and them. Football season was busy with games and helping at the concession stands. Friday or Saturday nights saw the house filled with three or four extra boys, watching videos. The chatter reassured me all was well.

Other changes happened. Alaska moved into the twentieth century. McDonald's came to Juneau and the boys were excited. A big controversy over 'Mickey Ds' golden arches was finally resolved. Juneau told the corporate bosses, no golden arches. After much back and forth Juneau won, but so did McDonald's. They didn't realize how desperate people were for fast food in Juneau. Millions of Big Macs were sold without the golden arches. The boys thought it was 'cool' to have Big Macs in their hometown.

Once in a while I met up with girlfriends to go dancing. Dancing was a great way to handle stress. It was cheaper than drinking and deterred depression, plus it was great exercise. In the mid '80s the Baranof Hotel had a bar where a group of us met on Friday nights at 10:00 p.m. Some had husbands that babysat and a few of us were single moms who hired babysitters. One drink and a glass of water kept us going for a couple of hours.

SERRC seldom held staff meetings, but one spring morning we were called together by the executive director. There were donuts and coffee, the typical first-thing in the morning food. The meeting was short and to the point: "Currently, we are unsure of our funding status so each of you might want to consider updating your resume to look for a 'real' job." People told me this was his annual reminder about the importance of grant writing. When I heard the speech it made me nervous.

I constantly worried about money. Grant work was unpredictable. I knew good grants weren't guaranteed funding. The condo needed a new roof so I had to come up with $2,000 quickly. *Who has an extra $2,000 sitting around?* My dad was a compulsive gambler and here I was gambling on having a job.

Part IV: Juneau, Anchorage, and Beyond

A friend told me the new successful, innovative aerobics studio was for sale. The owners were in the middle of a divorce and the wife, Darcy, was looking for a new business partner. The investment price was low. After investigating its potential for a sound investment I moved forward. People in rainy Juneau wanted an option for indoor exercise, especially state workers. Monthly expenses were small. Darcy and I divided up the business responsibilities.

SERRC and Studio 221 were only three blocks apart. I juggled the boys' school and sports, as well as my work schedule. Life was busy and productive when CRASH, the 1985 Alaska recession hit. Alaska's boom and bust business mentality happened four months after investing in the aerobics business.

The State over spent. Hundreds of jobs were gone and oil prices dropped substantially. Houses were foreclosed on and more people left Alaska than moved into the state. Some banks closed and people existed on bare essentials. Lawmakers made cuts, state workers lost their jobs, and Darcy disappeared with the money I invested, as well as leaving me with several debts she hadn't disclosed. My friends couldn't believe her and I felt like an idiot. Juneau was small. People attending classes knew something was wrong. Situations like this happened in big cities or in the movies, not in Juneau.

A lawyer friend told me it was in my best interest to change the name of the business.[29] My friend, Amy and I brainstormed new names for the business. After a few glasses of wine we agreed on Infinite Fitness. Studio 221 had debts, but not Infinite Fitness. She designed a logo and business cards were printed. I hoped the bad luck would pass.

I worked hard but closed the business a year later. I never saw a dime I put into the business and lost thirty thousand dollars. The teachers were paid twice in the year I kept it open. I learned a lot, more than I wanted about running a business with someone I didn't know. The great friends I had, and made while owning the business helped me get through a difficult time.

In Juneau people did everything in the rain. I loved that people I met were hikers, cyclists, kayakers, and runners who enjoyed being outside despite inclement weather. Many people hiked the Chilkoot Trail and I wanted to do it. The summer Zach turned twelve I asked if he was interested in hiking it. He thought it was a great idea. I camped, mushed dogs, and packed water so I felt confident we could survive a four-day backpack trip. Both boys had frame-packs and I had an Osprey backpack. We had camped in the snow during a late spring trip. It went well, so I figured we just needed to learn everything we could about the Chilkoot. Jeremia was nine so I felt he was too young.

The school counselor mentioned the boys would benefit from some one-on-one time with their dad and this was a perfect opportunity. Jed agreed to the plan for their summer visit. The boys thought it would be great to have alone time with their dad.

Zach thought 'preparing' for the big hike was a strange idea, but was willing. He walked three miles a day for three solid weeks carrying his backpack. I wanted him to become accustomed to the weight on his back. Running four to five miles a day was good conditioning for me. The night before we left, I weighed our packs. Zach's was twenty-five and mine was forty-five pounds. I was tipsy so I decided to carry some weight in a small front pack. Maybe we had too much of something, but I felt everything was essential. Friends told me getting water was easy so the weight of our packs didn't include much water.

Part IV: Juneau, Anchorage, and Beyond

The LeConte ferry to Skagway, our departure point, was one of the smaller boats in the Alaska State Marine System. The Alaska ferries traveled 3,500 miles of coastline with stops to over thirty communities. The water highway system had begun when three men decided Alaska's coastal communities deserved a dependable marine transportation system. The smaller ferries still provided showers for people and a cafeteria area with over priced food. I loved traveling on the ferry.

Boarding the ferry July 14 at 5:00 a.m. made the first day long, but that was part of the adventure. We arrived in Skagway around 2:00 p.m. and took a small van to Dyea where the trail officially started. Zach loved history so an essential item in my pack was a copy of the *Chilkoot Pass: A Hiker's Historical Guide to the Klondike Gold Rush National Park*.[30] Our boots hit the trail around 3:00 p.m. We could have camped in Dyea for the night, but we were eager. The plan was to hike four to five miles before setting up our tent.

The first site was the Slide Cemetery where the remains of sixty-eight people from the 1898 Good Friday avalanche were buried. We read about it in the book. We crossed the steel bridge over the Taiya River and then the work began as we moved up Saintly Hill. My friends mentioned the steepness of the climb, so I warned Zach the first quarter of the mile would seem like forever. It felt extra tough because we were barely warmed up when we approached the incline. We passed an area called the Beaver Pond. Some years it was bigger and wetter than others depending on the winter. It was close to Finnegan's Point where we decided to stop for the night. After dinner we hung our food, hopefully out of any bear's reach.

During the night it rained. We woke to a wet tent and damp sleeping bags. I knew I didn't want extra weight from wet gear or climbing into a damp sleeping bag after a long day of hiking. Someone mentioned a log shelter built by convicts in the 1960s at Canyon City, about four miles up the trail. It had a wood stove people used to warm up or take a break. Maybe we could dry out our gear there?

When we arrived at the log shelter we were the first hikers of the day. We spread the tent and sleeping bags in the warm midday sun, filled our water bottles, and investigated the artifacts from the past spread out around the area. While repacking I realized we did have too much food. A couple of hikers came through and welcomed the food I offered. My back was much happier.

The five miles to Sheep Camp included a mile-long steep climb followed by several up-and-down paths. In Sheep Camp several of the hikers who passed us were setting up their tents for the night. Everyone mentioned the great weather, 'Alaska warm' with clear skies. Sometimes people waited in Sheep Camp for the clouds to clear in order to hike over the Scales and Golden Stairs to cross the Summit. We felt the weather gods were good to us.

The demanding eight to nine mile segment to Happy Camp took many hikers ten hours or more. Everyone who hiked the Chilkoot cited the 3,200 foot elevation climb and the difficulty in traversing the rocks. Zach and I set up our tent, fixed dinner, and walked around the area before settling in the tent. We reviewed the next day before closing our eyes for the night. We wanted to get an early start the next day.

Zach was the only kid I saw hiking. We had discussed that the hike was a commitment. I explained that once we had started quitting would be difficult and at some point not possible. I was proud of him and glad we were on this adventure together. I was also scared. I had never done anything like this and here I was expecting my twelve-year-old to just keep moving forward.

At 7:00 a.m. we were the last hikers out of Sheep Camp. Zach was first and I was right behind him. My pack felt like part of my body and I was really enjoying the early morning light when Zach stopped and turned around. His eyes were as big as saucers. He was silently mouthing the word bear, as he pushed me back along the trail. Before I turned around I looked over his shoulder and caught a glimpse of a grizzly as he sat upright on his haunches stuffing blueberries in his mouth. We walked quickly for about two to three minutes and then for some strange reason we both started singing, "Oh, say, can you see? By the dawn's early light. . . ." We walked for another ten minutes before we looked back to see if the bear had tracked us.

Grizzly bears love blueberries and the season had just started. We waited another fifteen minutes before we returned to the trail. I was in the lead, Zach was in charge of ringing the bell we carried, and we talked loud about everything and anything. Why hadn't I bought bear spray? Both of us were relieved the bear was gone. The elevation started to climb, when we realized we were on the Long Hill. The adrenaline from the bear sighting helped us hike and crawl over boulders, as well as slip along the water covered rocks. We found snow pockets where we stumbled along icy slopes and sank into the deep snow. We read about the artifacts in the book left along the trail that coaxed us to linger. I looked at my watch and realized we needed to keep moving.

I was tired and feeling the extra weight on the top of my pack. Friends said putting extra weight at the top of the pack during the steep elevation gain helped the pack when going up. *What did I know? I took every piece of advice given to me.* Zach was doing a great job maneuvering

Hiking the Golden Stairs
Summer 1985

Part IV: Juneau, Anchorage, and Beyond

over the rocks as I struggled to match his speed. Maybe I should have put more weight in his pack. I was happy it wasn't raining and wished there was time to stop and take pictures but taking off the pack and finding the camera took time. I could barely find a spot to stand up without falling backwards because my pack was so heavy. The cables wedged in the rocks saved me a couple of times. After falsely thinking we were at the top and passing many relics of the Gold Rush days, we reached the summit. We stopped and took in the many vistas before we started the 2,486-foot descent.

The clear skies made the panoramic view breathtaking. We saw Crater Lake and smaller islands close to it. If we had brought binoculars we might have sighted the head of the Yukon River, but all I could think of was getting down to more level ground. Zach was excited and moved quickly as we left the top of the summit. I told him not to get too far ahead of me because there was something in the book about going the wrong direction. Thoughts of rearranging the pack crossed my mind. The strenuous hike wore me out and I wasn't steady.

All of a sudden, I fell, saw blood, and started screaming hoping Zach would hear me. I felt I hit my head and mouth. The pack made it impossible to get up. The blood trickled by one eye and my jaw throbbed. I was frustrated because I couldn't get up. I was stuck between two large rocks that in some ways protected me. Suddenly, I heard Zach say, "Shut up Mom." He never talked to me like that. I became quiet and realized he was trying to help me.

My screaming and fidgeting made me unaware of my surroundings. He helped take the pack off my back. It seemed there was blood everywhere. I had a hanky around my neck that Zach used to wipe my head. I asked how deep he thought the cut was. He said he really couldn't tell.

With so much blood I was sure I needed stitches. I remembered two Band-Aids in my pocket so I handed them to him. He crossed them over the cut like a big X. I rinsed the hanky and tied it over the wound as a headband. We hoped the pressure would stop the bleeding. I found an ibuprofen to take before we continued. The area around us was rocky and wet with no place large enough to sit, let alone set up a tent.

Happy Camp was the closest place to camp. It was less than five miles. All I could think of was how I wanted to lie down and rest. But that wasn't happening in the rocky terrain. *How could five miles take so long?* My head and jaw hurt, we were exhausted, and our bodies needed food.

I was numb from walking when I looked up—there was a pit toilet. We had made it to Happy Camp. It was 8:00 p.m., thirteen hours since we had started the nine-mile trek from Sheep Camp. We took our packs off and set up the tent. I insisted we eat some cheese and crackers before I bagged up our food. Being the only hikers in the camp, I decided to put the plastic food bag in the outhouse. We climbed in the tent and settled into our sleeping bags. I told Zach how sorry I was for putting him in a situation where he could have been left all alone. I tried not to cry but, being exhausted, the tears poured out. I hugged him tight and thought about how stupid I was for planning a hike like this with only the two of us. What if I had cracked my head open and died? I was so angry with myself I could hardly contain the fear I thought of after the fall.

We woke starved and happy no bears stole our food. We were twenty-one and a half miles into our thirty-three mile hike. There were five to six miles to Lindeman City where a Canadian ranger was located. I ached a bit. Maybe it was the hike and weight on my back, and not the fall. My head felt pretty good and the headband had stayed on all night. When I felt my head I could tell the headband was caked with blood. I was concerned it was stuck to my head. Zach didn't see any fresh blood so that was encouraging. My jaw was still sore, but no teeth were loose. I felt rested after a good night's sleep. The sun was out, no rain in sight, and we were done with the roughest part of the hike.

We checked the book's description of the next part of the hike, "Hikers must scramble over loose talus the next two miles to Long Lake." Zach asked, "What's talus?" I told him I really didn't know, but figured it was a form of shale rock. We agreed to be cautious. I had rearranged the pack with the weight evenly distributed, looked at my watch, and figured with five miles to Lindeman City I hoped we would be there by noon.

An hour and a half later, we passed Long Lake headed to Deep Lake where many hikers camped when coming off the Summit. The landscape changed as we traveled north. The cairns guided us through the trees. I was glad to see the green of fir, pine, alder, and willows gently waving us along. We stopped and filled our water bottles with fresh water running from Moose Creek. Moving along the side of a mountain we carefully watched our footing as we stepped over slick rocks.

As we hiked into Lindeman City I spotted the wall tent area when I saw the Canadian flag. We walked into the information area and told them about my fall. One of the rangers offered to take a look at my head. She poured some water over the headband before she removed it. I was grateful it wasn't ripped off my head. Zach was standing next to me when the ranger asked, "Who put the Band-Aids on your head?" Zach, sheepishly answered, "I did." The ranger congratulated him on doing an excellent job. "You saved your mom a larger scar on her head." Zach and I looked at each other.

The ranger explained I should have had stitches, but twenty-four hours later was too late. The next best thing to stitches was sealing the wound by 'butterflying' the Band-Aids. Zach did that. He intently listened to the ranger. The big surprise came when she offered to let us stay the night in one of the wall tents and use the makeshift shower to get all of the blood out of my hair. She warned me it wasn't a hot shower, but it wasn't cold. We thanked her and briefly discussed the rest of the hike.

The shower felt fantastic. We fixed dinner, slept on the cots, and were on the trail bright and early the next morning for Lake Bennett. The path followed Moose Creek until we came to a footbridge. There were areas where we walked through small streams and over bridges. The biggest difficulty was the sandy soil we found in the Bare Loon Lake. We didn't have time to stop and look at the cemetery and read about the men buried who helped with building the White Pass and Yukon Route railroad. We felt lucky to be walking through history.

We stopped in Lake Bennett long enough to eat our lunch. I was getting anxious about catching the ferry departure back to Juneau. In 1982 the White Pass railroad stopped running because the zinc mines in the Yukon closed. When the railroad ran it was common for hikers to catch it into Skagway. Now hikers arranged for people to pick them up or stashed a car along the Klondike Highway. Others hitchhiked into Skagway. We talked to someone in Lindeman City who guessed it was somewhere between two to four miles out to the highway from Lake Bennett.

It was easy walking along the railroad track. To keep us going, I asked Zach what he wanted as a treat when we arrived in Skagway. It was a warm day, probably in the mid-eighties. We talked about something cold to drink because we were thirsty, then he blurted out "Hot fudge sundae." For the next thirty minutes we described the different ways of making the sundae better and bigger. One of the couples we had seen earlier in the day walked past us, heard our conversation, and added toasted coconut flakes.

Twenty minutes later we walked past their car as they offered a cold beverage. A friend dropped their car with a cooler of cold beers, pop, and a bottle of champagne. We took off our packs and accepted the offer. Zach selected a Mountain Dew and I shared champagne with them. We told each other trail stories and agreed how lucky we were with the weather.

We thanked them for their hospitality and headed to a spot on the highway to look for a ride. Within ten minutes a motorhome stopped. A nice couple with a sleeping child looked safe enough so we jumped in. They were from Montana and visiting Alaska and Canada for the summer. We chatted about the Chilkoot Trail and before we knew it we were in Skagway headed for the ice cream parlor and that hot fudge sundae.

SERRC received a request for someone to conduct presentations on state-mandated information for new teachers. Rural districts needed this assistance because they had one administrator, the superintendent, who was responsible for everything. It was easier to hire a person trained to present the information than for them to attend the various training sessions. Federal and state mandates required districts to train staff members on child abuse and neglect, fetal alcohol spectrum disorders, drug free schools, AIDS, gender/cultural equity, sexual harassment and Title IX.

Larger districts, such as Anchorage, Fairbanks, Matanuska-Susitna Borough, and Juneau-Douglas Borough, had support administrators who conducted the in-services. Rural districts constantly had turnover. Even superintendents only lasted two to three years. SERRC received phone calls in July from new-to-Alaska superintendents trying to figure out compliance and in-service requirements. Over a few years I had received training in all topic areas and developed different agendas to handle two topics in one day or six topics over three days.

One August I delivered in-services for eight districts located in four corners of the state. The work was done over two weeks. Fortunately, I was able to schedule the boys' summer trip to see their dad during that time. The first week I traveled from Juneau to Barrow to Aniak, back to Anchorage. Two rural districts chose to have their in-service presentations in Anchorage. This decision cut down on my travel. I completed one district on Friday and the second district on Monday. Early Tuesday I flew to Dillingham. The long daylight hours allowed for time to get through both sessions and still make the flight back to Anchorage and on to McGrath. I worked long and hard to coordinate all the flights. The districts needed the in-services completed so schools could start and I needed the travel concluded while the boys were gone. I even planned a weekend in Anchorage visiting friends to save me two flights.

I was feeling smug about how well every thing was going until I arrived in McGrath to present to the Iditarod School District. The box with my materials and food that should have accompanied me from Dillingham to McGrath was sitting in Anchorage. Flights to and from Dillingham and McGrath were not on small planes so I hadn't helped load the luggage. The box couldn't be delivered until the next day on the same flight I was to depart on back to Anchorage.

Part IV: Juneau, Anchorage, and Beyond

What was I going to do? I did have a folder in my daypack with some of the information but not all of it. I needed to think quickly. A principal of one of the Iditarod School District schools heard me present at a State meeting so he had additional information. The problem was the packet sat on his desk back in Nikolai. The stars were aligned—he owned his own plane. He offered to fly to Nikolai and get the materials for me. He was back in an hour and I pieced everything together ready for the presentations the next morning.

When I finished my presentations in McGrath and climbed on the plane to Anchorage I was exhausted from the added stress of the box stuck in Anchorage. Eight districts in two weeks located in four corners of the state were too many and I still had one to finish. I vowed I would never do this crazy travel schedule again. I made it into Anchorage, grabbed my box in the baggage storage area and flew on to Unalaska. The in-service went well in Unalaska. I called to check on the plane before heading to the airport for Anchorage and found out the plane had a mechanical issue. The person on the phone said they still hoped to leave on time. The plane left late, which meant I missed the connecting flight home to Juneau. I was bummed as I checked into a hotel close to the airport.

SERRC received a contract to work with Kashunamiut School District (KSD), a small single-site district in Chevak, located on the north bank of the Niglikfak River, in the Yukon-Kuskokwim delta. People in Chevak had a tri-lingual system, Cup'ik (Chew-pick), a dialect of Central Yup'ik, English, and a mixture of the two languages. They were a unique separate Eskimo group, which allowed them to form a single-site school district.

An exciting part of the contract was its length. A video project with the Alaska Commission on Aging was finished. It had only lasted six months, but this contract was for five years. Even though it was still only part of my job I began to feel more stable. The Kashunamiut SD received a Title IV, Indian Education federal grant to align the Cup'ik culture with Alaska state mandated curriculum. I was selected because of my master's degree in cross-cultural education and experience in rural Alaska. The focus of the work involved teaching staff members to incorporate Cup'ik culture. Part of my job was writing the federal reports. The work involved three to four visits each school year to conduct staff training on culture and curriculum.

When Mark told me about the project I shared my hesitancy regarding care for my sons while traveling. He encouraged me to check with friends about arrangements for the boys. With all of the state workers, Juneau was full of people who traveled for work and were accustomed to supporting each other. The distance involved three airplane rides each way, which meant trips would be three to four days. I talked with friends and a childcare plan materialized. The trips were spread out over the school year, making arrangements easier.

I called the Kashunamiut superintendent to discuss the first visit. He told me Chevak had limited services, so 'plan accordingly.' The school was old and only parts of the village had running water. I knew the drill—sleep on a gym mat in the school and cook with the school's microwave oven (if they had one). I asked about his staff and what they thought of bicultural programs. He explained several were 'old school educators' still utilizing a missionary teaching approach. He hoped the grant would change their current behavior since the community was traditional in their ways. We established potential dates for my first year visits, but agreed the weather could change them.

The second week of October I loaded my backpack (sleeping bag, small pillow, and clothes) and filled a box with some food and supplies for the staff training. The flights into Bethel were on time. The mail plane to Chevak included two stops, Hooper Bay and Scammon Bay. Mail plane travel depended on passengers and amount of freight. I was the only passenger traveling today so I was the first stop.

When the plane landed in Chevak no one was there to greet it, not unusual for a village. The pilot deposited the mailbags, a couple of boxes, and me on the landing strip before he took off. As the pilot unloaded the mail he said, "I radioed the postmaster the mail plane is unloaded and leaving." Eventually, someone would pick up the mail, but I decided to start walking into town. The mile hike to town was muddy in spots due to the rains, but not bad. I was glad I opted to wear what some referred to as my Alaskan sneakers, or as we said, Juneau 'tennies' (knee-high rubber boots). A truck went by as I came around a corner. I waved, stepped off the road, and fortunately didn't get sprayed with mud.

The K–12 staff was composed of twelve teachers and one principal. A few teachers had been there a couple of years and one was new to Alaska coming from Hawaii. During the lunch break, the new teacher and I found out we had both graduated from Roosevelt High School in Honolulu. I was shocked. I never met anyone who knew there was a Roosevelt High School in Hawaii, let alone graduate from it.

During my visit, I met and talked with the teachers and other staff. Before leaving I reviewed the cultural work ahead with John Pingayak who facilitated the Indian Studies bicultural program. John Pingayak was an Alaska Native educator known throughout the state for his expertise and humbleness in sharing what he knew. I felt honored to have an opportunity to work with him. His staff was reserved for good reason. I was another white woman given the task of instructing them about their culture. What they didn't know was that I had planned on them doing the talking, not me.

I flew out of Chevak feeling good about the visit, but knew I had a responsibility to 'walk my talk.' This was just the first visit of many. I am sure they wondered if I would come back. Alaska Native villages were familiar with turnover and people that never returned.

The weather was kind and I made both flights into Anchorage. At 7:15 p.m. I climbed on the jet for the one hour, twenty-three-minute flight to Juneau. Feeling tired and anxious to be home, I eagerly listened for the captain's words about flying conditions. Juneau was famous for its weather[31] that cloaked the airport with heavy fog and low clouds that kept flights from landing or taking off. It was normal for pilots to make several attempts to land and, as often as not, give up. No one talked when the pilot tried to land through the shroud of clouds, but everyone cheered when he did. If the plane couldn't land then a decision was made to fly to Sitka, Seattle, Fairbanks, or back to Anchorage. No one knew how the choice was made. It always seemed random. Sitka was the closest, but that didn't influence the decision.

It was a Thursday night and the flight was full of people who worked for the State and had been in Anchorage for business. I heard the conversations and occasional bets about whether the plane would make it into Juneau. A couple of people, including me, called family or friends to ask about the cloud conditions. Somehow we felt by making the call, and hearing, "It's cloudy, but not bad," would help the pilot land. We all were aware the weather could close in quickly.

Part IV: Juneau, Anchorage, and Beyond

The camaraderie felt with the pilot and other passengers during the two attempts to land was bonding. Everyone rejoiced as we disembarked relieved the familiar form of travel we all accepted as 'normal' once again was successful. I grabbed my backpack and box and headed for the car, a yellow 1975 Honda Civic. Seeing the car made me realize how much the boys were growing. I needed a bigger car. I smiled. It felt good to be home.

Zach and Jeremia wanted a dog. A dog was additional responsibility and I felt full, but it was time. The first Saturday in October 1987 we headed to the Gastineau Humane Society to investigate rescue dogs. A small litter of puppies was entertaining everyone. I was hoping to adopt a dog already house trained, but no such luck. While they were busy playing with the puppies, I checked the size, breed, and price. The pound volunteer said the breed was a mix of collie, retriever, and spaniel and would be midsized with a shorthair coat. The price included a round of shots and the neutering procedure at the vet next door.

Since it was Saturday and the pound was closing, I told the boys we needed to think about it. I assured them nothing would happen on Sunday. The black and white male puppy they kept referring to, as 'theirs' was safe at the pound until Monday. We definitely needed a doghouse. Alaska wasn't like the lower 48 where there were places to buy doghouses.

Conversations Saturday evening and Sunday morning were consumed with chatter about the dog. They agreed on the name, Mattingly. Zach loved Don Mattingly of the New York Yankees. I was never sure if Jeremia gave in to the name or if they truly selected it together. After breakfast they looked at me and once again asked, "Can we get the puppy Mom? Can we?" My heart melted, "I said yes." We went to the store to buy wood for a doghouse. Jed built many doghouses, but I never watched or asked the details. I figured someone at the store would know what I needed. No such luck. I knew more than the clerk and that wasn't much. The tools we had were minimal. I wanted the wood cut at the store so I tried my best to determine the pieces we needed. We bought nails and started back home to build the doghouse

Jeremia and Zach insisted they didn't need my help. I think they wanted to demonstrate how responsible they were. I reminded them to work as a team. We reviewed how to put it together. They started hammering away. I checked on them a couple of times. Everything was going along well until, I heard, "Oh no." I went outside to see what happened. The top piece didn't quite touch the sides. I remembered there were wood scrapes under the eaves of the condo. They ran down to grab a couple of pieces. The roof wasn't perfectly flat, but I thought it was the most beautiful doghouse I ever saw. I knew Mattingly would love it.

Monday morning started with a fight over who would sleep with Mattingly first. I reminded them he had to be house broken. When I arrived at work I called the Humane Society. The woman remembered us. She said she would save the black and white spotted male puppy. An advantage of traveling for work was flexibility when I was home. SERRC supported families and allowed for employees to do things especially involving their children. None of the evening hours missed at home with family was ever replaced.

After school I picked the boys up and we headed to the pound. Zach and Jeremia listened intently as the volunteer explained proper care and training for puppies. I watched their brains absorbing it all. They put the leash on him and attempted to walk him next door to the veterinary clinic. Somehow I kept from laughing. The puppy stopped, chewed on his leash and walked two steps, before going in a different direction. Zach finally picked him up. They talked to him, as he chewed on their fingers, about walking with a leash as I set up dates for the shots and his neutering procedure.

We talked again about Mattingly sleeping in the bathroom until he was house broken. I told them I would take Mattingly out before I went to bed and again early in the morning. Over the next month each time I took him out, I told him he had a responsibility to take care of both of the boys. I was afraid he would favor one of them over the other and I would be dealing with a broken heart.

Mattingly loved his boys

Mattingly didn't let me down. When the time came for him to sleep with the boys he understood his role. The first night a coin was flipped, Jeremia won. The next night Mattingly headed to Zach's room. Each night I patted his head and told him what a good dog he was. When he looked at me, I was sure he winked. He understood his job and did it well. The boys had worked hard to build the doghouse with love. He certainly endeared himself to me. Sometimes during football or soccer practice, I would say, "Come on, Mattingly, let's go for a run." He would look over at his boys to make sure they were OK before going with me. They were his focus.

Did I hear the question correctly? The pilot asked if I knew where we were. It was Tuesday morning and we were headed to a logging camp I visited regularly. When I realized he was talking to me, I thought, *Are you crazy? Passengers sit quietly and pilots fly the plane.* This was 1988. When would small airlines quit hiring people from out-of-the-state to fly in the bush? It made me crazy and this was one of those days. This had happened in 1975 but Jed responded. He helped the pilot become schooled in landscape landmarks (the Alaskan way of flying in the early '70s). I was busy in the back seat with a toddler I hoped wouldn't throw up.

Flying in small airplanes doesn't allow for stops at a gas station or convenience store to ask for directions. When the pilot asked the question we were also out of range for radio assistance. I traveled to this community often, but that didn't mean I knew the flying route. It was now time to focus on landmarks.

When he asked the question my mind was thinking about the lesson I was to teach when we arrived in the logging camp. One of my responsibilities at SERRC was as guidance counselor for Chatham Schools, a district that comprised fishing communities and logging camps located on the Chichagof Island[32] in southeast Alaska. Chichagof's claim to fame was that it had the highest population of bears per square mile in the entire universe.

As the guidance counselor, I was to talk to students about plans for life after high school, encourage their interest in advanced classes, and inspire them to think about earning a living. One time I asked students what they might do after high school and not one of the eighteen students in the group responded. *Wow!* Scanning the room I thought, *Wake up and be present.*

Throwing out the prepared lesson, I asked what was needed to keep the logging camp running. They all sat there for a moment as I started writing everyday tasks done by someone on the white board. It was exciting to watch them evolve into helping me list the duties needed to keep the logging community going. They began to see the different jobs, as paid and unpaid. It was an incredible conversation.

The current pilot situation was another example of a small charter service hiring an inexperienced pilot from the lower 48 eager to gain hours. Eighty percent of Alaska was accessed only by air travel. Flying in small planes was the most efficient way to get around Alaska—but had its dangerous moments. This was one of them.

Maybe I should have been embarrassed I couldn't help or direct the pilot, but I thought, *What is wrong with you? Your job is to get me to the destination and my job is to be quiet and enjoy the ride.* Walking was my preferred form of travel. To me, walking got me there easier and faster than finding an address by driving around and around.

With Alaska's questionable weather I always carried a few extra items like a sleeping bag, toothbrush, and a change of clothes, but those were used if I was stuck in a school, not stranded in a lost airplane. Weather in southeast Alaska was easier to deal with than other parts of the state. In winter there were low clouds and rain but generally it was acceptable flying weather. The Taku winds *might* get strong; the clouds *might* become a darker gray and extra thick variation; or everything *might* become socked in creating hazardous flying conditions.

Looking again at the pilot I saw his question wasn't a joke. When I arrived at the airport in the morning I was greeted with this new pilot. I traveled three to five times a month with this company so I knew most of their pilots. Newbies unsettled me. I learned early if I was going to keep flying in Alaska it was best to think positive when boarding an airplane. In the fall I heard about a pilot I flew with out of Bethel who crashed and burned. Even the good ones go down and that never sat well with me.

Flying in Alaska was always stunning and today was no different. The skies, mountains, terrain, snow, and water changed color with the light and shadows. These features were dependent on the time of day, the month, and season of the year. Despite the picturesque and amazing photographs created by these moments a quick look played with one's mind when trying to remember land cues.

For some reason I can't explain, I took a deep breath and began using brainstorming skills to help the pilot determine where we were and how to proceed. I looked at my watch and asked, "How long have we been in the air?" I talked to him about the flight plan he was given. Based on this information, we talked about his best guess where we were just as we rounded a bend revealing a familiar landmark. I felt we were close as I saw smoke rising, not a low cloud.

Part IV: Juneau, Anchorage, and Beyond

He kept the smoke in sight as he regained his ability to function as the pilot. Flying in floatplanes allowed for low-to-the-ground flying, a helpful strategy for this type of problem. As I scanned the horizon and water, I saw one of the logging crewmembers next to the logs. It confirmed we were in the normal landing area for this logging camp. Sometimes the logs were tied up ready to be transported, which always made deplaning more challenging. This was one of those occasions. Unloading a floatplane onto logs and transporting luggage and boxes to the dock was tricky. It was critical to be careful or items landed in the water.

I recognized Ted, a camp representative who I knew and liked. He was helpful. Last month Ted was gone and couple of new guys had greeted the plane. They were feeling a bit ornery and didn't offer to help with the unloading. It was the same arrangement for deplaning by traversing the logs, never easy. I had the school district's Alaska Career Information System computer to share with students. I ended up sitting on my butt over each log to be sure the computer didn't fall in the water. The two guys just stood there acting like they were doing something. I was fuming but didn't say a word.

Ted carefully guided the pilot and plane into a tie-down position and helped get my gear off the plane. My backpack and box of teaching supplies was part of what was on the plane. As I started up the ramp carrying my box with the backpack on my back I heard the pilot and Ted talk about other items in the plane that needed to be unloaded. It was easy to identify this was the pilot's first trip because he was unsure if someone representing the postal service was picking up the mailbag. He didn't know if anyone would be signing for the items delivered.

Whenever I arrived in a logging camp or fishing village it was a toss-up if I started my lesson immediately or had thirty minutes to regroup. Today I hoped for a few regroup minutes. Reaching the school, I heard the familiar buzz of the bush plane taking off and wondered about my pick-up later in the day. I never saw him again so I can't say if his first flight was his last, a 'one and only rural pilot experience' or if he continued to fly charters in Alaska.

My return flight to Juneau was smooth with a pilot I knew. Hopefully, the pilot for the trip next week to Eight Fathom Bight, another logging camp in the Chatham School District, would be one I knew.

In early December 1989 I rescheduled a trip to Akiachak leaving January 11. I wasn't excited about a trip in January. This was the third attempt to this village, the first two cancelled due to weather. Trips like this one I tried to do in the fall or spring. The information I was presenting to the school staff was to meet federal equity requirements. The district needed this off their required list. Rescheduling around student sports and community activities was difficult but we found the January date.

Akiachak, a small Yup'ik Eskimo village twelve miles northeast of Bethel on the Kuskokwim River, was the largest of the three in the Yupiit School District. All three schools in the district, Akiachak, Akiak, and Tuluksak, were fishing and subsistence lifestyle communities. Travel to Akiachak was primarily by airplane in the winter or boat in the summer from Bethel. Local residents sometimes took the water taxi from Bethel or used their snow machines.

Water taxis weren't my favorite way to travel. In March the previous year I had worked in Napasikak, another village close to Bethel. When I made travel plans I accidently booked the river taxi from Bethel instead of the air taxi. I knew that to drive on the river people waited until it was frozen and checked for a depth of two to three feet, but I still was uneasy.

Upon arrival in Bethel the reservation clerk told me there was no availability on the air taxi. She gave me my water taxi ticket and told me to head to the store where a Chevy Suburban left at 11:00 a.m. As I climbed into the Suburban other passengers joined me. Their boxes and bags from purchases at the Alaska Commercial (AC) Store were loaded into the back. Finally, we took off. No one said a word, just settled down for the ride home to Napasikak. I was the only 'gussak' and probably the only nervous person. Driving along the frozen river I saw spots of open water that stressed me out. I read about people who fell into icy waters. I tried hard to relax, but it was difficult. I needed to become comfortable with river taxis and have confidence that experienced drivers were selected.

When setting the January trip to Akiachak, the superintendent and I discussed the weather. Often it was way below zero in January. I came prepared with my Arctic Sorel boots and thick parka. My backpack and box were checked through to Bethel. The plane from Anchorage to Bethel was a midsize commuter airplane. As we took off, the flight attendant told us the flight was to be bumpy and rough. She was correct. I am sure I wasn't the only person ready to be off the plane.

As I walked out the door of the plane and down the short stairs, I was almost knocked over by gusts from the wind. I was glad to put my backpack on because it gave me more weight. I picked up the box and struggled against the wind as I walked next door for my final flight. I was told the winds were too rough to fly into Akiachak. FAA weather service predicted the winds would be gone by early evening, but too late to fly.

I called the district superintendent who didn't skip a beat—he told me to be ready around 6:00 p.m. for a river snow machine pick up. I must have said OK. My mind was racing. *Do I get paid enough to take this kind of risk?* January, darkness, and open water on the Kuskokwim River—wonderful traveling conditions. I called SERRC and told them the situation. My office mate asked, "Are you really going?" I hesitated, but said, "I guess I am."

Riding in small airplanes was very normal in Alaska; however traveling by snow machine on the frozen Kuskokwim River wasn't. Time to assess my situation. Did I have the right clothes? Yes. What was the weather temperature? I asked the clerk at the desk. She told me currently the lows at night were in the twenties above zero. This was excellent weather, for the time of year. Two factors were out of my control: the wind-chill and the open water spots on the river. Sometimes when temperatures went up more open water was created. I was uncomfortable, but realized I was committed. My goal was to believe the snow machine driver was experienced and knew the safest route.

The meet up spot was the AC store. I arrived and found the crew loaded and ready to head out. The winds had stopped and it was a balmy twenty-nine degrees above zero, with no clouds in the sky and a magnificent full moon. Someone brought an extra pair of moose hide gloves for me to wear that made it easier to hold onto the sled. I was grateful. We were on our way by 7:00 p.m. I preferred standing on the sled runners than sitting in the sled, which really made the sled travel better. Ours was the second of three snow machines with sleds. The teacher driving the snow machine was happy to hear this wasn't my first rodeo driving a sled and I felt confident he was familiar with the frozen river.

Everyone was relaxed and confident it would be an easy trip back to Akiachak. I felt my inner spirit letting out a deep breath. The tension in my body was gone. I relaxed, looked around, and immersed myself in the snowbound wonderland of the evening. The low roar of the snow machine and the stillness of night was spellbinding. The ice crystals glimmered from the snow with light from the moon creating a clear path that seemed endless into the landscape. Stars danced in the night sky and teased me, "Didn't you know night travel was like this every night?"

A wolf announced his presence and shadows flickered as we rounded a corner. The sled effortlessly skimmed along the frozen river trail, occasionally jarred by a small bump. The stunning trip on the Kuskokwim River was beyond my imagination. I could have said, "No," and headed home, but what a loss.

Zach and I were at the Glory Hole Emergency Shelter and Soup Kitchen preparing dinner for the homeless when I received a call. Jeff, a fellow working on my kitchen, called to tell me Mattingly was missing. He had left the door open. I knew Jeremia was arriving home any minute. Thank goodness two moms arrived to help with the volunteer event. I told them the situation and they said to go.

I called the pound to see if they had a missing dog. They told me a midsize dog hit by a car was next door at the veterinary clinic. I called Jeff and he offered to bring Jeremia to us. Zach called the vet to confirm it was Mattingly and told them we were on our way.

Driving was difficult. I was churning with anger and frustration at Jeff, as well as the possible loss of Mattingly. How could I handle the unimaginable grief of three people? Jeff arrived the same time we did. The boys and I walked into the clinic. The vet technician recognized us and walked us to the back area. A couple of cats meowed and a sleeping dog looked up at us, when the boys saw Mattingly. They went right to him. Seeing his boys he tried to wag his tail. The young man said that was the first time he showed any signs of life.

Dr. Logan explained the person that hit Mattingly brought him to the clinic. Although the accident was at a slow speed the car hit his head. Mattingly was sedated to rest for the night. Injuries to the head were harder to assess. We felt helpless, but relieved there were no signs of internal bleeding. We were told to return in the morning.

Early Saturday morning we were there. Dr. Logan clarified the head injury caused him to lose the ability to control his right front leg. He dragged the leg because he didn't remember he had it. The hope was that by six months he would regain management of his leg. He needed to heal and our job was to watch him.

We left feeling confident Mattingly would be fine in a few weeks. After six months of bandaging and re-bandaging his foot with old socks and ace bandages a decision was made to amputate the leg. Dr. Logan assured us he would adjust. We heard numerous stories about three-legged dogs, although it was more rare for a front leg to be amputated. For the first year after his leg was removed Mattingly seemed depressed. He never had an accident in the house and was always eager to see his boys, but mostly he slept. The bedrooms were upstairs in our condo and he maneuvered them like a pro right after he came home.

Part IV: Juneau, Anchorage, and Beyond

One year, almost to the day, of his leg being amputated, a change occurred. He returned to his pre three-legged self. He was interested in longer walks and told us he wanted to go in the car. We helped him get in, but soon he jumped in by himself. He ran with me on short two to three mile outings. The three of us were overjoyed. We named him the 'three-legged wonder dog'.

Susan, a friend at work, asked about hiking the Chilkoot Trail. She had a friend in Fairbanks who wanted to hike it with her two nephews from New Jersey. I told her my youngest son and I planned to do it in a couple of months. Susan called her friend, Jane, and we agreed to all meet in Skagway in July. Jeremia had a friend, Liam, who joined us.

I wanted this trip to be different and it was. There were three adult women, two Alaska fourteen-year-olds, and two kids from New Jersey, Tom and Alan, who had no idea about backpacks. Susan and I had hiked together in Juneau, so I knew she was capable. She hiked with Jane who ran, skied, and lived without running water in Fairbanks. *That made her hardy in my book.* Jeremia and Liam were active in sports. The wild card was the boys from New Jersey.

Liam's mom located a backpack and sleeping bag for him. I knew I had the remaining gear. Jane arranged to meet us in Skagway on Monday, July 23. Her nephews, ten and twelve, were excited. She borrowed gear and made sure their hiking boots were broken in. While milling around the new Klondike Visitor Center, a woman came up to us and asked if she could join our group. *She was obviously smarter than I was in 1985.*

Our comfort level with her was immediate. We asked about her experiences and made sure everyone had enough food and gear. Karen was from Oregon with plenty of hiking and backpacking skills. We boarded the van to Dyea. Jeremia and Liam talked about the picture of a woman on the kiosk in the Visitors' Center carrying a cast iron stove on her back as she hiked up the long hill before the Golden Stairs. Liam said, "People were tough back in those days."

It was 1990, five years since my first trip. The timing was the same, but warmer. When we reached the trailhead we loaded up and off we went. All four boys were energized and eager. We hiked three miles when we came to a large patch of open water—Beaver pond. During the previous trip with Zach there was very little water in this spot. We read about the water when reviewing the trail conditions. Jane estimated the water was eighteen inches deep. We brought large garbage bags to use to put on our feet for situations like this. Wet boots created blisters when hiking and none of us wanted that. Karen, from Oregon, had a pair of Teva sandals she put on to cross. She offered to throw them back for us to use. They worked beautifully. The older boys reluctantly put on the plastic bags, which lasted maybe four steps. Jeremia tore them off followed by Liam. One of us yelled, "Don't complain when you have blisters." They both said, "Yah, we know." The younger boys waddled across in the bags.

We took a break at Finnegan's Point for a late lunch. I walked with the younger boys to see the artifacts from a bygone era. I felt again I was in a 'living museum'. Suddenly, the older boys started to herd us along and get everyone moving. We didn't understand the abrupt movement until Jane overheard their muffled conversation. She shared the boys were anxious to get going because they heard from the hikers coming from the Canadian side there were three young women ahead hiking topless. We chuckled and agreed *"whatever keeps them moving,"* meaning the boys.

Early in the afternoon on the second day we came to a creek to be crossed. I was bringing up the rear, not unusual for me. I enjoyed the scenery. Suddenly, I was frozen as I started to walk over unsteady, slippery rocks and wasn't sure I could continue. I didn't know what was happening to me. Each rock seemed more unstable, precarious, and treacherous. *Maybe I was thinking about my fall in the earlier trip.*

Focused on keeping my balance I heard someone call to me and saw Jeremia. He gently reached his hand out, and quietly said, "Mom, I have you. You're going to be fine." My fourteen-year-old son guided me across the creek, gave me a hug, grabbed his pack, and off he went to catch up to Liam. They were the self-delegated trail leaders. His eyes told me he knew I was embarrassed. I stood there for a moment thinking how proud I was of the man he was becoming. Susan asked if I was ready to move on. I said, "Yes, let's go."

We reached Sheep Camp about 4:00 p.m. The next day would be the longest and hardest day of the hike. Being rested and prepared was important. Liam went to help Tom get water while Jeremia and I set up the tent. Each evening the boys worked together filtering water and helped with other chores. We heard them talking about the video they saw at the Visitors' Center. Jeremia mentioned, "Many of the people who signed on to cook and clean worked just as hard as the ones carrying fifty to sixty pounds of provisions over the pass." Tom, the ten-year-old, said he remembered the Chilkoot Trail was called the 'meanest thirty-three miles in the world.' I told him the 'meanest' part was coming up tomorrow. We all laughed.

Jane told the boys the goal was to make Happy Camp tomorrow or Deep Lake. During dinner Alan, the twelve-year-old, talked about the picture of the fifteen hundred ice steps carved into the frozen snow mountain. He said, "That is a lot of steps." I explained aspects of the hike—the long gradual hill, climbing over small rocks, stepping through patches of snow, and endless boulders that went on forever. Someone added the boulders led us to the Canadian side. After reviewing safety precautions we settled into our tents.

Before going to sleep I told Liam and Jeremia that one of the adults would lead the next day. At breakfast I reviewed the bear incident I had on the earlier trip. We all agreed to talk a lot and make noise. The four boys did a great job. They moved carefully across areas that intimidated many adults. When someone (kid or adult) slowed down another person offered help. Breaks were taken but we were at Happy Camp earlier than predicted.

Made it to the Chilkoot Peak in sunshine
1990

Part IV: Juneau, Anchorage, and Beyond

We had a snack and decided to hike the three miles to Deep Lake. After dinner the exhilaration of the day's feat finally subsided as exhaustion kicked in. No one had trouble sleeping that night. The next day we hiked the ten miles to Lake Bennett. The weather was so warm all of us were in shorts, the women in jog bras and the boys shirtless. Jeremia and Liam had long given up on the topless ghosts and enjoyed time with the other boys. We were all giddy with how well the hike had gone, the glorious weather, and the incredible opportunity to participate in a special era of time. After setting up the tents, the boys went swimming.

The next morning we climbed on the White Pass and Yukon Route Railway into Skagway. We were all happy the route had reopened in 1988 as a heritage railway. I was pleased there were no accidents and bear sightings on this revisit to the Chilkoot.

Juneau averaged seventy-one inches of rain per year almost double the national average. The varying shades of gray closed the city in and held everyone captive with precipitation. There were periods of several days when planes didn't come in or go out. With 236 days of some type of water or snow falling and only eighty-five to ninety sunny days each year, people either loved Juneau or became fed up and left. The mist felt comforting on my face. Juneau taught me the beauty of rain, being in rain, and its many rewards.

I ran, walked, and hiked with the boys and my friends in the rain. After Zach started to drive I often gave him the car and walked the two miles home from work. I became an avid runner in Juneau. I ran alone and with friends. I wasn't fast, but enjoyed the training, especially hills. People thought I was insane because I enjoyed going up more than the faster speed of going down. The motto that encouraged me was 'just get out the door' and everything will be fine. I hated having my feet wet, but learned about proper socks and ways to dry the shoes between runs. The boys played football, soccer, and baseball in pouring down rain and mud. They didn't complain because it was their norm.

The Drug-Free Schools and Communities Act (DFSCA) of 1986 created new projects for me at SERRC. For five years, I was the Drug Free Schools Coordinator for twenty-two of Alaska's fifty-two school districts helping districts with smoking, chewing, huffing, and alcohol issues. Before the DFSCA smoking was a norm for teachers and students in many villages. With the new requirements in school buildings, smoking by staff and students was to be stopped. Villages tried to meet the letter of the law, but it wasn't easy.

Carrying a gun to school for protection from polar bears was a norm in Barrow and other villages. How do these actions stop when they have been approved for so long? Many adjustments were difficult. The one I worked hardest to change was allowing the star basketball player to continue playing after he was caught drinking. It was more often than not overlooked. I tried but wasn't very successful.

Grants were awarded to educators for issues related to Co-Dependency. SERRC knew how easy it was for teachers and administrators to become overly involved with students. All the cultural and economic changes in rural communities were problematic. They happened fast and created alcohol problems that took time to understand. Teachers needed to grasp the difference in good self-care and appropriate help for students.

Alaska's suicide rate was higher than other states, especially for Native men age 21–28. The role for Native men had shifted with the changes in the villages. Many people struggled to adjust and chose alcohol to take the edge off. There was a fear or concern someone else would follow in the footsteps leading to another suicide. Funding was made available to help communities when a suicide occurred. Everyone in a village was either related to or friends with the person who died. A neutral person was vital in helping communities process the grief, anger, frustration, and sadness.

Across the state, six to eight of us were selected and hired to work as community mediators. It required being comfortable in a village, working with Native people, and moving through procedural steps. It was draining work. When people talked and worked together to process through the stages of grief, emotions surfaced. There was a need for humor to be added to the activities to help people relax and balance the feelings of sorrow. Connecting people to resources inside and outside the communities was critical to the mediator's community plan.

No place in Alaska was spared the sorrow and anguish of suicides. When Jeremia was a sophomore at Juneau-Douglas High School three suicides occurred, all students sixteen years of age. The deaths were spread out over the school year: August, November, and April. Even though the boys weren't best friends, they were classmates. Juneau had one high school. Jeremia was closest to the third boy. Friends were important to him.

I watched him closely. His friends' parents were people I knew. We all checked with each other a little more often. I enjoyed hearing laughter at the house when Jer and his posse of friends were there. They seemed to gain strength from each other and I knew where he was. Juneau made adjustments and suicides decreased, but they didn't go away.

With the many obligations and stress in my life I continued to find outdoor activities to decompress. Kayaking was one of them. A friend suggested I try it and I was hooked. I kayaked to Oliver Inlet where I saw starfish in colors that made me gasp in excitement. I couldn't believe what I was seeing. In Berners Bay I watched humpback whales jump high and land sideways in the water making waves that moved the kayaks. My arms became stronger as I learned kayak skills crossing a strait or along a coastal area when the wind came up. I loved kayaking!

The boys were in Fairbanks visiting their dad and I was going on a weeklong trip with Dick, a guy I was dating. We loaded our kayaks and gear in Juneau. It was cloudy and gray when we left Juneau on the early ferry, but sunny and warm when unloaded in Sitka. We had two sea kayaks, six dry bags, and five other bags of various sizes. After several trips hauling gear and kayaks across the road we sat down by the put-in spot.

We had studied maps to determine our route for the seven days. Sitka was nestled on the edge of the Baranof Island with access to the outer coast, as well as shielded inlets. It was a paradise for sea kayakers. This unspoiled marine wilderness was best explored in a sea kayak because of its many narrow passages. We now needed to decide—were we venturing into the open waters or remaining within the protected waterways around Sitka?

The excitement of the sunny day encouraged us to select the open ocean water route to Goddard Hot Springs. As we loaded the kayaks we checked for wind and looked at the ocean. We discussed the approach to reach the opening of the canal to avoid rocks and move into the open water. We knew the time in the ocean was short and then we would return to protected area. We secured our life vests and settled into our kayaks. I was nervous, but focused.

We crossed the bay to the other side to enter the open water. The closer we came to the Sitka Sound the choppier it became making it difficult to maneuver our boats. I concentrated on my kayak and kept moving in the direction we discussed. Dick was over to the right of me when a wave came toward us. One option in kayaking in rough waters was to meet a wave straight on, which was what I did. I didn't capsize, but was caught off guard when the kayaks moved in an unplanned direction. Suddenly, the two boats were locked together making them unsteady. The plastic handles located on both ends of the kayak connected. If we didn't want to be upside down we needed to correct the situation quickly.

Dick started yelling at me, "You stupid fucking idiot." I was thinking *Where did that come from? Did he think this is my fault?* He was out of control. I started paddling backwards in hopes of loosening the tangled handles. I was disoriented and felt sick to my stomach. I needed to think, stay calm, and remain level headed. I wasn't sure where my strength came from as I moved the boat back toward the calmer water. Dick was six foot and twice my size. I wasn't sure what he was doing besides being angry and yelling.

Another small wave rose as I paddled hard to untangle and release the kayaks. It worked they broke free. I felt the tension leave my body as I moved into sheltered waters. I was totally exhausted and drained. When I felt safe I stopped, tied my boat securely to a rock, climbed onto another rock and fell asleep.

I never kayaked with Dick again. I found a new group of kayaking friends who were mentally stable and shared responsibility when unexpected things occurred.

As I boarded the flight to Nome the last week of January 1991, I realized Zach's high school graduation was five months away. Jeremia was a freshman. *Where did the years go?* The Alaska Department of Education had contacted SERRC and asked if I could go to Nome to conduct a Title I assessment. The person responsible for the job recently quit. When people applied for jobs in Alaska they didn't understand the definition for cold. Like me they had never heard of fifty degrees below zero.

Flying to Nome in January wasn't the perfect time. March was better and might include seeing the Iditarod. I left early Monday morning and would be home late Wednesday night. Flights to Nome were a regular part of Alaska Airline's schedule. The city of Nome had places for people to stay when on school district or city business. Nome was a big city compared to most of the places I visited. I made arrangements for one of the rooms.

A formal federal Title I visit involved a conference session with school administrators followed with classroom observations and meetings with teachers and paraprofessionals. I was given a checklist from the state and briefed on what to cover. Monday went well and Tuesday started off on schedule. After lunch a teacher from the high school picked me up and took me out to the high school. As I climbed into his Jeep I noticed how windy it was. He said an unplanned storm was brewing. After all, it was January. I thanked him for the ride.

Part IV: Juneau, Anchorage, and Beyond

At 2:30 p.m. someone interrupted the interview and told me to get my stuff. I gathered my materials and put on my parka when I heard the PA system. "This is an emergency announcement. Gather your belongings and head to the assigned doors of the building. I repeat..." The teacher, along with the paraprofessional I interviewed, helped students gather their things. We walked to the front entrance and were ushered into a huge Army carrier at the front of the school. We settled into benches along the edge of the belly of the beast. No windows in the vehicle meant we couldn't see out.

When the carrier started to move the teacher sitting next to me explained the emergency procedures. It felt surreal. When we arrived back in Nome I was dropped close to the apartment. I pushed through the blowing wind and snow to get to the door. The blizzard conditions and wind continued all night and the next day. Late Wednesday the snow stopped, but the wind continued until Thursday morning. The drifts were as high as the building. The building I was in had a door to enter and exit that wasn't entirely blocked by snow. Another person staying at the apartment and I found a snow shovel in the entryway of the building and started taking turns digging out.

By noon we found out the status of Nome's situation. The airport and schools were closed, but the city offices were functioning. Phones worked off and on. Alaska Airlines predicted flights in and out on Friday morning. I was able to call home and gave them a status report of my return. I talked with the superintendent and told him I needed to leave when the planes were flying. He understood. I flew out of Nome Friday and made it home to Juneau with no weather incidents. As I stepped off the plane I was happy to see rain and no winds.

Zach graduated from high school. He started taking classes at University of Alaska Southeast and volunteering for the Fire Department. He was interested in EMT classes and all the various CPR certifications. The following fall he left for the University of Alaska Fairbanks to attend their Fire Science program where he received an Associate of Applied Science (AAS.) degree. I knew he was serious about his decision and wasn't surprised when he started a bachelor's degree in Emergency Health Services at the University of Maryland–Baltimore.

Suddenly Jeremia and I were alone. Being the second child he had always shared the spotlight with his brother. I picked up a couple of rackets at a garage sale and suggested we try playing tennis. Jer loved to do anything involving movement so he agreed. We talked more, relaxed into new routines and I learned more about him.

In late March 1992 I had another trip to Chevak. People recognized me because I kept coming back. Sometimes individuals stopped me and said, "You are the lady that works with the teachers at the school and runs on the road to the dump." I did run but never thought anyone noticed. Fall was my favorite time to visit because I ran outside. A road connecting to a neighboring village was in an open area, a perfect running trail. The exhilarating feeling of being outdoors in the crisp air never grew old. On many trips all I could do was run laps around the gym and dodge basketballs.

Weather in Chevak, and everywhere in Alaska, was often tricky. March meant longer days, more sunshine, and surprise storms. When I left Juneau earlier in the week, the weather was predicted to be in the twenties with no storms. Understanding spring snowstorms arrived all the way into late May and early June, I knew better than to travel without my snow pants. Since it was the last week in March and my final trip until August, I took a chance.

The day I was return to Juneau I was sitting in the school office when the call for the plane came in. Planes in bush Alaska were unpredictable. Buying a ticket and having a seat didn't guarantee anyone would remember. I learned the hard way to call the day before and again the day of departure. A couple of times I was left and couldn't leave until the next day. When the secretary got off the phone she said the plane was landing and the pilot was anxious to leave because of a storm. She added, "Grab your stuff. Fred is on his way to take you to the airport." My friends kidded me for not bringing my snow pants. Linda insisted I wear her pants to the airport so I wouldn't get soaked. Spring snow this late was usually heavy and wet. I reluctantly agreed and said I would give them to Fred. We threw my backpack and box into the sled. I jumped on the rails and off we went!

The wet snow blinded me as we traveled the ten minutes to the airport. The pilot grabbed the box and backpack out of my hands and said, "Get in the plane." I told him I needed to take the snow pants off. The look on his face was pure irritation. He yelled at me to sit on the edge of the plane and told Fred to start pulling on one pant leg. None of us questioned his orders. I knew they would come off faster if I took my boots off, but we did it his way. The other passengers sat quietly looking straight ahead. The pants came off and were thrown into the sled. As I climbed into the plane I yelled over my shoulder, "Fred, please give the pants to Linda."

I felt embarrassed, relieved, and angry as I buckled my seat belt. Snow pants would never be left behind again. The pilot wasn't on my Christmas card list.

Running leg seven on LaBamba

In September 1989, I was asked to be on a Klondike Road Relay[33] team, La Bamba, a Masters Team. I knew about the race and was told it was fun. Many of my running friends did it. The Tourism Industry Association of the Yukon created it to attract visitors to the Yukon. A ten-person team started in Skagway, Alaska and finished along the banks of the Yukon River in Whitehorse, Canada. Each leg was different. They varied from 9km/5.6 miles to 25.6km/16 miles, starting at sea level with an elevation gain of 3,294 feet. La Bamba was a mixture of men and women, teachers and other individuals.

Most of the running was at night. Each team was allowed a car to follow and support their runners. Occasionally coyotes in the Yukon nipped at the ankles to hurry a runner along. We never understood why they showed up one year, but not the next. Before I agreed to be on the team I told them I wasn't fast, but willing to do long distances. The group agreed having fun and being safe were the important goals.

I was nervous the first year, but then relaxed. The fun teammates made it enjoyable.

After two years I transferred to the Juneau Women Masters team, the One Knight Stands, which I participated in for the next eleven years. They had one additional goal—to beat the Pink Flamingoes, the Anchorage Women Masters team. The Klondike started Friday evening in Skagway and ended in Whitehorse Saturday afternoon. The race often started in rain in Alaska then shifted to clear skies in the Yukon with trees in full fall foliage. It was an incredible weekend I looked forward to each fall. The best part was the spirit of friendly competition.

Jeremia was a senior in 1994. Watching him struggle with high school was painful at times. When he was junior he was selected to be on Juneau Douglas's first soccer team, which he enjoyed. I had hoped it was enough to keep him motivated, but it didn't. I investigated the alternative high school program as an option, but found it targeted gifted students. He needed his interest piqued and nothing had jolted him yet. Many high school students need to investigate their skills through vocational training or real-world experiences. He was one of those students.

In March of his senior year his attendance problems climaxed to the point it was obvious he wouldn't graduate with his class. GED graduates faced an unwarranted stigma, but it was the best option. Jeremia took the tests and passed them all. He explored construction, food service, and small business opportunities. A company for resort areas hired him to go to Vail, Colorado.

Flying out to cabins for camping and hiking

Life at Fifty Below Zero

Leaving Alaska

August 1998

After the boys graduated and moved into their lives, I was on my own. I had always lived with roommates, a husband, or children. My need to please caused me to focus on others, which didn't always end well. I now traveled a lot so I relocated to Anchorage in 1998. SERRC opened an office there and I knew living in Anchorage would reduce my travel out to many of the rural villages. I loved Juneau but the constant rain took its toll. Anchorage's climate was drier and colder and included more opportunities for cross-country skiing and new kayaking areas. The city was full of connecting trails for biking, running, walking, and cross-country skiing. The trails were lighted during the many months of darkness.

A friend from Juneau had moved to Anchorage a year earlier than I. We ran and kayaked together. She introduced me to friends more experienced in kayaking than me. I was included in multiday trips out of Seward, Whittier, and Prince William Sound. We left in one place and were picked up in another by boats large enough for four or five sea kayaks. The environment and endless birds we saw never ceased to take my breath away. Janice was an avid birder so I purposely guided my boat close to her to hear the names of the birds.

Over the years, backpacking and kayaking friends taught me about camping and being in wilderness—setting up tents under trees to stay dry in torrential downpours, locating clean water from streams or waterfalls, and washing my hair in cold streams and not salt water. As much as I missed a shower when on a twelve to fourteen-day trip, my spirit became refreshed in the quiet beauty of the outdoors. I loved to watch the evening light and varying gray hues of the sky. When storms threatened, the sun created vivid colors bursting through the trees and bushes. Experiencing nature helped me realize how fortunate I was to visit the pristine and seldom-visited areas of Alaska. The experiences increased my confidence and abilities to care for myself.

One of my running friends introduced me to the Chugach State Park, the 495,000 acres of parkland located minutes from downtown Anchorage. The majestic foothills quickly gave way to the mountains of the Anchorage skyline. The incredible trails provided access to Flattop Mountain (3,500 feet), Bird Ridge (3,505 feet), Rendezvous Peak (4,101 feet), and Wolverine Peak (4,455 feet) where a person could go for an hour run or hike, or spend a few days out exploring.

The huge park was home to moose, bears, wolves and lynx. I respected this fact—*humans were guests*. A mama moose and her babies or a male moose during rutting season were the ones to leave alone. Oddly, Anchorage residential areas were built on or close to moose breeding grounds. Moose were known to kill those that got too close. My opinion was to avoid them and go the opposite direction.

One evening as I drove home, I saw a large moose with a rack of antlers in my rear view mirror. He looked as if he was coming from the movie theatre and meandering behind my car to the other side of Northern Lights Blvd. There were no woods close by so I wondered where he slept. His tall legs allowed him to easily step over fences and keep moving. Maybe it was someone's backyard or a small neighborhood park. I laughed, wondering if he enjoyed the movie he saw.

The darkness and lack of light finally wore me down. In 2001 I noticed I was obsessed with watching the *Anchorage Daily News*'s forecast. It included the number of seconds, minutes, and hours lost each day as Winter Solstice approached. For one to two days, zero seconds were neither gained nor lost.

My favorite day of the year became the first day of winter. I felt like a 'solstice fairy' because internally I was dancing for joy. It seemed so ridiculous to call December 21 the first day of winter. The first dusting of snow arrived on the mountains in mid to late September. If it stuck around, local Alaskans called it termination dust. By December snow and cold temperatures were the norm. Nevertheless, the winter solstice date marked another year of darkness done and light returning. No one really noticed a significant difference until February, but I knew exactly how many seconds, minutes, and hours of light increased each day. *Why didn't anyone ask me?*

A friend from Juneau, Cynthia, came to visit. I told her I was thinking of leaving Alaska to help care for my mom and be closer to the boys. She was having similar thoughts. She asked if I wanted to accompany her to Oregon to visit friends for Thanksgiving. Her friends were retired Coast Guard, previously stationed in Alaska—Juneau, Sitka, and Kodiak. My mom was on a cruise and the boys were busy with their lives so I agreed.

We started the trip by driving through the Willamette Valley before arriving at Bill and Danielle's on the northern Oregon Coast close to Astoria. Bill was a retired Coast Guard helicopter pilot. The visit and conversations included stories about Bill's rescues and missions in Alaska before retiring to Oregon. We walked the beaches and once again I felt drawn to Oregon. Cynthia knew this area well. It had half the rain of Juneau. We discussed buying a house together to help each other with the transition out of Alaska. Somehow the decision felt right. In January 2002 we made an offer on a house and it was accepted.

One extra challenge for me was that I had recently started a Doctorate program through the Fielding Graduate University. It was a distance program that served students all over the world so I figured it would work in Oregon. My end-of career dream was for a university to hire me to work in teacher education. I felt my wide breadth of experience would make me a good candidate, but a doctorate was needed. Despite being in my late fifties, I wasn't ready to quit working. I investigated a doc program when the boys were twelve and fifteen, but realized I had one opportunity to be a parent, so I waited.

SERRC agreed to continue my contracts if I paid for my travel to Alaska. I sold my place in Anchorage. Mattingly, Anna (a friend), and I drove the Stewart–Cassiar Highway in July 2002 out of Alaska. While driving we saw moose, sang to loud music, and camped in fun spots. Mattingly warned us about bears before we saw them. In Stewart we stayed at an old brothel and shared a bottle of wine. From the porch we looked west and saw *Hyder*, advertised as 'The friendliest Ghost Town in Alaska' accessed going south to Alaska.

I felt confident about finding work in Oregon. Cynthia and I believed the combination of our skills would sell us. A fallacy neither of us predicted—we knew Alaska and had connections, but not in Oregon. Breaking into a new state was difficult.

My mom moved to Oregon to be closer. She knew I was looking for a job. After a year of not finding work I made the only realistic decision—return to Alaska. I needed work to pay the bills and my dissertation research was easier in a state where I knew education. At least with my mom in Oregon the trips to check on her were shorter than California.

In July 2003 I drove back to Anchorage alone. Mattingly passed away in December. His ashes were with me to sprinkle in Alaska. I located a small condo on the east side of Anchorage to purchase and gathered together some furniture. With one and a half mortgage payments to pay I beat myself up over the mess I created. I was focused on finishing the doctorate and returning to Oregon.

Driving back to Alaska filled my mind with memories and reflective thoughts. Alaska was familiar and easy in many ways. I thought of a trip I had made in August 1999 to St. Paul in the Pribilof Islands. *Once again I was traveling to a place many people never saw, to present state mandated professional development.*

The Pribilof Islands were unique. St. Paul didn't allow dogs or cats, because of the small Arctic blue gray foxes that ran free. The day I arrived I saw the foxes moving like farm dogs protecting their turf. It was odd to see, but interesting. Ornithologists rated the Pribilofs as one of the exceptional birding sites. Endless varieties of migratory birds and sea mammals were abundant on the islands. St. George was the key location for the red-legged kittiwakes. They mated, nested, and delivered their babies each year on the island. The Pribilofs were the most northern point for fur seals to gather and give birth to their pups, sometimes close to a million. The huge males went without food for several months as they guarded their harems.

After I arrived, I put on my running shoes and investigated the island before dark. I ran along the islands' rugged cliffs and grassy hills.

I heard the call of the common murres and saw cormorants sitting in the grass as I ran. Visitors who came to the islands to see the seals weren't allowed access to their rookeries. When I was close to the observation blind, I stopped and walked quietly to the viewing section. As I watched and listened to the seals and their pups climb off and on the rocks, I was mesmerized in the moment. I left as quietly as I arrived. This area was their home for thousands of years and hopefully would continue.

Many memories floated around in my mind when suddenly I was jarred by a couple of buffalo. In all of my previous trips on the ALCAN I never saw buffalo. Now in a desolate part of the Yukon highway with no cars in sight for hours, I was seeing a whole herd of them blocking both sides of the road. I was stunned by this image. They were big and not in a hurry. I stopped, turned off the car and watched them as they moved slowly forward. Who wants a buffalo to get upset and have his or her buddies surround their car? After about thirty minutes I continued driving slowly until I was sure there were no more buffalo. I had been driving all day without talking to anyone and only had seen a couple of cars. Maybe it was just a figment of my imagination, but I know I saw buffalo.

My life became consumed with working (to pay the mortgage payments) on evaluation projects and completing the doctorate. The Bering Strait School District (BSSD) was agreeable to the dissertation research. They allowed me to travel on their district plane, when empty seats were available; if I paid for my ticket to Unalakleet. I traveled to four of their villages. Rural districts saw many changes, but running water was still not consistent. Several schools in BSSD had wireless Internet access, but not indoor plumbing.

Part IV: Juneau, Anchorage, and Beyond

Exercise was a way for me to keep balanced and not work twelve hours a day. I missed Mattingly and decided it was time for a furry friend. Cynthia was visiting and noticed a golden retriever rescue in the paper. She knew I was interested in the breed. When we went to see him they let us take him to a park. I felt I needed to be sure that getting a dog was the right decision so I asked for the night to think it over.

As we backed out of the driveway 'my rescue buddy' jumped up on the fence and looked at me, "Where are you going without me?" I instantly fell in love with him. He weighed eighty pounds, was a year and a half old, with lots of puppy energy. I named him Anchor. His job was to keep me grounded with all of the mind work I was doing. He nuzzled me each day to remind me it was time to go outside. We had an agreement, five miles a day, minimum—it was good for him and me. We quickly bonded, as only an animal lover can fully understand.

On March 31, 2004, two weeks after Anchor entered my life, I called my son Jeremia to wish him happy birthday. It was 6:30 p.m. when we finished talking and I still needed to walk Anchor. The day had started with an early meeting and several other tasks. I was exhausted, but it was 'Anchor time.' I decided a short jog would be enough.

I grabbed the car keys, my drivers' license, and a light running jacket, fleece headband and gloves. Off we went two miles down the road to Chugach State Park. It was five above zero so I felt confident I was well dressed. As I got out of the car in the parking lot I noticed the daylight was longer.

The Chugach State Park had several entry points. The parking lot I pulled into was on the east side of town but within a thirty-minute run I could be on the south side of town. There were rumors of a bear sighting in the park earlier in the week. When Anchor and I were there the day before he had acted a bit squirrely, but tonight he seemed mellow. Anchor was good about coming when I called. His golden retriever traits made him anxious to be close to his human.

Venturing out alone on Anchorage trails was still difficult for me, but I was determined to overcome my problem with directions. Most of my friends knew I was directionally challenged. I made a pact with myself that the risk of getting lost was worth the opportunity to be in the incredible magnificence that encompassed all areas of Alaska.

A friend, Becky, made a suggestion I tried to follow to keep from getting lost—"look at the mountains and they will help guide you back to the car." The move to Anchorage had increased my need to improve my navigation skills. Becky's words comforted me and kept me focused. The problem was that winter snowstorms created blankets of snow on the mountaintops, resulting in the terrain looking similar. I shrugged off the thoughts of getting lost and said to myself "no worries tonight because I am taking the easy loop trail and I won't get into my habit of adding an additional mile or two."

I devised a two to three mile circle run that went past the science center and hooked up to another trail going up a small hill. If I waited until this time of the evening most of the skiers were done for the day or had gone to the lighted trails over on the south side of Anchorage. With Anchor running free he accomplished twice the mileage I did.

Reaching the top of the small hill I noticed Anchor wasn't with me. I worried about the bear, when he appeared. I reprimanded him, reminding him to stay close. When I looked at my watch I realized we had been out forty-five minutes. What happened to my short loop? Waiting for Anchor had disoriented me a bit. Confidently I said, "OK Anchor let's find the car." After ten minutes I knew we were lost. Darkness was closing in when I began to panic. I knew tomorrow someone would find us, because people used the trail to ski to work.

This wasn't a good situation. I was upset with myself for not being better prepared. My phone was at home charging so I couldn't call anyone. It surprised me the things that flashed through my mind. Did I tell my son I loved him? I should have paid all my bills this morning. I was mad at myself because I knew better. Just as I was starting to cry, a gentle calmness came over me and a soft smile appeared. I was outside doing what I enjoyed and wanted to do as long as possible. This thought pushed me into survival mode and summoned internal energy that helped me think.

Hearing a noise Anchor barked. Around the corner came a skier with a dog. His dog and Anchor greeted each other as I yelled, "I am lost and need help getting back to my car." The skier was great. He asked questions to determine where my car was and assured me I was less than ten minutes away from it. He was on his way back to a different parking lot so I couldn't follow him.

It was hard for me to feel confident I could follow his direction but I knew I would be OK. I memorized his direction—right, right, left, and right into the parking lot. We reached the car as a partial moon came out from a lone cloud. I gave Anchor his cookie after he jumped in the car and smiled at the beauty of the cold, brisk night. When we arrived home I made myself a cup of tea and sat in silence thinking about how different the night could have been.

At the end of October 2005, I finished my dissertation research, as well as the contracts I was working on. It was time to leave Alaska again. I toyed with the idea of staying because it was easy to find work. I felt a responsibility to my mom. Friends thought I was crazy leaving in November. *Is there ever a good time to leave?* It was bittersweet. The last couple of days I stayed with my friend Amy. She too had moved to Anchorage from Juneau.

On November 22, 2005, the evening before I was to leave, snow started falling. It was normal Alaskan weather for November, maybe a little heavier snowfall. The next day was Wednesday, the day before Thanksgiving. Amy suggested I stay since the snow was becoming thicker. I thanked her. Somehow leaving in a blizzard seemed appropriate.

The next morning Anchor and I were up early for a short walk. The snow was deep and steadily falling. We returned to the house, gathered our few things, and left. Amy gave me a hug and looked at me like I was crazy. I told her I would stop in Glennallen if the snow continued. The wipers barely kept the snow off the windshield. It was thick, wet, clumpy snow that made the car feel like it was driving through sand. The snowplows tried to keep the roads clear for the Thanksgiving traffic. I saw several fender bender accidents as I drove out of Anchorage.

The Glenn Highway was desolate after leaving Sutton. About twenty miles before Glennallen the snow slowed down and the clouds lifted. I took a break and felt confident we were fine. My plan was to drive to Tok, spend the night, and head to Haines Junction the next day. Anchor nuzzled my head to ask me when we were going to stop for our 'daily 5.' I whispered, "We'll get a short walk when we reach Tok." He wasn't happy but laid down when I noticed the car's outside thermometer. When we left Anchorage it was twenty-eight to thirty above zero, but now the reading stated ten degrees below zero. It felt cold even with the heater going. I usually tensed up driving on snow and ice, which didn't help circulation.

When we pulled into the motel in Tok the temperature hovered at twenty below. Cold weather temperatures were normal there, so they had plugins for cars. It had been a long day with lots of excitement from the snow and now it was dark and icy. Anchor and I ran the length of the motel parking lot a couple of times. I told him that was as good as it gets. I was pooped. He sulked for the next hour while I watched TV.

Day two was Thanksgiving morning. We left early for the 290 miles to Haines Junction. I figured this would be an easy day. It was still twenty degrees below zero, but we were headed south so it would warm up. I was looking forward to the drive along the Haines Highway to visit the Alaska Chilkat Bald Eagle Preserve. The Preserve covered 49,320 acres along the Chilkat River. Established in 1982, it was a state park and wildlife refuge. I visited the bald eagles there once before and was astounded at the number of them sitting in trees and along the water. Most people were lucky if they saw one bald eagle in their lifetime and there it was possible to see a hundred at one time. I saw it as a magical spot—many bald eagles in one place created a special type of energy. From Haines we would catch the ferry to Prince Rupert.

Listening to the CDs I had brought, I tried to relax, which was always difficult for me. Most people referred to me as a white-knuckle driver. Despite over thirty years of driving in Alaska, the fear of other drivers hitting me was fresh each time I was on icy, snowy surfaces. The imposing mountains covered with snow closed in from both sides. The edges of the road were barren with no signs of life, so different from summer driving. It was grandiose and unnerving at the same time.

Cell service didn't always work along the ALCAN. I was so glad to be driving my trusty Subaru.

The roads were clear, but icy in spots. The car had solid snow tires and I was driving about forty miles an hour when I hit black ice. Anchor felt a change in the car so he stood up to watch out the front window. The car was out of control and I was desperately trying not to put my foot on the break. My mind kept saying, 'remember go with the flow of the car.' I saw one car earlier and hoped none were coming from either direction. The embankment we were headed for was the focus of my attention. I hoped it wasn't a steep cliff. Anchor interrupted my trance with a quiet whimper that startled me. My foot came off the clutch and the car turned off. We slowly slid backwards in a side-to-side movement over the ice.

The slight incline led us back to the center of the road before we stopped. My entire body shook. We hadn't gone over the embankment. I released my tightly wrapped fingers from the steering wheel. I wanted to get out of the car and jump for joy, but decided to get the car started and out of the way. The icy conditions made the tires struggle to gain traction. The rest of the drive to Haines Junction was slower with my hands wrapped even tighter.

As I checked into the motel the desk clerk noticed the license from Alaska and mentioned the café had a Thanksgiving dinner special. I thanked her. I knew Canada celebrated their Thanksgiving in October, but appreciated the reminder of Turkey Day. I was thankful I wasn't sitting in my car down an embankment hoping someone would find me.

The next morning we found out the Haines Highway was closed due to weather. It was too icy for driving. Anchor and I drove to White-

Part IV: Juneau, Anchorage, and Beyond

horse and on to Skagway where we caught the ferry to Prince Rupert. During the ferry's stop in Juneau, Anchor and I got off to sprinkle Mattingly's ashes. I cried thinking about the years with Mattingly and his boys. Anchor understood and comforted me with his gentle nudges and loving eyes.

Time to move forward.

To the lover of pure wildness Alaska is one of the most wonderful countries in the world.

—John Muir,
Travels in Alaska, 1879

Afterthoughts

Friends gave me this book when I retired. When I read the above statement in the second chapter I smiled. The sentence captured Alaska and helped me understand why I loved it. The remoteness and harshness scared me and drew me into its quiet and majestic environment. I never planned to live there, and yet, without a doubt it impacted my life. So many times I felt grateful I lived through an experience that could have ended differently. I never looked for these moments, for the thrill of being on the edge, but they did find me. I respected Alaska for all of its wildness.

Alaska was the catalyst that moved me from a childlike girl to a fully matured woman. Despite being twenty-six as I crossed the state line, I was very naïve. I knew little about surviving life with its twists and turns. It was demanding and hard to be in Alaska, yet painful and difficult to leave. There were moments I was so cold I felt my bones were going to crack like glass.

The women I met in Alaska were powerful role models. They varied in ages from sixteen to ninety-plus. Some were students and women in villages, larger communities, and remote areas all over the state. They helped me survive and be smart in the wilderness. One woman, Mary Hervin[i], traveled in a sixteen-foot outboard motor boat on a six-hundred-mile trip down the Yukon with her friend, Phyllis, when they were twenty years old. They decided forty-two years later to repeat the trip. I met Mary in the '90s after the repeat trip when she was the cook for the Governor's Student Health and Safety conferences project I had coordinated. She was just one example of many women I was lucky enough to meet.

Alaska Native women I met in Kotzebue and Togiak invited me into their tents for tea and stories. I learned about caring for my toddlers, how to cook wild meat, and keep food for the winter if the electricity quit. I watched women labor on building houses and roads, working as equals with men in homestead situations. Even my mom finally took her three-inch high heels off to become the second crewmember for a forty-nine-foot boat that traveled from *San Diego to Skagway and Back in 42 Stops*[ii] (go Mom).

Alaska bequeathed my sons the gift of nature as an innate part of their being. Both understand and take time for the quiet solitude of being outdoors. I understand it in myself and see it in the choices they have made and continue to make in their lives. The need to step away from urban living as a regular part of life to reenergize is powerful. In today's world many people have "nature deficit disorder."[iii] I doubt the three of us will ever experience that disorder.

My life had turning points and forks in the road I never could have predicted. Sometimes these were daunting and left me unsure whether I had made the right decision. Each of these situations took me in directions unimagined. The paths I selected helped me explore and build understanding about the world. I am glad I went to Alaska to empty honey buckets in the small village of Marshall.

An Alaskan Memoir on Teaching and Learning

Life at Fifty Below Zero

Endnotes

1 Now known as Denali at the request of the Athabaskan Koyukon people.

2 http://www.nativefederation.org/about-afn/history/

3 http://www.ankn.uaf.edu/curriculum/articles/CarolBarnhardt/HistoryofSchooling.html

4 WEIO promotes the cultural expertise and traditions of Alaska, Greenland, Siberian and Canadian Inuit, and Native Americans. The games require skill, strength, agility and endurance and will test their ability to the highest level. This is an exciting time for competitive tournaments, traditional dance, beautiful artwork, stunning regalia and the Miss WEIO pageant.

5 *Qaspeqs*, commonly called *kuspuks* in English, started in the late 1800s because of flour sacks in trading posts. They were dresses and shirts with hoods made of cloth, originally worn over fur garments because cloth was easier to replace than fur.

6 When whale blubber is not available people used Crisco to make *akutuq*.

7   https://iditarod.com/joe-redington-sr-remembered-for-his-service/
    https://alaskasportshall.org/inductee/joe-redington-sr/

8   When the bishop bequeathed his pectoral cross, which resembled a relic of the 'true cross,' to Father Robaut he asked for a promise. The bishop wanted a Northern Alaska mission to be given the name 'Mission of the Holy Cross.'

9   Molly Hootch was the name of one student who represented all students fourteen years and older in rural Alaska that did not have access to schooling.

10 Tryck, K. (December 1975). *Rafting Down the Yukon*. National Geographic. Vol. 148:6.

11 Wallis, Velma. (2002). *Raising Ourselves: A Gwitch'in Coming of Age Story from the Yukon River*. Kenmore, WA: EpiCenter Press.

12 https://alaskasportshall.org/inductee/george-atla/
    https://www.adn.com/outdoors-adventure/iditarod/2019/09/25/another-movie-about-alaska-mushing-icon-george-attla-set-for-release-next-month/

13 Hensley, W. L. (Iggiagruk). (2009). *Fifty miles from tomorrow: A Memoir of Alaska and the Real People*. New York, NY: Farrar, Straus and Giroux.

14 Fejes, Claire. (1996/2016). *Cold Starry Night: An Artist's Memoir*. Kenmore, WA: Epicenter Press Inc.

15 Fejes, Claire. (1981). *Villagers: Athabaskan Indian Life Along the Yukon River.* New York: Random House.

16 I spelled Zacharia and Jeremia without an h because it was a silent letter. As a kindergarten teacher I felt it was easier for a child to learn to spell letters they could hear.

17 Fur cradles that hung from the ceiling were used by Tsilhqot'in Athabaskan, the most southern Athabaskan in British Columbia.

18 Yukon-Koyukuk School District village

19 Yukon-Koyukuk School District village

20 http://www.alaskool.org/projects/ANCSA/reports/rsjones1981/ANCSA_History71.htm

21 Tanana Chiefs Conference was a consortium of forty-two villages in Interior Alaska, founded in the mid-1960s.

22 Alaska Federation of Natives was formed in October 1966, when more than four hundred Alaska Natives representing seventeen Native organizations gathered for a three-day conference to address Alaska Native aboriginal land rights. From 1966 to 1971, AFN worked primarily to achieve passage of a just and fair land settlement. On December 18, 1971 the Alaska Native Claims Settlement Act (ANCSA) was signed into law

23 http://www.alaskool.org/projects/ANCSA/reports/rsjones1981/ANCSA_History71.htm

24 Mount McKinley, the highest mountain in North America, was officially renamed Denali in 2009. The name Denali, based on the Koyukon word for mountain, (Deenaalee meaning "the high one"), was requested by the Alaska Native people in 1975. Denali National Park became the accepted and most often name used in reference to the Park in the second half of the '70s.

25 Plugging in a vehicle was part of living in Alaska when the temperatures dropped to fifteen to twenty degrees below zero. No one in the rural villages worried about their vehicles being plugged in they just used their snow machines or dogs until the weather heated up (which could be most of the winter). Long outdoor cords were attached to the batteries to keep them warm enough for the car to start.

26 https://www.fws.gov/nativeamerican/pdf/tek-barnhardt-kawagley.pdf

27 Alaska Native Brotherhood and the Alaska Native Sisterhood Grand Camp is the oldest known indigenous persons' civil rights organization in the world. Our mission is to better the lives of Native people and their families; to continue the fight for civil rights and land rights of all Native people; to share the cultural knowledge, wisdom, and artistic beauty of Native Tribal Societies and strive for a spirit of Brotherhood and Sisterhood among all people!

28 His Holiness the Dalai Lama and Cutler, H. C. (1998). *The Art of Happiness: A Handbook for Living*. New York, NY: Riverhead Books.

29 Lucky for me my name was not on any of the paperwork. Darcy had not followed through with having me sign anything. A few years after I closed Infinite Fitness a rumor surfaced a bear had killed Darcy. I always wondered if it was true.

30 Satterfield, Archie. (1983). *Chilkoot Pass: A Hiker's Historical Guide to the Klondike Gold Rush National Park*. Portland, OR: Alaska Northwest Books.

31 An unusual crash in 1971 that killed 111 passengers resulted in Juneau being considered one of the most dangerous airports in the United States. The mountains on both sides and frequent gray sky were reminders to be extra cautious.

32 Chichagof Island was comprised of 2,050 square miles with 742 miles of coastline. It was the fifth largest island in the United States. The island was bound by Chatham Strait to the east, *Icy Strait* to the northeast, *Cross Sound* to the northwest, and the Gulf of Alaska to the west.

33 https://klondikeroadrelay.com/

i Hervin, Mary & Martinsen, Karen. (1991). *Yukon Re-Run: A Last Frontier River Trip Repeated by Two Women Forty-two Years Later*. Mary's Road Press: Gustavus, AK.

ii Sworde, R & R. (1990). *San Diego to Skagway and Back in 42 Stops*. San Diego, CA: Mission Graphics.

iii Boyst, Beth. (2018, Fall). *A Letter to My Favorite Trail on Your 50th Birthday*. Pacific Crest Trail Communicator. Pacific Crest Trail Association: Vol. 30: 3, P. 4.

The only journey is the one within.

—Rainer Maria Rilke

Acknowledgements

Several years ago, I read this quote in a meditation book, but it wasn't until I wrote the memoir that I truly understood its significance. A memoir is a person's *journey* and this was mine for thirty-three years. Alaska will always feel like home to me, because of the way it influenced me. Some dates and itinerary of locations may be obscured somewhat because years can be confused in memories. Names of people in villages have often been changed to protect their privacy.

Many people encouraged me and assisted me in writing this book. Hopefully, these words acknowledge each of you. Please forgive me if I left anyone out.

First, to my wonderful sons, Jeremia and Zach: Thank you for your patience with me as your mother, the greatest honor I will ever have.

Thank you, Sean for all of the conversations and infinite reading of the many, many versions. You were so encouraging and supportive, more than you will ever know.

Thank you, Jed for taking me to Alaska. I thought we would be there for a year. I am so glad that we wrote letters to our families and friends. They were extremely helpful in filling in the endless details time had lost.

Thank you to Harold and Peggy Reagle for the letters they wrote about our first years in Alaska.

Thank you to my sister, Nancy—you are the strongest woman I know. So many times, I wanted to call when I had no access to a phone. I knew you would have encouraging and comforting words when I felt confused or frustrated.

Thank you to Dan and Genie St. John for reading the Chapter on Allakaket to help ensure my memory was intact during that wonderful and critically difficult year.

Thank you to all the Alaska Native people that shared their homes with me while living and working with rural school districts. Many of you taught me so much and I was honored to learn from you. There were many turbulent times in Alaska in the 1970s and I have tried to be respectful of all that happened.

Thank you to Drs. Ray and Carol Barnhardt—your endless research and articles, as well as the respect for Alaska Native people you taught and exemplified in your work and daily lives helped me in my commitment to encourage Alaska Native leadership in education.

Thank you, Matt Love for encouraging all writers not to be self-deprecating. You were a disciplined writing coach, content editor, and persistent in comments about cutting out the unneeded words.

And, finally to three people who assisted in the final steps of the book. Thank you to Jason Storey and Vanessa Couto of Otterburn & Co. for the book layout, website, and countless ideas on publicity for the book. Thank you to Shannon Carson for the final edits and endless hours of getting into my head through reading and rereading the very long manuscript.

Reading Paulo Freire (1970) helped solidify my desire to teach. When really engaged as a teacher it is impossible to separate teaching and learning. Each group of students I had the privilege to teach taught me so much. I am hopeful they left knowing they were capable learners. The curiosity of children and the intrigue of how individuals learn hooked me into education years ago and I still maintain that interest. My work spanned a variety of educational positions, which allowed me to see different learning perspectives. I am proud I chose education as my career. Although many problems exist and perhaps always will, I am grateful to be a part of the work for fifty-two years.

Life at Fifty Below Zero

About the Author

Christina was born in California. She became an Airforce brat traveling to different states before ending up in Hawai'i in 1956 where she was graciously accepted into families of friends from varying cultures. The warmth of people increased her interest and appreciation for diversity. After graduating from Roosevelt High School (go Rough Riders!) in Hawai'i, she returned to California to become a teacher.

After teaching in California she and her husband were hired to teach in rural Alaska. Comfort with diverse groups became a valuable resource and increased her effectiveness as an educator over the thirty plus years she worked in rural Alaska communities. Despite fifty below zero temperatures the immenseness of Alaska's wilderness captured her heart. Taking time to play outdoors with her sons and friends hiking, running, backpacking and kayaking led to amazing memories and fun stories. Events she experienced and landscapes she saw many people only read and dream about in the pages of *National Geographic* or outdoor magazines.

Christina was in the enviable position of being in the right place at the right time to observe transitions both in Hawai'i and Alaska as they were rushed into full statehood. Her motto continues to be 'adventures are out there just waiting for us to find them.' Being in the woods is much more fun than shopping in a mall. Her career in education spanned more than fifty years.

Life at Fifty Below Zero